FOOD, CLIMATE, AND MAN

EDITED BY

MARGARET R. BISWAS
AND
ASIT K. BISWAS
BISWAS & ASSOCIATES, OTTAWA, CANADA

A WILEY–INTERSCIENCE PUBLICATION

JOHN WILEY & SONS
NEW YORK • CHICHESTER • BRISBANE • TORONTO

Library of Congress Cataloging in Publication Data:

Main entry under title:
Food, climate, and man.

   (Environmental science and technology)
   "A Wiley-Interscience publication."
   Includes bibliographies and index.
   1.   Food supply—Addresses, essays, lectures.
2.   Crops and climate—Addresses, essays, lectures.
3.   Human ecology—Addresses, essays, lectures.
I.   Biswas, Margaret R.   II.   Biswas, Asit K.

HD9000.5.F594   338.1'9   78-15154

ISBN 0-471-03240-9

Printed in the United States of America

10 9 8 7 6 5 4 3 2 1

To Elmore Jackson
without whose inspiration and support
this book would never have been started,
and without whose encouragement
it could never have been finished.

CONTRIBUTORS

Dr. Asit K. Biswas
Director
Biswas & Associates
3 Valley View Road
Ottawa, Canada

Margaret R. Biswas
International Institute for Applied
Systems Analysis
Laxenburg, Austria

Dr. F. Kenneth Hare
Director, Institute for Environmental Studies
University of Toronto
Toronto, Canada

Dr. Victor A. Kovda
Institute of Agrochemistry & Soil Science
Academy of Science of the USSR,
Puschina-on-the Oka
Moscow Region, USSR

Dr. Helmut E. Landsberg
Institute of Fluid Dynamics & Applied Mathematics
University of Maryland,
College Park, Maryland

Professor Gunnar Lindh
Institutionen för Teknisk Vattenresurslära
Lunds Tekniska Hogskola,
Fack 725, S-220 07 Lund, Sweden

Dr. David Norse
OECD-Interfutures
176 Avenue Charles de Gaulle,
92200 Neuilly-sur-Seine,
France

Dr. Aurelio Peccei
President, Club of Rome
Via Giorgione 163,
Rome, Italy

Dr. David Pimentel
Department of Entomology
Cornell University,
Ithaca, New York

SERIES PREFACE

Environmental Science and Technology

The Environmental Science and Technology Series of Monographs, Textbooks, and Advances is devoted to the study of the quality of the environment and to the technology of its conservation. Environmental science therefore relates to the chemical, physical, and biological changes in the environment through contamination or modification, to the physical nature and biological behavior of air, water, soil, food, and waste as they are affected by man's agricultural, industrial, and social activities, and to the application of science and technology to the control and improvement of environmental quality.

The deterioration of environmental quality, which began when man first collected into villages and utilized fire, has existed as a serious problem under the ever-increasing impacts of exponentially increasing population and of industrializing society. Environmental contamination of air, water, soil, and food has become a threat to the continued existence of many plant and animal communities of the ecosystem and may ultimately threaten the very survival of the human race.

It seems clear that if we are to preserve for future generations some semblance of the biological order of the world of the past and hope to improve on the deteriorating standards of urban public health, environmental science and technology must quickly come to play a dominant role in designing our social and industrial structure for tomorrow. Scientifically rigorous criteria of environmental quality must be developed. Based in part on these criteria, realistic standards must be established and our technological progress must be tailored to meet them. It is obvious that civilization will continue to require increasing amounts of fuel, transportation, industrial chemicals, fertilizers, pesticides, and countless other products; and that it will continue to produce waste products of all descriptions. What is urgently needed is a total systems approach to modern civilization through which the pooled talents of scientists and engineers, in cooperation with social scientists and the medical profession, can be focused on the development of order and equilibrium in the presently disparate segments of the human environment. Most of the skills and tools that are needed are already in existence. We surely have a right to hope a technology that has created such manifold environmental problems is also capable of solving them. It is our hope that this Series in Environmental Sciences and Technology will not only serve to make this challenge more explicit to the established professionals, but that it also will help to stimulate the student toward the career opportunities in this vital area.

Robert L. Metcalf
James N. Pitts, Jr.
Werner Stumm

FOREWORD

I believe that the fundamental question that confronts mankind at present is how to meet the basic human needs without simultaneously destroying the resource base—that is, the environment—from which those needs must be met. Hence an understanding of the interrelationship between environment and development is absolutely essential to any strategy for the protection and improvement of the environment. This is the process I have often termed *development without destruction*, and in a book entitled *Food, Climate, and Man*, it is desirable to discuss this important concept.

Many of the negative aspects of development have so impressed themselves on the minds of those concerned with the environment that the question has often been asked, "Why development?" Some have even advocated arresting economic growth in the interest of promoting environmental protection.

It is true that, in the past, industrial and agricultural development have created such environmental problems as water, soil, and air pollution, with consequent costs to human health and well-being, spread of the deserts through the mismanagement by man of natural ecosystems, and so on. Such problems are seldom localized and, through their interactions with other factors, frequently become matters of regional or global concern. What, for instance, is the possible impact on global climate of the continued combustion of fossil fuels to meet energy demands? There is no doubt that there are "outer limits" to the ability of the biosphere to absorb the impact of man's activities, and such limits must be respected for man's own long-term well-being, even for his own ultimate survival.

It should also be realized that the environmental problems are caused by a lack of adequate development. Today there are hundreds of millions of people without the basic human necessities like adequate food, shelter, clothing, and health; hundreds of millions more lack access to even a rudimentary education or regular employment. This is not only an intolerable situation in human terms, but it also has serious environmental consequences. The relentless pressures that arise when basic human needs are not met can reduce the resource base from which man must inevitably gain his sustenance. The destruction of forests, the loss of arable soil, the loss of productivity through disease and malnutrition, and the increasing pressure on fragile ecosystems that so often result from poverty—these things are as significant as the pollution created by industry, technology, and overconsumption by the affluent. All of them lead to the rapid depletion of basic natural resources, as is discussed by Margaret Biswas elsewhere in this book.

With these thoughts in mind, I would say three things in commenting on the question "Why development?" First, for the developing countries of the world, in which more than two thirds of mankind live, there is no alternative to pursuing economic and social change so as to meet the basic human needs and secure better prospects for their citizens. What is more, the lesson of the United Nations Conference on Population, held at Bucharest in 1974, is that only when the poor in the world have a more satisfactory existence will the rate of population growth—itself a major contributory factor in environmental problems—begin to slow down. Next, it has often been noticed that the manner in which development takes place is too often destructive to the environment, and the basis for continued development is thereby threatened. The third point is that, far from being in conflict, environmental and developmental objectives are complementary and should be viewed as two sides of the same coin.

This last point needs a little elaboration. A few years ago, the environmental problem was thought of solely in terms of pollution, whereas economic and social development were measured solely in terms of growth in gross national product. Given these premises, the pursuit of environmental objectives through pollution control was seen as a check on development. But there have been significant advances in recent years in our understanding of what is meant by environmental and developmental objectives, and there is a growing acceptance that these converge. We should look on environment as the stock of physical or social resources available at a given time for the satisfaction of human needs and on development as a process pursued by all societies with the aim of increasing human well-being. Thus the ultimate purpose of both environmental and development policies is the enhancement of the quality of life, beginning with the satisfaction of the basic human needs. We should therefore not query whether to develop; we should establish a new kind of development related not only to the opportunities offered by the natural resource base but to the limitations imposed by that base on various activities. It is now clear that the past patterns of development in both developed and developing countries have been characterized by such serious environmental damage that they are simply not sustainable on a long-term basis.

What are the features of this new kind of development? I believe that there are three that are particularly relevant: it is needed by all countries, rich and poor; it presupposes new directions for growth and development, not their cessation; and it incorporates the environmental dimension.

There are, however, certain important differences between the form and the new kind of development might take in industrialized countries and that which would emerge in developing countries. In the industrialized countries, it will be necessary to reorient society's aims so that the entire population will have more opportunity for self-expression in the fields of culture, education, the arts and humanities—those nonphysical areas of development that represent the highest levels of human achievement. This new orientation must be less demanding on the environment, particularly on natural resources and energy. Present patterns of production and consumption, based on waste, extravagance, and planned obsolescence, must be replaced by conservation and reuse of resources. I am encouraged by signs from several industrialized countries that such a reorientation of life-styles and societal aims are now being discussed seriously, though clearly the change implied by this approach is immense and will take many years to carry through.

In the developing world, which still lacks the infrastructure and readily useable resources required to meet the growing needs and aspirations of its peoples, the new kind of development must continue to have a strong physical orientation. But each country should be helped to follow a path to development that is best suited to its own human skills and natural resources and responds to its own needs and accords with its own culture and value systems. Developing countries should have access to the technologies they require and should be enabled to adapt these technologies to their own needs, rather than have their development processes distorted by the dictates of imported technologies. Most of all, the new forms of development in the developing world should be based on practices environmentally sound in relation to each country's natural resources of soil, water, and plant and animal life, with care taken to avoid the destruction of the resource base.

The new kind of development should avoid the irrational and wasteful use of resources. Development is irrational if resources are not used in the best known ways to further the aims that a given society has set for itself and account is not taken of all effects known to follow from such action. It is also irrational to waste resources by using more of them than necessary for a given purpose. I will illustrate this theme by one or two examples.

Effluents from industry are commonly regarded as threatening to human health and well-being. It has been remarked that a pollutant is a resource in the wrong place, and certainly the well-known example of sulphur, which can be retrieved from factory chimneys and used for industrial purposes, is a case in point. I do not think it rational to lose more and more resources as pollutants and then to use other resources in even greater quantity to offset the effects of that pollution.

Another example: It has already been demonstrated that resources, like wildlife, if wisely used, can provide food in a manner less destructive to the soils and vegetation of the area than the "traditional" pastorage of cattle and that, through tourism, wild animals can bring to a country valuable foreign exchange. Yet, despite the efforts of governments, this resource is being steadily destroyed the world over for short-term profit—used, that is, irrationally and wastefully.

These new approaches to development also have international implications. The debate around the New International Economic Order, with its emphasis on meeting basic human needs, making fairer use of the world's natural resources, and meeting the need for development in a form appropriate to each country's requirements, shows that there is already some sense of these implications. I hope that the international community, especially the developing nations, in advocating and designing the much-needed new economic order, will not forget that there will be no sustained development or meaningful growth without a clear commitment at the same time to preserve the environment and promote the rational use of natural resources.

I have tried to clarify what I mean by *development without destruction*. I mean sustained development, which takes due regard of environmental constraints. Nowhere is that need more in evidence than in the provision of food, an important theme of this book.

There has been mounting concern in recent years about food, the world's number one problem. We in UNEP share this concern, and feel deeply about the necessity of moving toward solutions that maximize food production yet do so without destroying the ecological basis for sustaining such production.

Any strategy to increase food production on a sustained basis should take explicit account of the complementarity of environment and development. The urgency and magnitude of the task of more than doubling food production by the end of the century and at the same time assuring the supply of basic food requirements to all should not be underestimated. It is vitally important that the measures taken to increase food production on a short-term basis be sustained and effectively integrated with long-term policies. To achieve this, the following considerations, many of which are discussed in greater detail in this book, need to be borne in mind.

One, pressure to expand areas under agriculture—frequently aggravated by the loss of good agricultural land and by industrial and human settlements requirements—has often resulted in serious environmental disruption. To cite but a few examples, the expansion of agriculture to steep hillsides has led to serious erosion in Indonesia; increasing pressure of slash-and-burn agriculture has adversely affected tropical forests in the Philippines; deforestation in the Himalayas has contributed to the increasing frequency and severity of flooding in Pakistan, India, and Bangladesh; and overgrazing and deforestation has assisted the southward march of the Sahara in the Sahelian Zone of Africa. Experts estimate that the land being lost to agriculture by such processes may now exceed the acreage of new land brought into production. Thus rational management of arable and pastoral agricultural land is becoming an increasingly urgent need.

Two, technology transfers in the field of agriculture have often not taken root because proper account was not taken of local, cultural, economic, and ecological conditions. Equally dismal has been man's frequent inability to use locally available technology. For instance, simple, inexpensive countermeasures known over centuries, like terracing to prevent soil erosion, are often ignored. Existing technical and scientific knowledge must be better mobilized and more effectively applied to ensure sustained rather than short-term benefits.

Three, there is an intimate relationship between inputs of energy and output of food. Scientifically planned inputs of energy to the land can yield extraordinarily favorable results, though a saturation point can be reached where any extra inputs are wasted, and serious environmental degradation may result. Large amounts of the energy spent on producing packaging materials like paper and plastics and on transport, storage, marketing, and the like could be conserved so that the energy is available to apply on the land.

Four, fertilizers are indispensable for increasing food production, but their excessive use has occasioned much concern as a possible environmental threat. Production and environmental aims require that fertilizers be used with maximum efficiency on the farm, but it is never efficient to create dangers for man or his environment. New types of nitrogen fertilizers must be developed that release their nitrogen as nitrate into the soil solution during the growing season at a rate comparable to the crop demand for nitrates; biological sources of fertilizers, especially microbiological nitrogen fixation and compost, need to be further developed and applied.

Five, pests cause significant losses of crops throughout the world despite continued and ever increasing use of pesticides. This has resulted, through the processes of natural selection and evolution, in the appearance and proliferation of new strains of pests that may be more vicious and less susceptible to control by chemicals. Neither larger doses nor the use of different pesticides provides a permanent solution. Another major problem is that existing modes of applying chemical pesticides have extremely low efficiency rates. Several studies indicate that a very high proportion of pesticides applied by aircraft never reaches the target and creates totally unnecessary ecological hazards. A third element of concern is that the distribution of pesticides through ecosystems takes place most commonly by selective concentration as the pesticides pass through successive levels of food chains and food webs; thus high pesticide levels accumulate in the higher animals and in man. It is therefore essential to develop effective new methods of integrated pest management, incorporating an ecological approach to pest control; where the use of pesticides cannot be avoided, the efficiency of their application should be increased. The motto should be "efficient use of pesticides: more on target, less outside."

Six, vast losses of food stocks occur each year during storage, processing, and handling. According to some estimates, rodents eat or destroy an amount sufficient to feed nearly 200 million people. Federal authorities estimate the cost to the United States economy of losses due to rats at well over one billion dollars per year. In Africa, almost 30% of all crops are lost in storage. Thus new and better techniques to conserve food by preventing loss and waste could play a major part in improving the world food situation.

Seven, weather and climate have always been important to crop production, often outweighing the factors subject to human management. Today there are increasing signs of possible changes in climate and weather patterns. Man's ability to predict and to anticipate these changes has greatly improved, and he may soon develop a new capacity to influence them as well. Improved long-term forecasting is needed to make crop planning more efficient. There is also an urgent need to develop mathematical models to explain how climate and agriculture interrelate.

Eight, irrigation schemes are undoubtedly needed in the developing countries, but after several years salinization of the soil may render it once again unproductive. In some cases, moreover, they result in the spread of waterborne diseases. The application of ecological and environmental principles, beginning at the planning stage, would avert these hazards and improve the health, well-being, and productive capacity of the population.

Nine, we know that the world can produce a surplus of food and that much more can be produced where the skills and capital are available. The international community must develop mechanisms to distribute surpluses from the favored regions so as to prevent or remedy the unjustifiable coexistence of overconsumption and starvation.

Ten, strategies to solve the world food problem must be developed in full knowledge of the web of interdependence that exists between this and the other major problems facing mankind—those of population, energy and other raw material shortages, underdevelopment, and environmental degradation.

I have stressed the food issue because it is not only the central theme of this book, but it also illustrates so well the importance of assessing the environmental impact of various forms of development and the necessity of adopting an environmental approach to the management of activities within the development process generally.

In the years ahead, we face the task of meeting the minimum human needs of mankind and of avoiding environmental castastrophes. I have spoken encouragingly about the prospects, because I am convinced that disaster is not inevitable. But the urgency is extreme; we have very little time in which to set right our approach to the environment and to meet the legitimate demands of the world's poor. We shall need to act far more thoroughly and speedily than hitherto to redress environmental and human grievances, and we shall need to harness the energies of all sectors of society in the effort. No sector has a more important role than the scientific community. It is the duty of science to bring the problems and solutions to light to display them with appropriate objectivity. Through the diligence and thoroughness that is the mark of all sound scientific endeavor, scientists can help man to see dangers that confront him, and to understand that it is essential that he adopt wiser and safer approaches to managing his planet.

For the above and other reasons, I consider *Food, Climate, and Man* a very timely and important book. Edited and written by nine of the world's leading scientists, the book provides up-to-date information and thinking about the interrelationships between food, climate, and man. As the Executive Director of UNEP, it gives me great pleasure to note the close connection between the editors and most of the contributors and UNEP. I am further gratified to note, as the editors have pointed out in their preface, that the idea of this book originated at the World Food Conference, which both of them attended on behalf of UNEP under my leadership. I am convinced that this book will be read widely and will be a major contribution to our understanding of food and climate, as they relate to man. I wish the book every success.

MOSTAFA KAMAL TOLBA
Executive Director
United Nations Environment Programme
Nairobi, Kenya

PREFACE

And he gave it for his opinion, that whoever could make two
ears of corn or two blades of grass to grow upon a spot of
ground where only one grew before, would deserve better of
mankind, and do more essential service to his country, than
the whole race of politicians put together. —JONATHAN
SWIFT, 1667–1745

Food crisis is undoubtedly one of the major crises facing mankind at
present. With increasing population, and rising affluence of certain segments of that population, the world demand for food has been steadily
increasing in the past. Unfortunately, however, in the "Poverty Belt" of
Asia, Africa, and Latin America—where most of mankind lives—
malnutrition is a chronic problem, and the number of people suffering
from malnutrition has also been steadily increasing in recent years.

Food problems of the world cannot be solved in isolation—without
consideration of their interrelationships with other important problems
facing mankind today, such as those of population changes, economic
development, availability of adequate energy and raw materials, development of new technology, high inflation rates, and shortage of investment capital. All these factors have significant impact on food production, some beneficial and some adverse, and food production, in its
turn, affects development in those areas.

In addition, there are the problems of forecasting future political and
technological developments and the difficulty, often near impossibilty, of
predicting the secondary and tertiary effects precipitated by these developments. For example, few scientists predicted the effectiveness of the
oil boycott, and even fewer foresaw its effects on the price and availability
of fertilizers and the resulting food shortages in many parts of the world.
The process is further complicated by the fact that there is generally a
time lag between an action and the development of secondary effects, and
the side effects of a proposed action are seldom totally anticipated at the
time action is taken. It is not exactly unusual to find that the combined
effects of the secondary developments could even be worse than the

original wrong the action was intended to correct, as discussed elsewhere in this book. Thus it is important to realize the necessity of long-term planning, because during the present era of rapid social, economic, political, technological, and institutional changes, short-term forecasts are likely to be very deceptive and could even be diametrically opposite to the long-term development goals of mankind.

Even though many aspects of the problems considered in this book are interdependent and global in nature, in their magnitude they vary widely from region to region, and even from one part of a country to another. For example, some parts of the world may be more concerned with excessive protein intake and problems of obesity, whereas other parts suffer badly from a lack of protein and the resulting malnutrition and diseases. Thus two of the most important factors to consider in any analysis of global problems are the diversity of circumstances and the vastly differing magnitude of problems to be found around the world. In addition, we must remember that the nation state is, and will continue to be, the central repository of power and has the primary responsibility for the action that must be taken to deal with these complex issues. International cooperation is necessary to establish the global frameworks required, but if the action taken by nations is to be effective, only the exercise of national sovereignty and acceptance of national responsibility can provide the basis for such action. Naturally, the action taken will reflect the nation's relative priorities as well as the complex interaction of each society's own social, economic, cultural, political, institutional, and religious motivations and goals.

All of these major issues form a complex system of cause-and-effect relationships in which the dynamics of our future will be shaped. They increase by many orders of magnitude both the potential for conflict and the need for cooperation. It is in their interaction, not in any one of them, that the future of mankind will be decided. Increase in population and provision of basic human necessities to each individual mean more food, energy, and raw materials; intensifying the supply of food means more land, water, energy, and fertilizers; the energy crisis and higher oil prices mean less energy available to increase food production and to alleviate fertilizer shortages; and the common denominator in virtually all responses to these problems must include more capital, more technology, and more cooperation. It is here that these concerns inevitably merge with the important issues of war and peace and monetary and trade relations. Each affects and is affected by the others. This system of relationships is global in scale. That is not to say that all global problems can be met with global solutions; there are few global solutions. But they can only be understood and dealt with in a global framework, within which there can be a wide variety of national and regional responses.

The major problems we are now facing, including that of food, are urgent and complex, and if appropriate action is not taken immediately, they are bound to proliferate, making conditions even worse. Since these problems are often multidimensional, no nation, however powerful, can cope with them individually and unilaterally. Many problems go far beyond the capacity of even small groups of the more powerful nations to solve. Action taken to combat these types of problems must be well planned and coordinated, otherwise, steps taken to alleviate the problems in one part of the globe could create negative reverberations in another. The so-called "food crisis," "energy crisis," and "raw materials crisis" dramatize the finiteness of our earth, a sober reality that should be accommodated within the context of social, economic, political, and institutional frameworks.

Faced with these serious problems, a series of major world gatherings has been held under the auspices of the United Nations, which have attempted to develop workable "Action Plans" for the resolution of the problems. Among these are the Conference on the Human Environment at Stockholm (1972), Special Session of the General Assembly on Raw Materials and Development (1974), Law of the Sea Conference at Caracas (1974), World Population Conference at Bucharest (1974), World Food Conference in Rome (1974), the Special Session of the General Assembly on Development and International Cooperation (1975), Conference on Human Settlements at Vancouver (1976), World Water Conference at Mar del Plata (1977), World Desertification Conference Nairobi (1977), and Conference on Technical Cooperation Between Developing Countries at Buenos Aires (1978). All of these conferences deal with particular aspects of the complex issues affecting man and his quality of life on this earth.

The idea of this book originated when both of us were at the World Food Conference in Rome, with Dr. Mostafa Kamal Tolba, Executive Director of the United Nations Environment Programme for that organization. We developed the framework and invited leading international authorities to write specific chapters. The need for such a multidisciplinary book was immediately obvious, since all the contributors we approached, very busy as they were, readily agreed to prepare the chapters—a most unusual phenomenon under the best of circumstances. Furthermore, Dr. Tolba, despite his many commitments, both as the Executive Director of UNEP and the Secretary–General of the UN Conference on Desertification, consented to write an introduction for the book. We are very grateful for this and for his constant support and encouragement throughout the preparation of the book.

Ottawa, Ontario, Canada   MARGARET R. BISWAS
July 1978   ASIT K. BISWAS

CONTENTS

FOOD, CLIMATE,
AND MAN

1

FOOD, CLIMATE, AND MAN

F. Kenneth Hare, Director
Institute for Environmental Studies
University of Toronto

It was in 1972 that we began to suspect that something was going wrong with world climate. There were reports of heavy ice in Canadian arctic waters, and along the Greenland coast. The summer was remarkably cool and wet over much of North America. Reports kept coming in of a failure of winter snow-cover in the winter wheat lands of the Soviet Union; and as the summer went through there were stories of drought in the same areas. In Ontario, Canada, all our tobacco crop was lost through a severe killing frost in mid-June, unprecedented even in Ontario's erratic climate. The southwest monsoon failed to produce the needed rains over much of peninsular India. And we began to comprehend the full scale of the Sahelian tragedy then entering its bitter climax.

It was a year that exposed illusions, and gave birth to new policies and new strategies of research. In point of cold fact there was nothing revolutionary about 1972's climatic anomalies. All of them resembled things that had happened before. What was extraordinary was the list of places they happened to hit, and the chaos they were to cause in the world food system. There were crop failures in both exporting and importing countries, in advanced as well as in subsistence economies. The overall impact was a less than 1% fall in world cereal production, after many consecutive years of steady advance. So precariously balanced, however, is the world grain trade that a 1% loss of supply instead of a 3% gain (which rising demand requires) threw markets into disarray throughout 1973, and began a price inflation that has only recently subsided. New policies and new strategies of research have indeed followed—but have not established a new stability.

Orthodoxies need to be challenged by events, and both economic and meteorological orthodoxies in the early 1970s were ripe for such a chal-

1

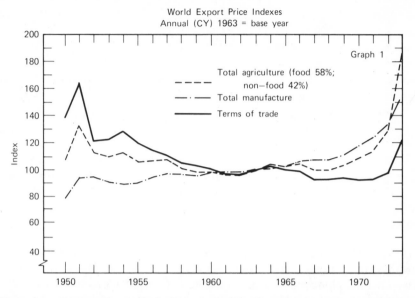

Figure 1-1.   Progress since 1950 of total agricultural and manufacturing prices and the terms of trade (i.e., the ratio of one to the other). The curves show that price changes were restricted following the Korean war, but that a slow change against the farmer began about 1964. The abrupt rise of agricultural prices following the climate-induced crop failures of 1972 restored the farmer to a better situation—which has begun to deteriorate again since 1976 (Harris, 1974).

lenge. In 1971, all three of the major grain exporting nations—Canada, the United States, and Australia—were committed to a restriction of cereal acreage. Stores of most grains were embarrassingly high, and prices correspondingly low. The terms of trade (Figure 1-1) had lain against the farmer for over a decade (Harris, 1974). The orthodox view was that supply had outrun demand because of the rising productivity of world agriculture, notably of the cereal crops. There had been a brief period of anxiety in the mid-1960s, when there were fears of famine. But in 1971 the talk instead was of the success of the miracle grains and Green Revolution technology. It was held by many economists that production would continue to outstrip rising demand. Western countries, at least, thus entered the decade in a mood of pessimism about their ability to sell their farm surpluses, and to maintain farm incomes. For a year or more after the dramatic transformation of 1972–73 was established history this pessimism continued. Even in 1976, many farmers were reluctant to sow and harvest wheat, because they were afraid that the surpluses will return as, indeed they have in 1977.

Nor can the meteorologist be happy about his performances. The bad weather of 1972, and that which has followed, was not forecast, since meteorology has no skill on the time scales that matter for farm strategy. Indeed climate was not a concept that had much appeal to the leading meteorologists, with only a few notable exceptions. The profession had its eyes still set on extended range forecasting, and on understanding the general circulation of the atmosphere. The Global Atmospheric Research Program—GARP—was conceived in the 1960s along these lines. The ability to comprehend and conceivably predict climate was added much later, barely ahead of the spectacular events of the 1970s. Indeed it was the orthodox view that world climate was at root a stable system that possessed enough degrees of freedom to exhibit regularly some large departures from average. There was no need, on this view, to consider the possibility of climatic change. This was a subject best left to geologists, geophysicists, and biologists, for it was not likely to be of importance to modern man.

This book is written by a group of research workers who were among the first to recognize that a new stance was needed, and that the situation demanded an approach towards world food supply that differed strikingly from these orthodoxies. Each author gives his own perspective from the viewpoint of his own specialization. We raise some questions in this chapter. Not all of these will be answered, and it will still be easy to raise others.

First we must ask: is the climate really changing? Or are the events of the past 5 years merely random expressions of the capacity of the *existing* climate to generate great extremes? Obviously our economic strategies depend on a good answer to this question. Unfortunately a good answer is hard to come by.

The conservative view, widely held by dynamic meteorologists and by some climatologists, is that nothing new has happened. All the disturbing extremes of rainfall and temperature since 1971 can, on this view, be accommodated within the statistics of the existing climate. Even the Sahelian drought can be so treated. One of the present writers, Landsberg, analysed the long rainfall record at Dakar, and concluded that

> The drought of the 1970's was not unprecedented. It has to be accepted as part of the normal climate of the region. Locally it may have been a rare event that should be expected only once in a century . . . . There is no indication of a climatic change and the fact that the Sahel had, in part, abnormally high rainfall in 1974 attests to the fact that nature in her own peculiar ways initiated the alternative weather régime of the region (Landsberg, 1975).

A very similar conclusion was reached by Bunting, Dennett, Elston, and Milford (1976) in an analysis of five rainfall records from the central

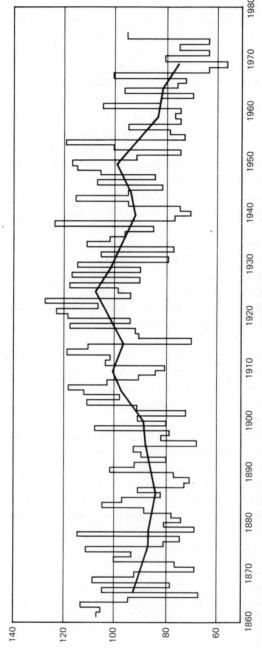

Figure 1-2. The number of days with generally westerly winds prevailing over the whole of the British Isles each year from 1861 to 1974 and 10-year averages plotted at 5-year intervals. This tabulation by Lamb shows that there were slow changes in atmospheric circulation in parallel with temperature changes over the northern hemisphere, accompanied by large interannual variability (Lamb, 1976).

4

Sahelian belt. They could detect no established trends or periodicities, and found that the recent succession of drought years fell within statistical expectation. Similar results have been reported by Davy (1974).

These opinions about the Sahelian drought stand in contrast to the results of Winstanley (1973, 1974) who saw in the statistics a long-term trend towards aridity in parts of the desert-margin countries that might culminate in the next century. Moreover he brought forward certain dynamical hypotheses as to cause, suggesting a relationship between the trend towards drought and the strength of the circumpolar westerly circulation in midlatitudes—a relationship tested and rejected by Bunting *et al.* (*op. cit. sup.*). Another meteorologist, R. A. Bryson (1974), went significantly further. He argued that the Sahelian effect was the result of a southward shift of the subtropical high-pressure belt, and that this shift was induced by two activities of industrialized man—carbon dioxide increase and a rising dust burden in the atmosphere, both leading to an altered radiative balance, and hence to the change in the general circulation.

The same sort of division of opinion exists as to events in midlatitudes. Lamb (1976), for example, has argued that systematic long-term variations have occurred in the northern circumpolar westerlies (Figure 1-2) more or less in phase with the widely-publicized variation in the hemisphere's surface air temperature. Lamb's parameter is the frequency of westerly-type circulation over the British Isles. He shows that this frequency has sharply declined since the mid-1920s and especially since 1950. A high interannual variability fails to obscure this trend, which has accompanied the widely reported decline of air temperature that began about 1940. Several authorities argue that highest variability in weather tends to occur in times of declining and low mean temperature. On this view the extreme weather of the past few years is the effect of the decline in temperature.

The importance of such a hypothesis for crop production is obvious. A decline of 0.5° C in mean daily temperature during the growing season, as has been reported in some northern areas, represents the loss of several days of the growing season (as much as 9–10 since 1940 in the English lowlands), a serious matter where this represents such a significant part of the total. Combined with a higher variability, this implies more frequent weather-induced crop losses in northern countries, affecting most notably wheat. Two recent bad harvests in the Canadian spring wheat belt (Figure 1-3, after McKay, 1976), together with renewed drought in the winter wheat belt of the U.S. in 1975–76, have revived discussion of this issue in North America. The lamentable performance of the U.S.S.R. crops in 1972, 1974, and 1975 are still more noteworthy and disturbing.

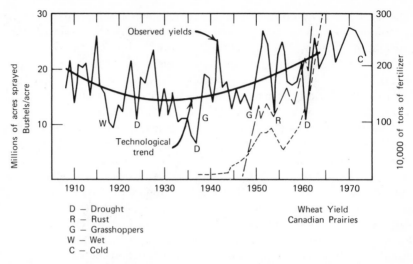

Figure 1-3. Variations in spring wheat yield over a 70-year period from the Canadian prairies. Causes of the large interannual variation are indicated, as is the rate of pesticide spraying and fertilizer application. Much of the variation about the technological trendline is climate-related. (McKay, 1976).

Bryson (1974) brings these effects home most vividly in relation to the Icelandic climate, which is uniquely well documented back far into medieval times. He assumes that growth of hay, the staple crop, has a yield proportional to accumulated temperatures above 5° C. He points out that a drop in mean temperature (growing season) of 1° C would decrease the growing season by 2 weeks, but the accumulated temperatures by 27%. A reduction of 2.4° C would decrease the season by 40 days (a quarter of the whole), and the accumulated temperatures by 54%. Iceland is indeed subject to large, prolonged fluctuations of this order, and in the past has suffered frequent famines. In the 204 years between A.D. 1600 and 1804 there were no less than 34 famine years—the little ice age. In the early decades of this century conditions were much more favorable, but the downturn since 1940—very marked round the North Atlantic—has caused a sharp deterioration only partly offset by increased nitrogeneous fertilizer applications.

But Lamb's hypothesis, and others like it, are frequently challenged. We do not have global statistics to confirm the long-term variability of the westerlies, nor do we have general circulation models that substantiate his correlation of these variations with temperature changes. Even the reality of such changes—or at least their homogeneity—is being questioned. Detailed analysis of the recent past by Van Loon and Williams (1975) has shown that there are large, persistent regional anomalies of differing sign that are unmistakably linked to advection; that is, to persistent abnormalities of wind over the regions concerned. In detail these connect with the long waves of the westerlies, notably with their phase and amplitude. It follows that one crop-growing region may suffer while another gains, and that sharp longitudinal differences of climatic anomaly may be more significant than the latitudinal shifts stressed by Lamb and Bryson.

This litany of conflicting views can be continued to the point of tedium, but no more detail is needed. The plain fact is that meteorologists have come to this problem too late, and with too little general commitment, to have got the right answers, and to have achieved agreement. Still less can they claim yet to have enough predictive capacity to influence future crop production. But the situation is now much better. Spurred on—goaded, in fact—by the pioneers like Lamb and Bryson, the dynamicists and numerical modellers are now fully aware of the need to concentrate on the climatic scale of atmospheric change. The recent U.S. National Academy of Sciences publication *Understanding Climatic Change* (N.A.S., 1975) and the G.A.R.P. document *The Physical Basis of Climate and Climate Modelling* (W.M.O., 1975) show that the lesson has gone home.

We will not presume to say whether as much can be claimed for the state of economic forecasting. It is clear from the literature that the major national and intergovernmental agencies concerned with the grain trade were taken by surprise by the events of 1972–73, and were very slow to adapt to them. A consultation between climatologists and agricultural economists held in 1974, under the auspices of the Rockefeller Foundation, made it clear that something had to be done to bring the two specializations closer together.

Another gap that has been partly bridged in the past few years is that which separates meteorologists from crop production specialists and plant breeders. In principle such a gap is inexplicable. There is, for example, a Commission for Agricultural Meteorology, of the World Meteorological Organization. The very recital of titles indicates that the problem is recognized and is being tackled. Yet the gap remains a reality. To quote a well-known crop specialist, Herbert W. Johnson (1976), at another Rockefeller Foundation conference:

> . . . I am supposed to share with you research information on the effect that changes of climate have on crop production, and I should admit at the outset that there is little such information to share. The crop scientist is much more limited geographically than is climate. A change in climate in one part of the world may be accompanied by a similar or opposite change in another, but the crop scientist usually is concerned with the effects in his small geographic area.

One suspects that Johnson's opinion reflects a relatively recent development. The 1950s and 1960s were favourable for crop production in many regions, notably the U.S. midwest. Work by McQuigg, Thompson, LeDuc, Lockard, and McKay (1973) and Thompson (1975) has shown that the high performance of the corn crop in those decades owed a great deal to favourable weather (for extensive discussion of this point, see Biswas, 1978). In earlier decades much genetic research went into the development of frost, drought, or pest-resistant strains of many crops, to push cereal cultivation out to the climatic limits. The fast-maturing spring wheats of the Canadian Prairies and the U.S.S.R. steppes are cultivars of this period. But in recent decades, when world climate has been better-behaved than it was, for example, in the 1930s, attention has shifted towards better-yielding varieties within the climatic limits. And Green Revolution research into "miracle grains" tacitly assumed, until quite recently, optimum water availability and fertilizer supply. Certainly the major objective was not an attempt to increase the climatic range of the cereals concerned.

What is needed in this area is a capacity for strategic, long-term decision making, rather than further emphasis on fine-tuning of crop varieties and farm practice to existing and future climates. It has become apparent that a major part of the world food problem arises from the vast areas of dry-land farming that can never be irrigated, and over which the episodes of drought to which the drier kinds of climate are prone must sweep with ever-increasing effects, as population and livestock densities increase. Hence a large part of the internationally-sponsored research effort will be devoted in the future to these poorer economies.

In fact, we have had to realise that world food problem is something far beyond the international grain trade whose statistics dominate most discussions. Grain moves primarily from wealthy producing countries to wealthy or powerful consuming countries. As an example, Table 1-1 shows the destinations of Canadian wheat and barley exports in 1974–75. The great bulk of the cereal and protein requirements of the world are locally produced, and do not enter into international trade (omitting movement within trading blocs like the E.E.C.).

Hence, it becomes important to focus attention on those parts of the world where climatic stresses are frequent and acute, and where imports of food on a large scale are not economically feasible. In practice this means the drier parts of the earth—not merely the arid zone so long studied by UNESCO, but semiarid and subhumid zones as well to the extent that they support dense populations largely dependent on locally produced food. A solution to the world grain deficiency will not help these areas if it is coupled with prices far beyond their capacity to pay.

Table 1-1. Canadian Wheat and Barley Exports to Major Markets—in Millions of Bushels—1974–75.

Countries	Wheat	Barley
China	82.4	–
U.K.	57.7	1.6
Japan	43.8	39.8
Brazil	32.6	–
Cuba	26.0	0.5
Italy	24.2	30.2
Algeria	20.8	1.5
India	13.5	–
U.S.S.R.	12.9	–
Bangladesh	12.2	–
Iraq	7.6	–
Lebanon	6.1	–
Philippines	5.9	–
Netherlands	5.7	1.1
West Germany	3.4	1.8
Peru	3.4	0.9
Pakistan	3.1	–
Poland	2.2	16.2
Morocco	2.1	0.1
U.S.A.	0.3	17.7
Iran	<0.1	9.2
Israel	<0.1	8.2

Unfortunately the recent phase of climatic extremes has affected many of these areas, most notably the Sahelian republics of Africa, together with Ethiopia, Somalia, and Democratic Republic of Yemen. Intense drought fell upon most of these countries between 1968 and 1973 (inclusive). Widespread desertification ensued—the loss of vegetation and topsoil resulting from overstocking and unwise cultivation under deficient rainfall (see Chapter 6). North and east Africa has in fact endured a dust bowl similar in many ways to the events of the 1930s in North America—with nothing like the resources to repair the damage that can be marshalled in Canada and the U.S.

These tragic events still more sharply define the need for climatic forecasting, or at least for a realistic estimate of climatic probabilities. Rising populations, rising numbers of domestic animals, and rising areas of dry-land farming have all combined to create high risks whenever climatic extremes arrive—as they habitually do in the drier climates, and as they have done with special frequency since 1972.

It becomes of prime importance, therefore, to arrive at better ways of incorporating climatic knowledge into decision making. This may take a variety of forms. At one end of the economic scale it is a matter of the individual dry-belt farmer learning that during a succession of favorable years he must avoid overstocking his land beyond carrying capacity, or ploughing soils that will blow away if the rains fail. It may be impossible for him to do this even if education convinces him that it is right. And at the other end of the scale it is a matter for great institutions to take better account of climatic variation in their choice of strategies. For the meteorologist, above all, it is a matter of a dogged search for that elusive entity—predictability.

References

Biswas, A. K. (1978). Climatic fluctuations and Water Resources and Agricultural Planning. Report to Land and Water Development Division, Food and Agricultural Organization. Rome, 145 pp.

Bryson, R. A. (1974). A perspective on climatic change. *Science* **184**, 753–760.

Bunting, A. H., Dennett, M. D., Elston, J., and Milford, J. R. (1976). Rainfall trends in the west African Sahel. *Quart. J. Royal Meteorol. Soc.* **102**, 59–64.

Canadian Wheat Board (1976). *Report to Producers on the 1974–75 Crop Year.* Winnipeg, 18 pp.

Davy, E. G. (1974). Drought in West Africa. *WMO Bull.*, **23**, 18–23.

Harris, S. (1974). Changes in the terms of trade for agriculture: New plateau or new precipice. *Aust. J. Agricult. Econ.* **18**, 85–100.

Johnson, H. W. (1976). The effect of climate change on crops. In *Climate Change, Food Production and Interstate Conflict.* Working Paper, Rockefeller Foundation, New York, 59–68.

Lamb, H. H. (1976). On the frequency and patterns of variation of climate. In *Climate Change, Food Production and Interstate Conflict.* Working Paper, Rockefeller Foundation, New York, 40–58.

Landsberg, H. E. (1975). Sahel drought: Change of climate or part of climate? *Archiv. Meteorol., Geophysik Bioklimat.* **B, 23**, 193–200.

McKay, G. A. (1976). Future climate and decision making. In *Atmospheric Quality and Climatic Change,* Kopec, R. J. (ed.), Studies in Geography, University of North Carolina at Chapel Hill, Dept. of Geography, 90–105.

McQuigg, J. D., Thompson, L., Le Duc, S., Lockard, M., and McKay, G. (1973). *The Influence of Weather and Climate on United States Grain Yields: Bumper Crops or Droughts.* National Oceanic and Atmospheric Administration, U.S. Dept. of Commerce, Washington, D.C., 30 pp.

National Academy of Sciences, U.S.A. (1975). *Understanding Climatic Change: A Program for Action.* Washington, D.C., 239 pp.

Thompson, L. (1975). Weather variability, climatic change and grain production. *Science* **188**, 535–541.

Van Loon, H., and Williams, J. (1975). The connection between trends of mean temperature and circulation and the surface. Part I: Winter. Typescript report, National Center for Atmospheric Research, Boulder, Colorado, 24 pp. plus 21 figs.

Winstanley, D. (1973). Rainfall patterns and general atmospheric circulation. *Nature* **245**, 190–194.

Winstanley, D. (1974). Seasonal rainfall forecasting in West Africa. *Nature* **248**, 464–465.

World Meteorological Organization, Global Atmospheric Research Programme (1975). *The Physical Basis of Climate and Climate Modelling*, Garp Publication Series No. 16, ICSU-WMO, Geneva, 265 pp.

2

NATURAL RESOURCES, DEVELOPMENT STRATEGIES, AND THE WORLD FOOD PROBLEM

David Norse
OECD—Interfutures

The food problem can be primarily considered as an increasing production deficit in certain developing countries over the past 10–25 years and a consequent decrease or inadequate growth in the per capita availability of food. Although the food deficit is confined to the developing countries it is nonetheless a world problem in that the economic, social, and ecological systems of the developed and the developing countries are closely connected.

Extensive food problems are not a new global feature. Throughout history famines have been a common but irregular feature in now developed and in developing countries, as natural crop failures or war reduced food production and/or supply (Russel and Russel, 1968; Mayer, 1975). In general these perturbations disrupted an already inadequate supply, and food shortages were a normal part of everyday existence for many people in Europe and the U.S.S.R. until 1920–1940.

Food production in various countries and communities of Western Europe failed to keep up with population growth during certain periods in the 11th–19th centuries. Much of Western Europe suffered in the major famine of 1315–1317, and in Germany during the 13th and 14th centuries overcropping of marginal soils as a result of population pressure led to crop failures and the eventual abandonment of the land by many pioneer settlements (Russel and Russel, 1968). Thus the present failure of some developing countries to expand food production at the same or at a faster rate than that of population, is similar to that which occurred in some developed countries when they were at an earlier stage of development.

Almost 200 years before Malthus wrote his famous essay, the English philosopher Francis Bacon proposed that generally it is to be ensured that the population of a kingdom does not exceed the stock of the kingdom, which should maintain them (Bacon, 1625). Some 350 years later many nations do not or could not fulfill Bacon's proposition.

In recent years many developed countries have moved away from food self-sufficiency and become major food importers, commonly because overseas suppliers could provide the commodities at less than the local price. Consequently, the self-sufficiency ratios of some developed countries have fallen considerably, and it is impossible for them to maintain current food consumption patterns from their own resources. The United Kingdom could provide a less diverse but nutritionally better diet from its own resources (Mellanby, 1975) without major cost increases, but it is doubtful if countries like Japan and Israel could produce a nutritionally adequate diet for their current population from their own land and water resources, except at extremely high cost.

Most developing countries are not in this position. They still have the land and water resources to be self-sufficient in all the essential foods required to maintain or improve on the existing consumption patterns. However, the fact remains that many people in the developing countries have inadequate diets, and the growing imbalance between food production and population growth has spawned numerous books and essays emphasising the dangers in current development pathways (Paddock and Paddock, 1967; Eckholm, 1976). Many of these studies stress the resource constraints and ignore the institutional problems which commonly constitute a more significant limitation to the expansion of food production (Lipton, 1977). Such studies are correct when they state the obvious fact that we live in a finite environment, but they commonly take the concept of a resource to be a static one, whereas it is dynamic and they emphasise stock limitations when many of the serious problems arise from flow limitations.

The failure of developing countries to buy or grow adequate food has been considered in many studies to be essentially a supply problem, which can be overcome by increasing production (UN, 1974; USDA, 1974; Klatzmann, 1975; Abelson *et al.*, 1975; Wortman *et al.*, 1976). These studies generally conclude that there are no major physical and technological limitations to the expansion of world food production to balance the likely. growth in population over the next 3–4 decades. Aggregate land resources are more than adequate (FAO, 1970; Buringh *et al.*, 1975), and the necessary production inputs could be made available. (PSAC, 1967; FAO, 1970).

That there is a large production potential in the developing countries is generally accepted. However, there are doubts whether the production inputs and the knowledge required for their use could be dispersed over the wide area involved in a short space of time given the urgency of the problem. Shortage of capital, the long training time required to produce staff for conventional agricultural advisory services, the adaptation of technology for local needs, all place a major constraint on rapid and widespread expansion of food supply. Furthermore with the present sociological and political structures and our current limited knowledge of the environment as an integrated ecosystem, it is possible that the numerous technological opportunities which are apparently available will not solve the food problem in the short nor in the long term. The latter conclusion is based on the supposition that (1) many subsistence farmers will not have access to the necessary production inputs, (2) the product may be too expensive for those most in need and/or (3) the ecosystem cannot support the widespread use of intensive agricultural technology. The environment's ability to receive manmade inputs is finite and this limit may be reached before all the technologic possibilities for expanding food production have been utilised.

Factors like (1) and (2) above are highlighted by those who consider the food problem to be one of demand and not of supply. They propose that it is ineffective demand (lack of purchasing power) and/or inequitable distribution which are the basic causes of the food problem (Josling, 1976). These analysts agree that there is a large potential for increasing the food supply but contend that without a redistribution of the means to grow or buy more food, the problem will not be solved. They point out that the overall supply is already adequate to provide a nutritionally balanced diet for all the developing countries population and propose various measures to bring about the redistribution, for example, more food aid, reduction in feedgrain use in the developed countries, improvements in the terms of trade of the developing countries, and land reform within them. The implications of such measures on the various development strategy options will be considered in this chapter.

The view that ineffective demand and not inadequate supply is possibly the major factor underlying the world food problem is supported not only by recent studies from the developing countries, but also historical evidence from the developed countries. Thus during the Irish famine of the late 1840s, when the low-cost staple crop (potatoes) was largely destroyed by a fungal disease, supplies of an alternative, but higher cost staple, wheat, were available. Wheat exports occurred during the famine while millions starved because they could not afford to buy wheat and many migrated overseas. Similarly, malnutrition was widespread in France in the late 19th century. The poor in some areas could not afford to buy grain and consumed a staple made from the fruit of the wild chestnut (Weber, 1977). As recently as the 1930s rickets and other consequences of malnutrition occurred among low income groups in the United Kingdom. In both France and the United Kingdom, adequate supplies of food were available, there was major potential for growing more, but the purchasing power was lacking among the affected groups; thus the situation was close to that currently prevailing in many developing countries.

The preceding discussion indicates that in assessing potential development strategies one must look not only at those which improve the food supply position, but also those which improve the ability of those in need to buy or grow more food. Increased purchasing power is largely dependent on the removal of unemployment and under-employment in rural areas among smallholders and the landless, and in the urban areas, whereas the ability to grow more food is dependent on various infrastructural improvements and institutional changes, such as land reform.

Most governments in developing countries have emphasised industrialization as the route to promoting economic growth and higher employment, and in doing so have neglected or have biased their policies against agricultural (Lipton, 1977). In following such policies they have ignored the fact that most countries need a dynamic agricultural sector, at least in the early stages of industrialization, both to supply surplus food for the urban areas and to provide capital to finance industrial development. The result in human terms has been severe food shortages and widespread undernutrition, while in economic terms it has meant low productivity growth in agriculture, limited flows of capital from agriculture, and growing import dependency for basic foodstuffs. The latter preempts the foreign exchange earned by the cash crop, mining, or industrial sectors and thus reduces purchases of capital goods from overseas, which are essential for the development of social and industrial infrastructure.

It is now widely accepted that even at rates of industrial growth over the next 25 years considerably greater than that of the past, the growth in labour demand will be inadequate to take up both the approximately 250 million currently unemployed or underemployed and the projected additional 750 million who will enter the labour force by the year 2000 (ILO, 1976). The only sectors in many developing countries, with the potential for significant and rapid expansion are the agricultural and agricultural support service sectors such as the agrochemical and secondary processing industries.

Agricultural development strategies therefore must recognize and allow for a range of environmental, infrastructural, and institutional factors, which are not common to all developing countries. What is appropriate for the arid areas of Upper Volta, Chad, and Niger, with limited roads and marketing infrastructure, is not suitable for Indonesia and the Philippines, where these ecological and infrastructural constraints are less important.

Agricultural and social scientists have commonly proposed agricultural development strategies to overcome the food problem which involve one or more of the following pathways:

1. Increasing the total area of cultivated land and the frequency with which it is cropped.
2. Changing the cropping pattern.
3. Increasing output per unit of land and water by the use of fertilizers, improved cultivars, irrigations, and the control of pests and diseases.
4. Reverting from intensive to extensive livestock production systems, thereby releasing feed grains for human consumption.
5. Increasing the production of fresh and saltwater fish, and other marine organisms; and
6. Developing nonconventional food production systems, for example, single cell protein culture or leaf protein extraction.

There are other important potential pathways that are sometimes neglected. Few analysts have suggested expansion or improvements in the livestock sector, even though many millions are wholly or partly dependent on them, and large areas are ecologically unsuitable for crop production, but can be used for livestock. There are also other areas where large positive gains can be achieved, such as reduction in storage and processing losses. These will be considered after examining the current agricultural resource base and the six pathways previously listed

Increasing the Total Area of Cultivated Land and the Frequency with which It Is Cropped

Current Agricultural Resource Base. The total area currently in the cultivation cycle and hence regarded as arable, is about 1473 million ha (FAO, 1975). This represents about 11% of the world's total ice free land of about 13,200 million ha. Approximately 55% of this arable area is in the developing countries. A further 23% of the earth's ice free land surface is grazed, but much of it is used only intermittently and at low livestock densities. The most intensively used pasture is commonly that classified as temporary meadows and fallow, which are used in rotation with arable crops and hence form part of the 1473 million ha of arable land.

Not all the arable land currently in the cultivation cycle is used each year, in order to allow a build-up of fertility or soil moisture. However, most is cropped regularly, particularly in temperate areas and in the humid tropical lowlands. In contrast, well-distributed rainfall or irrigation in certain areas, particularly in some developing countries, permits the use of multiple cropping systems, under which two or three crops are raised each year on the same piece of land (Dalrymple, 1971).

Much of the existing cultivated land is subject to important ecologic constraints on productivity. These constraints also affect the application and effectiveness of technology, the type of crops which can be grown, and the year-to-year variation in output. Thus over large areas of North America, U.S.S.R., China, and South Asia conditions are very arid, and in the absence of irrigation they can only be used for relatively drought tolerant crops such as millet and wheat. The response to fertilizer is limited (USDA, 1968; Gerardi, 1968), there is large annual variation in production, and the probability of crop failure is high (Gerardi, 1968).

The present stock of arable land is not a static resource; it is subject to both qualitative and quantitative changes. In both developed and developing countries the quality of some arable land has been improved over time by good husbandry (Cooke, 1971). Elsewhere mismanagement has resulted and continues to cause the loss of land through soil erosion and salination (Pereira, 1973, and also see Chapter 6), the reduction of soil fertility and damage to soil structure.

The short-term abuse of land has been a common feature in the past. Land in temperate areas was overexploited in advance of appropriate technology and then abandoned, but much of it was eventually taken up again into viable agroecosystems. The damage being caused in some tropical and subtropical areas may be greater than that previously caused in temperate zones, and hence redevelopment of such land may not be possible. However, provided some top soil remains, the limitations may be largely ones of cost and/or labour availability, and hence circumventable, as the Chinese have shown.

Although many countries apparently have large areas of cultivated land, on a per capita basis the area is commonly very low, particularly in some developing countries (Table 2-1). Such estimates can be misleading, because they do not reflect the ecological constraints affecting this land; for example, much of the arable land in Tanzania is subject to uncertain rainfall with drought possibilities greater than 30% (Robinson and Glover, 1954), and not all of it can be cultivated each year. The arable land shortage is given greater prominence when it is expressed in terms of that which can be used each year for staple food production (Table 2-1, column 2) rather than that used for food and nonfood crops and fallow (as in column 1).

Table 2-1. Per Capita Estimates of Currently Cultivated Land in 1974

	Arable Hectares of Land Per Capita	Harvested Hectares of Cereals and Starchy Roots Per Capita	Area Irrigated (%)	Multiple Cropping Index
United States	0.89	0.33	8	102
Japan	0.04	0.03	55	126
Netherlands	0.06	0.03	6	100
India	0.27	0.17	20	120
Bangladesh	0.10	0.12	14	115
South Korea	0.06	0.08	34	140
China	0.15	0.16	60	150
Tanzania	1.00	0.10	0.5	100

Additional Potentially Arable Land. Estimation of the size of these stocks is usually based on three criteria: (1) the duration of suitable weather to allow the completion of at least one crop cycle, (2) topography, and (3) soil type. There are large differences between some of the estimates which range from a pessimistic 2425 million ha (Mesarovic and Pestel, 1975) to 3419 million ha (Buringh *et al.*, 1975) with intermediate values of 3140 million ha (Norse 1976) and 3190 million ha (PSAC, 1967). However, it is clear that at the global level the potential area is large, and is at least double the current one (Table 2-2). Furthermore, many of the differences stem from the estimates of the land available in areas subject to one or more of the following constraints; uncertain potential productivity, high development costs, low population e.g., the Amazon and Congo basins, and the Steppes of Central Asia. These areas are likely to give very low marginal returns and hence may remain largely unused until after A.D. 2000. Consequently strategies for the next 25 years or so, probably will not be sensitive to errors in the estimation of the size of these resources.

The additional area in the developed countries is about 50% greater than that currently in use but its potential productivity is limited to some degree by low temperature and aridity constraints. The additional area available in the developing countries is about 150% greater than their present one, and water rather than temperature is the dominant limiting factor. Perhaps one-quarter of the developing countries' potential land area, particularly that in the wet tropical zone (Table 2-2) is not suitable for staple crop production (except possibly some root crops) given current technology, but can be used for the production of crops giving a much higher value/unit area than the staples, for example, oil palm, rubber, and certain beverage crops.

At the subregional or national level many developing countries are confronted by the lack of potential arable land, particularly in some of those countries with the greatest population pressure, such as India and Bangladesh. The latter can expand their arable area by perhaps 5%, although there are additional areas of formerly cultivated wasteland which probably could also be brought back into use. In some countries land is available but is located away from the main centers of population and there is little natural migration. Indonesia has 10–20 million ha of potentially arable land on certain sparsely populated islands, yet people are reluctant to leave Java and other heavily populated islands which have virtually no undeveloped arable land and where the pressure on land is acute. The largest resources are in Equatorial Africa, particularly Zaire and Brazil, where at the national level population pressure is not acute. In Zaire neither population nor economic pressures are likely to lead to major exploitation of the potential arable land over the next 25 years or more. Similarly, much of Brazil's potential may not be exploited. Official policy in Brazil is to develop about one third of Amazonia by the year 2000, but ecological, technological, human disease, and manpower constraints are restricting development (Jahoda and O'Hearn, 1975) and the target may not be met.

It is apparent that many of the developing countries with currently low land/man ratios have little additional land to develop. Furthermore, even in those countries with apparently large resources, the utilization of the additional land will be limited by (1) agroclimatic and edaphic constraints and (2) development costs.

Potential Productivity of the Additional Arable Land. The wide variation in primary biological productivity across the world can lead to serious distortions in the assessment of the production potential of the additional arable land resources. Two of the key factors determining plant growth and productivity are the duration of suitable temperature and soil moisture levels. The longer the period during which temperature and soil moisture are near the optimum for plant growth, the greater the productivity, the shorter the production cycle and the greater the likelihood of being able to grow more than one crop per year. Therefore, in recent studies on the present and potential productivity of the arable land stocks (Buringh *et al.*, 1975; Norse, 1976), the agroclimatic zone in which they are located has been specified (Table 2-2). Buringh *et al.* and Norse both use the FAO/UNESCO soil maps (UNESCO, 1974) as a starting point in their examination of most regions. The former authors then use a growth model

Table 2-2. Land and Water Resources—in Millions of Hectares

Agroclimatic Zone	Present Arable Area Non-irrigated	Present Arable Area Irrigated	Additional Potential Arable Area	Additional Irrigable Area in Columns 1 and 3	Total Potentially Cultivable Area
Developed Countries					
Wet tropics	1	0	2	0	3
Dry tropics	10	1	7	5	18
Warm humid	43	3	20	4	69
Warm dry	69	17	20	23	103
Cool humid	367	13	240	8	630
Cool dry	106	20	46	58	170
Cold temperate and polar	20	0	30	0	50
Total	616	52	315	98	1,043
Developing Countries					
Wet tropics	76	9	414	80	499
Dry tropics	373	40	733	105	1,146
Warm humid	28	26	58	6	112
Warm dry	94	44	90	9	228
Cool humid	26	32	12	20	70
Cool dry	20	11	10	4	41
Total	617	162	1,317	224	2,096
Grand total	1,233	214	1,632	322	3,139

to estimate potential productivity, whereas Norse fits a productivity curve to farm and case-study data from each agroclimatic zone.

Both these studies conclude that the crop production potential of much of the additional land is high if development costs and institutional constraints are ignored. Buringh *et al.* estimated that in some regions maximum dry matter production could reach 84 tonnes/ha/yr, and that if 70% of the additional land was used for cereals, total world production could increase to about thirty times current production. The other study (Norse, 1976) is less optimistic but nonetheless estimates maximum production in irrigated areas of the dry tropics to be equivalent to about 10 tonnes grain equivalent/ha/yr when multiple-cropping is taken into account.

In some areas of the developing countries low temperature will limit productivity; for example, in northern China and Korea, but in most areas the major constraint will be aridity. Globally some 300 million ha of land with suitable soils cannot be utilized because of the lack of water (Buringh *et al.*, 1975). Such land exists in areas such as Rajasthan State, India, where the population pressure on the existing cultivated land is very acute. Aridity constraints in the developing countries may severely limit the development of some 45 and 200 million ha of land with suitable soils in the warm dry and tropical dry zones, respectively. In the dry tropics it is estimated that nearly 700 million ha of the potential 1150 million ha of arable land require supplementary irrigation for maximum productivity, but only about 105 million ha could be served by water resources within a likely economic distance. Furthermore, the above estimates make no allowance for the water requirements for urban and industrial development, which may require 20% or more of the total supply. In some areas, desalination could overcome this problem, but the costs are likely to be too high except for specialized high value crops.

Many analysts believe that the potential is less than that suggested by broad agroclimatic and soil characteristics. They refer to (1) the current low fertility of some soils in the developing countries, (2) the problems of cultivating lateritic soils, (3) the shallowness of the soils in certain areas, and (4) question the suitability of rainforest areas in Amazonia and the Congo basin for agriculture.

The largest stocks of potentially arable land are in the tropical forest and savannah regions of the wet tropics and dry tropics, respectively (Table 2-2). Commonly, the soils in these areas are of low fertility at the present time as suggested by (1), but this need not persist. The soils of large parts of Western Europe and Japan were similarly infertile until man introduced soundly based agroecosystems and improved the fertility (Cooke, 1971).

It is frequently but incorrectly suggested that the organic content of the soils of much of the potential arable land is substantially less than that of the soils in developed countries. In areas where the mean annual rainfall, temperature, and periodicity is similar to that of the developed countries, the organic contents are comparable. Although high temperatures favor the rapid breakdown of organic matter in many developing countries, over large areas the extensive dry season reduces or stops biological activity for three or more months each year, and thus aridity fulfills a similar function to low winter temperatures in the temperate regions. The organic matter of tropical rainforest areas have equilibrium organic matter contents similar to heavily leached forest soils in the developed countries, such as the soils in parts of Michigan, Florida, and Western Europe which can only be used for forest crops. However, in some areas; for example, South Eastern U.S.A., such soils have been developed for very productive cropping systems (Sanchez and Buol, 1975). Outside the main humid rainforest area the soils are also commonly highly leached and although they have low nutrient contents they have good physical qualities. Once the fertility has been built up, as in south eastern China, they are very productive and can support large populations.

Soil type limitations such as (2) and (3) above are not as widespread as formerly thought to be the case. The areas of the tropics with soils which are likely to form laterites on exposure (i.e., the Plinthites) possibly occupy 7% of the total potential arable area (Sanchez and Buol, 1975). The main problem occurs if the topsoil is removed by erosion. Similarly the shallow soils only occupy about 18% of the tropical land mass. They are commonly further constrained by aridity or topography, and thus represent considerably less than 18% of the potential arable area; the useable area is possibly only 5% of the total.

Although in the drier areas conventional farming systems may be used, in the wetter areas such is not the case, as suggested in (4) above. In the high rainfall areas of the tropics, particularly in parts of Africa, East Asia, and Brazil, the expansion of food production cannot be accomplished using the package of improved seed and fertilizer which is appropriate for South Asia and other parts of the dry tropics.

Shifting cultivation is efficient given the prevailing constraints when adequate fallow periods are left between cropping cycles, but it is not when population pressures reduce the fallow period. Agroecosystems have to be developed which can replace shifting cultivation and at the same time provide an adequate income and food to the farmer. Rehm (1973) and Greenland (1975) have discussed some of the requirements and possibilities for such agroecosystems. Currently these possibilities are seldom considered in the development of marginal land. The ecologically fragile areas are commonly colonized by people having no legal rights to the land, and hence they consciously overexploit it before moving on (the commons paradox, Hardin 1968). Alternatively they are developed by people from urban or semiurban areas; for example, N.E. Brazil, who have little or no agricultural knowledge and therefore use unsuitable management techniques. However, in both instances the damage is largely avoidable given the removal of institutional constraints and the introduction of infrastructural improvements.

Cost of Developing the Additional Arable Land. Most of the easily developable land is under cultivation, except in parts of South America and Africa south of the Sahara, where man and his grazing animals have already removed much of the tree cover. By analysing a wide range of agricultural development projects assessed and/or financed by the World Bank, the Asian Development Bank, the Commonwealth Development Corporation, etc., it has been possible to make some general estimates of the likely development costs. For each project a thorough breakdown of land clearance and construction costs are given, together with information concerning the agroclimatic and soil conditions. From these one can determine the likely range of development costs for different types of land development.

The costs are generally very high. In 1977 prices, land clearance costs vary from about U.S. $300/ha for shrub savannah without drainage problems to over U.S. $10,000/ha in rainforest areas requiring drainage. A large proportion of the additional land is in the upper part of this range. Economies of scale are possible in some situations, but are unlikely to be a major ameliorating factor.

High development costs will be a severe limitation to the exploitation of much of the potentially arable land listed in Table 2-2, particularly in the sparsely populated areas where in addition to the agricultural development costs there are those for social infrastructure (such as schools and hospitals), roads and markets. Although labour intensive methods can reduce costs (particularly the foreign exchange component), much of the development is likely to be of the conventional capital intensive type.

Water Resources. Although irrigation appears under pathway (3) in the list on page 6 as a component of the intensive agriculture package, the size, location, and possible development costs of the water resources are examined under pathway (2) because they complement land resource considerations. Globally the resources are sufficient to at least double the current irrigated area (Table 2-2, see also Chapter 3). These estimates are largely derived from FAO data (Tsutsui, 1974) and recent national studies.

They indicate that the developed countries, with the exception of the U.S.S.R., have few possibilities for expanding their irrigated area. Certain important grain producing areas with aridity constraints are hundreds of kilometres from additional water resources; for example, the midwestern states of the U.S.A. and the eastern steppes of the U.S.S.R. Overcoming this aridity commonly involves long-range interbasin transfer of water which is often very costly (Howe and Easter, 1971; Precoda, 1975; Biswas and Golubev, 1978), with the possibility of high transmission losses.

In contrast, the potential for increased irrigation in the developing countries is great (Table 2-2) even in those with acute land pressure, for example, India and Bangladesh. Furthermore, groundwater resources have not been estimated in many countries and hence the potential resources may be larger than those indicated.

However, the most important potential lies in the existing irrigation systems. The developing countries have a gross irrigation command area of about 162 million ha, but almost half of it requires rehabilitation or improvement (UN, 1974), and much of the available flow is underutilized (Carruthers, 1976). As a result of the above, many irrigation schemes are operating at less than 50% efficiency, and in the Philippines, for example, it has been observed that the quartile of the command area most distant from the source may receive no irrigation in the dry season with a consequent 75% reduction in cropped area, and 80% reduction in yield when compared with those in the quartile nearest the source (Herdt and Wickham, 1974). The central problem is usually on farm development, that is, land shaping, field channels, and drainage, but in some cases the distribution canals do not serve all the potential command area. Inadequacies of this type not only result in a lack of resource use (Carruthers, 1974) but also cause deterioration of the land through waterlogging, salinity, alkalinity, etc. Rehabilitation or improvement measures generally have short lead times, low overall costs, and of particular importance, low foreign exchange costs. Thus at a relatively small cost and within a short period, the developing countries could increase their effective irrigated area by some 50–80 million ha (and their cropped area by a greater amount if multiple-cropping is practised) compared to the 4–5 million ha of new irrigation produced each year.

Cost of Irrigation Development. The costs of different forms of irrigation development were determined in the same manner as those for land development, namely by analysing projects funded by the World Bank and other agencies. Most of the smaller and/or easier irrigation schemes based on river capture have been completed, although some simple but very expensive schemes have been avoided because of the large capital requirements. The exploitation of ground water is commonly less expensive than that of surface water but the resources are not well known.

Although some forms of irrigation are less expensive than others; that is, tubewells or lowlift pump schemes are generally cheaper than gravity diversion schemes, there are few opportunities for low cost schemes. Current costs range from about U.S. $1,500 per ha for simple sprinkler irrigation schemes under good soil and topographic conditions to well over U.S. $10,000 per ha for interbasin transport schemes.

Given the hypothesis that the simplest irrigation projects are completed first, a time series examination of irrigation development costs should indicate increasing costs/ha with time as greater physical constraints are met and overcome. Regression analysis has been applied to observed changes in costs over time, using the actual costs/ha for completed projects and estimated costs based on engineering surveys for those in construction or at the project appraisal stage. Although there are obvious dangers in using estimated costs, post implementation surveys indicate that development costs are generally under rather than over estimated (IBRD, 1969), and therefore the analysis presented in Figure 2-1 for costs in developing countries is likely to error on the side of optimism. Figure 2-1 suggests that at constant 1968 prices, the unit costs of irrigation development are rising linearly at approximately $27/year. Extrapolation of such relationships too far into the future is not valid, but the irrigation development costs for 1976 implied by Figure 2-1 are close to the average estimated by the World Bank for that year (Biswas, 1978).

Partial compensation for these high costs via economies of scale seem limited. When net irrigable area was plotted against total capital cost for over 90 irrigation schemes varying in size from less than 1000 ha to over 1 million ha and in cost from about $500,000 (U.S.) to over $1 billion, no consistent economic return to scale was apparent (Figure 2-2). These are economies of scale from such factors as pump size, but these are generally dwarfed by other costs.

In contrast to the high cost of new irrigation, which is generally more than $2500/ha, rehabilitation costs are frequently in the range $200–300, and hence in many cases are of an order-of-magnitude less than new irrigation. Improvement costs may be considerably higher; although still less than new irrigation, with land levelling costs in the range $250–300/ha and main drainage and canal lining both costing more than $200/ha.

Not only will new irrigation be very expensive to construct, it will be increasingly more expensive to operate where pumping is required because of rising energy costs. These rising operating costs may be partially circumvented in the future by the development of wind and solar powered

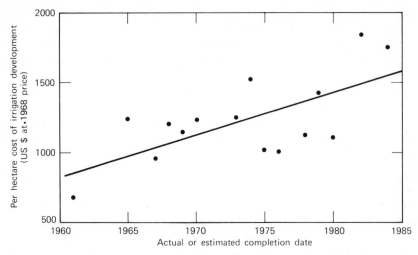

Figure 2-1. Increase with time in the cost of irrigation development.

pumps, which would seem ideally suited to the environmental conditions prevailing in the most arid areas, but major technological developments are required. Operating (and energy) costs may be reduced by applying less water more efficiently by such methods as drip irrigation, but these could lead to land loss through salinization.

Increases in the Frequency of Cropping. Farmers in those parts of the tropics or subtropics with well distributed rainfall or with irrigation available for much of the year are able to grow two or three successive crops each year, without deleterious effects on soil fertility. In contrast, soil fertility or aridity constraints in many developing countries prevent frequent cropping. The soil moisture in the arid areas has to be increased and conserved during 1 year in order to grow a crop in the following one, although certain technological improvements, particularly the development of minimal or zero cultivation techniques, are now making annual cropping possible in some of these areas.

Elsewhere in the tropics where shifting cultivation is practised, a fallow period is currently essential to maintain soil fertility. On the poorest soils the fallow period may be 20 years, although 8–12 years is more normal. When population pressure causes a reduction in the length of the fallow period, soil erosion is almost an inevitable result, but as discussed by Greenland (1975), there is significant potential for modifying the tra-

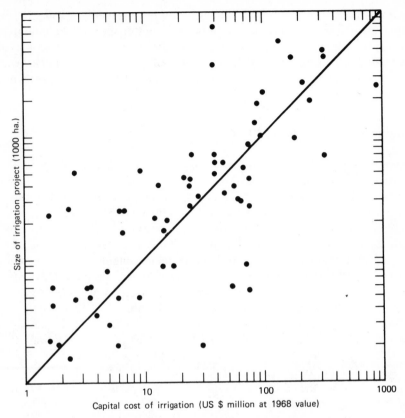

Figure 2-2. **Relationship between the size and cost of irrigation development.**

ditional shifting cultivation techniques and evolving sustainable new agroecosystems which eliminate or reduce the fallow period.

The expansion of multiple cropping is primarily dependent on the improvement of the existing irrigation systems and the construction of new irrigation; the development of short season cultivars is a secondary but very important factor. The potential for increasing gross cropped area and hence production in this way is very large. Revelle (1976) has estimated that the potential gross cropped area in Asia is about 1100 million ha implying a potential multiple cropping index of about 220 (see Table 2-1 for typical current values) and a potential 90% increase in cropped area without any additional land development.

Since additional irrigation will commonly be very expensive to construct, and capital or foreign exchange may not be readily available, the actual growth in gross cropped area is likely to fall short of the potential. However, constraints on the development of new irrigation could be partially compensated for by the development of multiple cropping techniques and the rehabilitation and improvement of the existing irrigation systems.

Changing the Cropping Pattern

Changing the cropping pattern by substituting high yielding grain or root crops for cash crops or food crops with low potential yields could undoubtedly increase the available food energy supply even though nonfood cash crops occupy only about 7% of the arable land. However cash crops and low yield, high unit value food crops are commonly more profitable than staple food crops, and while this is the case it seems reasonable to assume that there is unlikely to be any major change in the cropping pattern. Furthermore, the land used for certain cash crops; for example, cocoa, rubber, etc. cannot be used for annual food crops without greatly endangering the long-term productivity of the soil.

Some changes have occurred, particularly in India and Pakistan since the introduction of high-yielding varieties (HYV) of wheat. Initially that is, in the late 1960s and early 1970s, the HYV wheats were replacing pulses and millet on a significant scale, which was very deleterious because pulses are the most important low cost protein food, and wheat is much more·expensive than millet and hence the poor could not afford to buy as much grain. More recently in India, wheat has been displacing cotton and oilseeds, at least in relative terms, and the government has now embarked on a programme of incentives to encourage the production of these crops which are in short supply.

Increasing Output per Unit of Land and Water by the use of Fertilizers and Improved Cultivars, and the Control of Pests and Diseases

In recent years the primary mechanism for increasing output per hectare of arable land has been through the introduction of high-yielding varieties and the use of fertilizer, particularly in irrigated areas. This approach has been the major policy measure in the agricultural development strategies of most developing countries, and is commonly referred to as the Green Revolution. It is a convenient but misleading term. The technology is neither new nor revolutionary. The change was not unprecedented, it had been applied to rice in Taiwan, and South Korea in the 1920s and 1930s (Cho, 1970) and to hybrid oil palm in the early 1940s. The technical development involves the application of relatively standard plant breeding techniques to produce fertilizer responsive wheat, rice and to a lesser degree maize varieties for the tropics. The only revolutionary aspect was the extensive organisational effort which went into the production and dissemination of the seed of the new varieties.

The fundamental technological innovation underlying the Green Revolution package is a breakthrough in plant breeding techniques which occurred in 1908, but which was not widely applied in the U.S.A. until the late 1930s and 1940s (Griliches, 1957; Batelle, 1973). Maize yields in the U.S.A. were virtually static from 1870 to 1940 at levels at or below those currently prevailing in some developing countries, thus the technological gap between the developed and the developing countries is not as great as that commonly stated.

Technological changes of the improved seed-fertilizer type, are evolutionary, a fact largely ignored by those who proclaim the demise or deficiencies of the Green Revolution. Technological developments whether they are applied in developed or developing countries, are frequently most suited to a specific set of farm conditions and have to be adapted to suit different agronomic conditions before they can be widely used. Thus the full benefits are not received for a number of years.

This is exemplified by the historical pattern of agricultural development in Taiwan and Korea. The foundation for the successful post-1945 development of agriculture in these two countries was largely built during the 1920–1940 Japanese colonial rule. Certain HYV of rice were introduced from Japan, which were then adapted to local conditions and farmers progressively made the appropriate changes in their husbandry techniques. Similarly the rapid gains in rubber and oil palm productivity in Malaysia in recent years is in large measure the result of research and development programmes initiated in specialised institutes many years before.

There is extensive evidence to suggest that the potential for utilising existing technology is very large, and there is no reason to conclude that recent findings at laboratory level cannot be extended and developed for use in the field (OECD, 1976; Jennings, 1976; Rogers, 1976). Nonetheless there are significant gaps in our knowledge, particularly concerning certain technological developments which are required in the LDCs, for example, disease control in livestock, and solar pumps, all of which will have a long lead time.

Although the improved seed-fertilizer package has resulted in significant increases in food production in some areas, it has had little impact in others. In many developing countries the majority of farmers use little or no fertilizer and hence national average application rates are very low, particularly to staple food crops which generally receive 20 kg/ha or less (compared with 100–200 kg/ha in most developed countries). Commonly 50% or more of the fertilizer in developing countries is applied to rubber, tea and other nonfood cash crops (FAO, 1969). Only about 10% of the fertilizer is used for basic food crops in Latin America (Vega, 1971).

Various hypotheses have been proposed to account for the low use of fertilizers. Some analysts have suggested that there are no halfways in the use of the Green Revolution package (Brown, 1970), that is, farmers must use fertilizer in conjunction with improved cultivars and irrigation to benefit. These analysts propose that since the latter two factors are commonly not available to many farmers in the developing countries, fertilizers are not used.

However, such is not the case. The response to fertilizer under rainfed conditions can be large, even from unimproved traditional varieties. That such is the case is amply shown by the results of the FAO Freedom from Hunger Campaign (FFHC) Fertilizer Programme (FAO, 1972), which sponsored fertilizer trials and demonstrations throughout the developing countries under a wide range of soil and agroclimatic conditions, and with a large number of different crops and cultivars. The programme completed about 62,000 trials between 1961 and 1969. Many of them did not utilise the package approach, so that the large fertilizer response frequently observed in these trials does not represent the maximum potential response. Furthermore given that most of them were conducted on farms by farmers, they represent yields with indigenous management and traditional technology to a large degree, and therefore they indicate the potential for additional yield increases in the future as management standards rise.

The large fertilizer response of some traditional cultivars, particularly to nitrogen fertilizer (FAO, 1969) indicates the widespread potential benefits to be gained from intensifying production, even by a single input approach. However, although this simple strategy is effective, the benefits are greater when fertilizer is used in conjunction with other complementary inputs, particularly improved cultivars, irrigation, and pest control.

Irrigation generally increases the response to fertilizer by 25–100% compared to rainfed conditions (depending on the crop and the agroclimatic region). Field pests and diseases commonly cause losses in the range 10–50% (see Chapter 6). Suitable control techniques are not known for some pests and diseases, and for others the available methods are too costly, but for many important ones the losses can be markedly reduced at low cost and without damaging the environment.

Improvements in fertilizer utilisation and pest and disease resistance are commonly embodied in new cultivars. Not only are they able to receive more nitrogen fertilizer without lodging (toppling over), but they also utilise more of the fertilizer in the production of the consumable product rather than in waste by-products. Technologic developments of this type can be the dominant factor in yield increases. In Holland and in the United Kingdom during the period 1939–1964 the increase in yield from the introduction of new cereal varieties has been estimated to be from 0.7 to 1.4%/yr and was over 2.0%/yr towards the end of this period (Elliot, 1962; Dyke, 1968). Similarly the introduction of new cultivars into parts of India in the late 1960s was observed to cause a substantial (about 20%) upward shift in the production function (Sidhu, 1974), implying annual gains greater than those observed in the developed countries.

Traditional varieties are the outcome of an intentional selection process which in some cases has been going on for thousands of years. There are many of them, and some are adapted to specific, very local conditions. They generally possess a wide genetic base, and although lower yielding than most modern varieties, they commonly have greater tolerance or resistance to pests and unfavourable weather. It is therefore unrealistic to expect plant breeders to dramatically shorten the natural selection process and incorporate the key genetic elements into the new HYVs at the first attempt. Thus the first generation HYVs had a relatively narrow genetic base and met similar problems to those experienced when such varieties were first introduced into the developed countries. Nonetheless they made a major contribution to food production in Asia and parts of Latin America.

These first generation varieties were quickly replaced as local varieties were crossed with them to obtain others more adapted to the prevailing constraints. Thus the poor disease and pest resistance, and drought intolerance of the early HYVs has now been significantly corrected. In addition to these attributes, the latest HYVs complete their growth cycle more rapidly than the traditional cultivars; for example, the rice cultivar IR28 requires a growing season of only about 105 days, as compared with the traditional ones which need about 160 days, thereby increasing the opportunity for multiple cropping.

Reverting from Intensive to Extensive Livestock Production Systems

Such a change has been proposed together with a voluntary or imposed reduction in meat consumption in the developed countries because they used c.330 million tonnes of grain for livestock feed in 1975, that is, less than the early 1970s but still more than the total human consumption of cereals in India and China in that year. It is therefore apparent that a major reduction in the use of grains for livestock feed could greatly increase the availability of food, provided there was a parallel increase in the ability of grain deficit developing countries to purchase the resultant grain surplus at prices which would encourage continued production of this surplus. Without such an increase in purchasing power it is possible that restriction in the use of grains for feed would reduce the quantity available as production is cut back to maintain high prices.

In most developed countries it would be impossible or very costly to switch completely from intensive to extensive livestock production and maintain current consumption levels of livestock products. The price increase would generally be substantial, and this itself would markedly reduce consumption in the developed countries, and would probably cause substitution of vegetable protein meat analogues for meat (Gallimore, 1976). Such rationing by price would be effective, but socially inequitable in the absence of any compensating measures, for example, food stamps for low-income groups.

An important short-term consequence of a relatively rapid change to extensive livestock production might be higher fertilizer prices for developing countries as the developed countries use more fertilizer on their grassland. Within the developed countries there is the danger of environmental damage to the marginal land brought into use for grazing.

The possible shortfalls in the meat supply in developed countries, could result in increased trade with those developing countries who have the capacity to expand their production of grass-fed beef. This should increase the purchasing power and effective demand for food amongst those working in the livestock production and processing industries in the developing countries.

Increasing the Production of Fresh and Salt Water Fish and Other Marine Organisms

At the global level fish do not make a major contribution to nutrition. They provide only about 1% of the world's food energy, approximately 4.5% of the total protein, and about 11% of the animal protein. These gross figures hide the large regional and national variation in their importance. At least 25% of the animal protein in Africa is from fish, whilst in Congo and Bangladesh the proportion can exceed 70%.

The main drop in production during the early 1970s occurred as a result of overfishing. In particular this caused the temporary collapse of the Peruvian anchoveta industry, which is primarily organised to produce fish meal and not food for direct human consumption. Korea, Thailand, various Latin American countries and some other developing countries markedly increased their production of both marine and inland food fish throughout the period 1950–1975.

The traditional fishing grounds of the developed countries are over-exploited or close to their maximum sustainable yield for conventional fish. Much of the remaining potential lies in the southern hemisphere within the 200 mile economic zone of the developing countries. The long-term potential marine catch is only about double the current one (UN 1974) although a greater proportion could be used for human consumption. Given the likely growth of population and demand, such increases will probably have a negligible effect on the per capita supply in developing countries. Much of this additional output will have to come from unconventional species which may not gain acceptance as human food and will therefore be used for animal feed.

In addition to the fin fish resources, there are other marine organisms which are projected to be available in large quantities, for example, squid and antarctic krill. The latter is thought to represent a potential annual catch of 100 million tonnes/yr. However, krill fishing will be very capital and energy intensive (equivalent to about 1 tonne oil/ton krill) and thus inappropriate for most developing countries.

Currently 85–90% of the total world catch comes from the sea and the rest (5–6 million tonnes) comes from freshwater lakes and rivers; but at the national level the latter proportion can rise to about 90%, for example, in Bangladesh. It is projected that the sea fisheries will be unable to meet the likely long-term demand for conventional fish. However, the potential from inland fisheries is high (EEC, 1977); output may increase fivefold by 1985 (UN 1974) and tenfold by the year 2000 (Bardach, *et al.*, 1972). If this potential is realised, it would be an important contribution to the food problem in certain areas.

Inland fishing has many advantages. It provides the mechanism for utilising a sizeable proportion of the 10–20 million ha. of lakes, lagoons, and mangrove swamps in the developing countries. Output per hectare is considerably greater than that of deepsea (about 3 kg/ha) or estuarine fishing (15–150 kg/ha). Yields vary from 250–8000 kg/ha, within the wide range of traditional, improved traditional or modern fish management systems, many of which have low capital and fossil fuel energy requirements (Edwardson, 1976). Fish farming can be integrated with other activities in order to utilise crop byproducts, and to control weed growth in irrigation canals and ditches (Legner *et al.*, 1975). The fish can be cured by traditional methods (for example, sundrying or smoking), and in this form can be distributed more readily and at a lower cost than most marine fish. Thus they are less dependent on a modern marketing and distribution infrastructure.

Developing Nonconventional Food Production Systems

It has been suggested that as resource depletion causes the price of conventional foods to rise, there will be an increasing need to produce nonconventional foods which are independent of or less dependent on land and water resources, and which can substitute for or supplement the conventional foods. These foods can be placed into two main groups (1) those based on conventionally produced agricultural substrates like maize or soyabean, and (2) those produced in the industrial sector using fossil fuel substrates, such as the production of single cell protein (SCP) by culturing yeasts or bacteria on N–paraffins or natural gas (see Chapter 5). These can be further subdivided in terms of the primary end use, that is food for human consumption or feed for livestock. Key elements for the end use are price, palatability, and health hazards.

Their potential role as foods for human consumption has recently been reviewed (OECD, 1975). The greatest growth area has been and probably will continue to be the use of vegetable protein, primarily soyabean, as a supplement or replacement for animal products, particularly milk and beef. In the U.S. this may have significant implications for the growth of livestock numbers, and the availability of grain for export since less feedgrain and oilseed would be required if vegetable protein replaces a significant proportion of beef consumption (Heady, 1976).

The industralised production of single cell protein (SCP) is constrained by the high price of the fossil fuel feedstock, palatability and health risks. Current production is entirely for incorporation in animal feeds. Most of the growth is likely to occur in the developed countries although there is potential in the developing countries for producing SCP utilising simple technologies and using agricultural waste products as the substrate (Imrie, 1975). In most instances it is likely that the price of the unconventional industrial product in the developing countries will be too high for the majority of the population, and will be higher than the locally produced natural equivalent. The vegetable protein based nonconventional foodstuffs could make an important contribution to special weaning foods and to supplementary feeding programmes (Young *et al.*, 1976, Mondot Bernard 1976) but are currently constrained by the low level of development of the food processing industries in the LDCs.

Livestock Development. Livestock are a crucial component of agricultural development, and their current role is very important, yet the sector is frequently neglected in development strategies. A large number of people in the developing countries are partially or solely dependent on livestock for food and income. There are some 20 million nomadic pastoralists in the Sudano-Sahelian zone of Africa, and many millions of nonmigratory pastoralists in other parts of Africa, South America (particularly Argentina, Paraguay, Peru, and Uruguay), Asia (Afghanistan, Mongolia, parts of India and Northeast Thailand). Livestock are kept by a large proportion of the approximately 700 million people living on smallholdings of 5 ha or less. In some countries most of the livestock are on such smallholdings; for example, in the Republic of Korea and in Lesotho they rear more than 80% of all cattle, sheep and goats (Scoville, 1976). Generally livestock production is not integrated with arable farming but it is on some of these smallholdings and provides a valuable mechanism for utilising crop by-products.

Although at the regional or national level in the developing countries the contribution of livestock products to man's total food intake is commonly small, it is nonetheless vital, and there is great variation within and between countries in the size of this contribution. In Argentina, Paraguay and Uruguay, and certain tribal communities in Africa, beef is the staple food, but elsewhere it may be mutton or milk. Consumption in some societies in Africa is restricted to milk, sheep and goats, together with those calves and cattle who die naturally or are killed because they are old or diseased. In such societies cattle are kept as an embodiment of wealth or as insurance against drought and famine, rather than as a source of regular food and income.

Livestock, particularly the ruminants, have other important roles. They provide hides, wool, and hair for clothing and shelter, and in some countries these products are significant export commodities earning considerable foreign exchange, which can be used for the purchase of capital goods from abroad. In many areas they are the major power source for transport, land cultivation, irrigation, and grain threshing.

Livestock are almost the only way in which much of the world's arid and infertile land can be utilised by man. The current area of grazing land is about 3000 million ha. Much of the grazing land in the developing countries is very arid, and has not been improved.

Overstocking is widespread in many parts of Latin America, Africa and Asia. The reasons for the overstocking are complex and tend to vary according to the region. In Africa it is commonly the result of high-population growth rates and technological developments in a static social and economic situation. Thus improvements in disease control and in the availability of stock watering points have encouraged the build-up in numbers which have not been balanced by improvements in the pasture; by the expansion or development of marketing facilities (nonexistent in many areas); changes in the socioeconomic role of cattle; or integration of livestock production with crop farming. Overstocking has led to the desertification of vast areas of former grazing land in Rajasthan and other parts of Asia, in Africa, and in Latin America (Breach, 1977). Elsewhere under more humid conditions, although desertification is not occurring, the overgrazing has markedly reduced grassland productivity. Thus in parts of Kenya, which formerly could support one mature cow on 2 ha, now requires 8 ha. The areas involved are generally communally owned land, and improving the management of this land is a major social and economic problem.

Unless steps are taken to prevent this overgrazing, the problem will become more acute in the future, with a progressive reduction in grassland productivity, increasing land loss by desertification and soil erosion, deterioration of people's diet, and more severe and extensive famines during periods of unfavourable weather.

During the 1970–74 drought in the Sahel-Sudan zone, some 25% of the regional population were directly affected, with the 20 million nomadic pastoralists being most at risk. Some 25–30% of the cattle population died, but the remaining population was still possibly as much as 100% greater than the carrying capacity of the prevailing unimproved pastures under average rainfall conditions and 200% greater than the carrying capacity during periods of drought. Nonetheless, given the high sociocultural importance of cattle and common ownership of land, the paradox of the commons will prevail and cattle populations increase. Droughts of the 1970s intensity and duration are not unusual in the Sahel region, three or four have occurred in the past 70 years or so, and about 22 over the past 400 years. By the time the next major drought occurs, the regional herd will be even greater than that of the early 1970s, overgrazing will be even more serious, and therefore the collapse and famine greater than in the period 1970–74.

A cattle cycle of this type, induced by periodic droughts has been observed in the Masai area of Tanzania. Thus under normal weather the cattle population increases, leading to marginal overgrazing, which becomes acute during the next drought, and causes the population to collapse. When the more favourable weather returns, the population builds up again until the next drought. This cycle takes between 10–15 years.

There is potential for expansion both in the area of land grazed and in the productivity of that already in use. There is a further 3000 million ha that could be developed. Much of this potential grazing land is very arid, and in many areas watering points will have to be provided before it can be utilised. In addition its use will be limited or prevented by certain animal diseases; for example, trypanosomiasis and bovine rabies, until satisfactory control methods are developed, or known methods are applied. Although the potential benefits of developing the additional grazing land in the LDCs are possibly very high (UN, 1974) the costs will also be very high and suitable technologies for disease control are unlikely to be developed for sometime. In general, as in the case of potential arable land, it will be more economic to increase the productivity of the existing grassland rather than to develop new grazing land. There are many possibilities for such improvements, commonly involving relatively simple and low-cost technology (Blaxter, 1973; Scoville, 1976). One aim must be to introduce grass-legume mixtures. When the feed and forage supply has been improved, the full benefits of better breeds and animal health will be received.

Brazil is the only developing country undertaking large-scale development of grazing land (Jahoda and O'Hearn, 1975; Brandford, 1976). Part of the development results from spontaneous colonization following the construction of roads into Amazonia, but a major proportion is large scale development of cattle ranches by private companies receiving tax incentives from the government. Many of these companies initially used slash-and-burn methods to clear the jungle, ignored the ecological characteristics of the region and caused serious soil erosion and fertility loss (Brandford, 1976). Most of these companies are learning by their mistakes and developing appropriate land clearance and pasture establishment methods. These ranches are sometimes very large, that is, up to 0.5 million ha, and since 1965 several million hectares have been developed, with a possible carrying capacity of 5 million cattle by 1983.

Infrastructural and Institutional Constraints to the Utilisation of Natural Resources and Modern Production Inputs. Although land, water and labour resources in most areas of the developing countries were not a major constraint in the period 1950–1975, and suitable technologies were known, technological growth was very slow. Food production in terms of output per hectare grew at less than 1%/yr, that is, at about one-third of the annual gain in the developed countries. Most of the approximately 3%/yr increase in output came from the development of additional land and not from the use of fertilizer, improved seeds, and other components of modern agricultural technology. Furthermore, the increase failed to keep up with population growth in many areas, and in some food supply per capita declined.

A range of infrastructural and institutional factors have reduced or prevented the adoption of advanced technologies. Important features which have inhibited dynamic growth of LDC agriculture are:

1. Factor-product price distortions—urban bias;
2. Weak marketing infrastructure—merchant bias;
3. Limited credit facilities—large farmer bias;
4. Distorted distribution mechanisms for key inputs—large farmer bias;
5. Penal land tenure systems—landlord bias; and
6. Inequitable land distribution—large farmer and landlord bias.

Large farmers commonly only utilise a small proportion of their holdings, whilst subsistence farmers with 1–2 ha have insufficient land to adequately feed their families. The skewness of this distribution reaches extreme proportions; for example, in Peru 1% of the rural population owns 80% of the land, although more typically 10% of the population may own more than 50%. The lack of resource use is frequently compounded by the fact that output per hectare on the proportion cultivated is lower than on small holdings in the same area (IBRD, 1974a).

Fertilizers have not been widely adopted in the developing countries, although the growth rate in consumption is high, that is, about 12%/yr. They are essential to the modernisation of LDC agriculture and for increasing agricultural productivity. Their average price in the LDCs is often twice that prevailing in the developed countries, as a result of low and inefficient domestic production, and poor marketing and distribution infrastructure. There are also large price ranges within countries. Outlying farmers commonly have to pay considerably more for their fertilizer and receive less for the grain they produce with it, thus their effective price may be 60% or more greater than that for the farmers closer to the source and to the markets (David, 1976). These distortions together with the problems of credit availability, general risk and uncertainty about yields and market prices, result in the perceived price of fertilizer being considerably greater than the market price (Donde, 1970; Norse, 1976), and place a large constraint on fertilizer use in the developing countries.

Many developing countries have attempted to industrialise too rapidly. National investment policies have usually neglected agriculture in favour of industry and mining, even diverting most of the profits from the sales of concessional food aid away from agriculture. Comprehensive national account statistics are not available for many LDCs, but for 22 countries publishing suitable data it has been calculated that during the period 1950–1965 agricultural investment was on average only 20% of the total (Szczepanik, 1969 and 1970). Such investment strategies have prevailed in developing countries where 60–70% of the labour force are in agriculture, where agriculture produces 40–60% of the GDP and commonly where incremental agricultural capital/output ratios indicate returns 2 to 3 times greater than those from nonfarm investment.

Government investment in agriculture in the LDCs has not been supplemented by private investment to any significant degree because government policies have generally depressed agricultural commodity prices and distorted factor-product price ratios. Credit availability for the majority of farmers has been non-existent or only available at very high interest rates. Most of the credit facilities are for short-term loans and thus investment in capital goods is severely restricted.

This neglect of agriculture is probably the primary cause of the downward trend in agricultural production in recent years and the low growth in productivity. The downward trend will have handicapped industry by reducing the flow of capital from agriculture to industry. The increasing dependence on food imports has depressed local production in some areas, and the purchase of the food from overseas preempts foreign exchange, which is usually in very short supply and is required for the development of social and industrial infrastructure.

Development Strategies. Agriculture must not be considered solely in terms of what it produces. In the developing countries it also has a fundamental role in respect of employment creation, in the motivation to limit family size and hence in the reduction of their dangerously high population growth rates. Given the projected addition to the potential labour force upto the year 2000, that is, about 700 million, and the estimates of those currently unemployed or underemployed, for example, 300 million (ILO, 1976), it is impossible for industrial growth to provide sufficient job opportunities (Shaw, 1970). It follows therefore that much of the employment creation will have to take place in agriculture and the agroindustries.

The lowering of child mortality is a key factor influencing the motivation to limit family size (Taylor, 1973). Lack of income is the primary cause of malnutrition and therefore of high child mortality and high fertility. Most of the poor live in rural areas and must participate in

economic growth to bring about this reduction in family size. This partici-
pation will have to take place by greater productivity and increased
employment opportunities in agriculture and the agroindustries.

Employment opportunities in agriculture and the agroindustries depend
largely on how fast effective demand for food grows. It is essential for
most governments in the developing countries to promote balanced
growth of demand, supply and productivity, because such growth could
feasibly provide employment for a labour force growing at about 2%/yr,
but if productivity increases too rapidly unemployment may result (Shaw,
1970; Adelman and Morris, 1973). In those countries which are currently
importing food, for example, India, Indonesia, Tanzania, or are able to
compete on the world grain market, for example, Thailand, it is possible
for productivity to rise more rapidly than demand. But in the former, once
self-sufficiency is reached, unemployment may result (Adelman *et al.*,
1976), unless there is growth in the indirect demand for cereals from the
livestock sector or diversification into crops with more buoyant markets.

A number of developing countries have no minerals, no fossil fuels or
other depleting commodities required by industrialised countries. They do
not have the natural attributes required for tourism, and have not the
educational and general infrastructure to establish labour intensive industries competitive with those of the developed or the more advanced
developing countries. Thus their opportunities for employment creation
and economic advancement are far more limited. For such countries the
only sound option in the short- to medium-term and possibly longer is to
exploit ecological advantage and foster their agriculture, rather than
placing emphasis on industrialization.

The above aspects underline the importance, and the complexity of
agriculture's multifacetted role. It follows that the selection of development strategies is commonly complex, because the policy maker has to
try and determine both the primary and the secondary effects of particular
developments. Each potential strategy should be subjected to a number of
questions including one or more of the following:

1. Does it directly or indirectly increase the food purchasing power
   of those suffering from under-nutrition?
2. Is it employment creating?
3. Are the social costs acceptable?
4. Does it have neutral or beneficial effects on other sectors?
5. Is it scale neutral?
6. Is it suitable for subsistence farmers?
7. Does it increase the dependence on purchased inputs, particularly
   those from overseas?

8. Is it sustainable in the long term?
9. Does it increase the sectors' vulnerability to external perturbations; for example, in weather, climate, energy costs, etc.?
10. Does it require large amounts of foreign exchange?
11. Does it have net foreign exchange earnings?

The agricultural development strategies favoured by most national governments and international organisations during the 1950s and 1960s were those of additional land and irrigation development. Such strategies are still common. They are an important component of the plans put forward by the United National at the World Food Conference in Rome, 1974. Development costs are a major parameter in the selection of these strategies, and errors in the estimation of such costs markedly affect the marginal returns/net productivity of any given strategy. The limited financial resources for agricultural development in developing countries make it essential that they are allocated optimally. Under estimates of development costs will exaggerate the marginal returns and hence lead to the misallocation of the financial resources.

The UN World Food Conference proposed that some 34 million ha of new land in Africa and 85 million ha in Latin America should be developed during 1974–85 at a cost (in 1974 prices) of U.S. $44 and U.S. $150/ha, respectively. However, during 1970/71 land clearance costs alone were generally more than $200/ha and therefore although some land is already partially cleared, it seems unlikely that the average land development costs could be as low as $44/ha. Similarly irrigation costs in the Far East are set at $1500/ha, when land levelling costs were $250–500/ha during 1970–71. It thus appears that the development costs estimates used by the UN may have been too low. Under estimates of this type will result in further capital investment in new dams and land development schemes when the greatest marginal returns would come from the intensification of production from the existing infrastructure.

The optimal strategies derived from India, Bangladesh and Pakistan (Norse, 1976) all suggest that the largest marginal returns would come from such an intensification of production. A comparison of the input/output coefficients of different tranches of land available for improvement or development in India and Pakistan, suggest that the incremental food production in the next 5–10 years can be obtained at the lowest cost from the existing infrastructure. Following the projected optimum development pathway in these countries, the highest food output up to 1985–90, would be obtained by cultivating more intensively the presently irrigated or developed rainfed land with only low levels of fixed capital expenditure, for example, for on-farm development of irrigation. Not until the mid-

1980s would it become more economic to undertake further capital intensive developments. In contrast, the equivalent pathway for Bangladesh involves major capital expenditure from the base year 1970. If current levels of income and the distribution thereof are maintained, rather than the higher and less skewed ones assumed for these projections, the effective demand for food would be less and hence the requirement for new infrastructure further delayed than in the above cases.

Projected future capital requirements are greatly in excess of present levels; for example, completion of the development programme for Bangladesh would require the annual fixed investment during the period 1982–90 to reach about three times the amount proposed by the World Bank for the period 1973–83. Furthermore the optimal pathways involve major increases in the annual capital recovery costs of irrigation and land development, although currently these costs are often under charged or not charged directly to the farmer.

The above conclusions on the sequence of land and water development are supported by an examination of current product and production input costs. This examination indicated that it is unlikely that food crops could provide a rate of return, which, at current food prices and incomes, would justify the development of much of the potential land and water. New irrigation projects at the costs suggested by the UN, namely $1500–2500/ ha would require high rates of return to be financially viable, but at the current prices in Indonesia, India, Malawi, and other developing countries, the internal rate of return from food crops and some cash crops, for example, cotton, would be only 2–3%. Consequently the unsuccessful development of such resources would require a subsidy at some point in the production-marketing chain.

The lowest cost pathway may not be the optimal one in terms of long term food security, for example, in those areas which are subject to drought. Historical time series data on weather indicates that serious droughts of the degree prevailing in 1965/66 and 1972 can be expected to occur in the future. During such droughts areas with reliable irrigation do not have greatly reduced yields, but elsewhere grain yields may be reduced by 25–60% (Swaminathan, *et al.*, 1967), with yields in the most seriously affected areas being only slightly greater than the seed requirement for the next crop. Consequently investment in new irrigation may be justified in some instances, but only after the existing systems have been rehabilitated or improved where necessary, since the internal rate of return to rehabilitation in the projects analysed was commonly double to treble that of new projects, and the incremental food energy return to capital investment, 3 to 4 times that of new schemes.

Although the utilisation of the existing infrastructure is the optimum strategy in many situations, certain improvements and noncapital intensive additions have to be made to it before the maximum benefits will be gained. The lack of agricultural credit, limited farm advisory services (resulting in low farm management standards with late planting and suboptimal plant populations), and poor marketing facilities, are major constraints to the use of the existing infrastructure and to the expansion of food production. Inadequate knowledge on the storage problems of developing countries, and the limited storage facilities result in grain losses of > 15% and green vegetable losses of 30–50%. Only 10% of the livestock is formally marketed in some countries because of the poor roads, lack of stock-holding facilities, and limited marketing infrastructure.

Infrastructural improvements of this type are not costly in terms of capital or foreign exchange costs. Extension services have been expanded and credit facilities introduced in a number of recent World Bank projects. The capital costs of these improvements were about U.S. $40/ha with recurrent costs of $20–40/ha of arable land (in 1976 prices); that is, they were not high-cost developments.

A recent study in the Philippines (Herdt and Wickham, 1974) attempted to determine why national average yields were only 25% of those obtained by the best farmers and the experimental farms, that is, 8 tons/ha. Of the 6-ton/ha deficit, about half is amenable to government action, in particular the spatial and temporal availability of irrigation water, credit and market price uncertainties. Each of these have been recognised widely before and incorporated in development plans, but only if they are integrated will rapid progress be made. This integrated approach is particularly important in programmes to encourage the use of fertilizer and other modern inputs. It is estimated that some 80% of farmers in the developing countries do not have access to fertilizer because of the lack of credit or of supply following from deficiencies in the fertilizer marketing and distribution infrastructure. Farmers have to make a decision on fertilizer use on the basis of expected rather than actual returns, in that much of the fertilizer is applied at sowing time, whilst the return to fertilizer will not be received until after harvest. Thus for six months or more the farmers' investment in fertilizer is at risk, because weather factors, disease or pest attack may reduce the yield and hence the return to fertilizer. Furthermore between planting and harvest large changes in the market price of crops can occur. In most developing countries price guarantee mechanisms do not exist to cushion farmers against such uncertainties, yet farmers in such countries are exposed to much greater risks and uncertainties than farmers in developed countries where such mechanisms are common. Thus, although access to modern production inputs and credit may be improved, without suitable price policies farmers will not be encouraged to move from the subsistence to the market sector.

The integrated approach is also essential in the livestock sector. The introduction of superior livestock breeds from temperate zones to tropical or subtropical areas must be preceded by improvements in animal health, in forage and feed supplies, and in the marketing and distribution system. However, coordinated improvements of this type will fail or will be less successful if they are not accompanied by favourable pricing policies. In many areas such price policies are required to foster efficient resource use. For example they are needed to encourage cooperation between herdsmen and arable farmers, so that livestock can be reared in areas unsuitable for crop production and then fattened for the market in the arable areas using crop residues and improved temporary pastures.

Institutional changes are required to ensure an equitable distribution of credit and of production inputs, to remove factor-price distortions such as those which lead to inappropriate mechanisation, and to introduce pricing policies which give economic incentives to the use of modern agricultural technology without creating labour displacement. Land and tenurial reform are essential in some developing countries to encourage the technological and social development process (Cho, 1970; Barraclough, 1973).

Redistribution of land could increase the area under cultivation, the output per hectare, the rural employment, and rural incomes. This fact has been recognised in many developing countries, but the politicians and bureaucrats are commonly part of the same Western-educated elite as some landowners, and are landowners themselves with a vested interest in maintaining the status quo. In contrast subsistence farmers and landless labourers have little or no education and little or no political power. Thus, although large-scale land reform has been introduced in parts of Latin America and Asia, it has been partial or incomplete. In some instances initiating legislation has contained clauses which markedly limit the effectiveness, in others no time limitation is given on implementation.

Land fragmentation through the mechanism of inheritance is a severe problem in many developing countries, therefore land reform legislation should ensure that the land is not subdivided into small tranches which are unable to generate adequate family income. The legislation should also make provision for increasing the size of the smallest holdings, either directly or indirectly. Although cooperatives *per se* have commonly failed in developing countries (Hunter, 1974), there are alternative modes of cooperative development, for example, village development committees, and communes which have close affinity with the existing social structure.

A key factor in support of strategies to promote agricultural productivity and technological innovation is the favourable impact such developments can have on food prices. Technological growth stabilised the real price at the farm-gate of many foods and agricultural commodities in the U.S.A. from 1929 to 1973, during which time production doubled or trebled, and the total costs of production rose considerably (USDA, 1974). Thus technological growth can cause a progressive upward shift in the production function and a downward shift in the cost function, with postponement of the time when diminishing marginal returns to fertilizer and other inputs cause an increase in food prices. In India the introduction of the Green Revolution package for irrigated wheat, while greatly increasing output, reduced the unit costs of production by about 16% between 1968 and 1972 (Sidhu, 1974). Such changes are essential if the use of purchased inputs are not to raise food prices beyond the reach of the low income groups.

There are a number of important deficiencies in recent research and development programmes which must be corrected, for example, investigations on technologies which are scale neutral or are most appropriate for the small farmer (that is, with less than 5 ha) should receive priority. Thus the development of small solar pumps and nitrogen-fixing cereals would reduce production costs, credit requirements, fossil fuel requirements, etc. and increase labour productivity. Furthermore they would insulate the farmer from supply shortages, weather perturbations and reduce the risk and uncertainty of market price fluctuations.

Until recently the greatest emphasis was placed on producing new HYVs of wheat and rice for areas with controlled irrigation, and little attention was given to breeding new cultivars for rainfed or flood conditions. Consequently in many such areas yields have been almost static for the past 10–20 years. This error is now being corrected, but there are still serious omissions particularly regarding the requirements for arid areas. The estimates of land and water resources given in Table 2-2 indicate that much of the present and potential arable land lies in arid or semiarid zones and cannot be irrigated. Although there are several hundred million hectares with serious aridity constraints, recent technologic growth has had little or no effect on the susceptibility of crop production to low rainfall (USDA, 1974). Minimal cultivation techniques, and the new grain crop, triticale, may ultimately have a significant impact, but a research strategy aimed at the development of short season, drought resistance or tolerant cultivars, and water conservation methods should receive greater priority than is currently the case.

Many traditional crops are still largely neglected, for example, millet, cassava, yams, and pulses, all of which have a large potential for improvement (Coursey and Haynes, 1970), and which have important nutritional and ecological roles. In some developing countries important technical developments have taken place regarding these crops, but the results have had limited distribution both nationally and internationally. There are varieties of millet, groundnut, chick-pea, pidgeon pea, cassava, and yam which outyield traditional cultivars by 100% or more, and have better nutritional or agronomic characteristics, for example, higher protein contents or shorter growing season requirements. What is needed are development programmes comparable to those applied to irrigated wheat and rice to distribute the material and adapt it to particular local conditions.

There are some fundamental changes taking place in research and development methods and strategies which should have beneficial effects on the development of plant varieties and agroecosystems more suited to the needs of the subsistence farmer than those currently available. Thus plant breeders are now beginning to select plant varieties under average or below average farm conditions using no or few inputs, rather than under optimal management or above average soils. It is becoming widely accepted that the shifting cultivation and intercropping systems, which are widely used in the LDCs represent optimal management under the prevailing conditions. They did not evolve by accident. They were progressively adapted by observant farmers to suit the ecological conditions and their particular social system. These can be modified and up-dated using higher yielding plant varieties and certain modern agronomic techniques (Rehm, 1973; Greenland, 1975) to double or treble output without markedly increasing farmers' dependence on external inputs. Given parallel improvements in the marketing and distribution infrastructure such developments could lead to a progressive evolution to an ecologically sound continuous cultivation system and a shift from subsistence to market orientated production.

Comparative advantage may favour regional strategies for cropping patterns and resource allocation. For example, the largest land reserves lie in the equatorial forest zone, which given current technology can only support a limited range of crops, for example, oil palm, if soil structure or fertility is to be maintained. In contrast, the land resources of the dry and humid savannah are more limited, but the soils can support a wider range of crops, for example, cereals and groundnuts. The yield potential of the oil palm is far greater than that of groundnuts, and in terms of vegetable oil production the former is likely to give a greater response to fertilizer. On the basis of the cross elasticity/substitutability of groundnut oil and palm oil, optimum resources allocation would entail the expansion of oil palm production in the rain forest areas, thus freeing land in the savannah areas for cereals and other food crops.

Certain development strategies cannot be pursued by the developing countries, without the cooperation of the developed ones, particularly with regard to the harmonisation of their respective agricultural development pathways. In the past the developed countries have commonly responded to technical improvements and changes in consumption patterns, without giving serious consideration to the natural endowments of the developing countries, or to the mutual benefits which would flow from the economic advancement of the developing countries. Thus the expansion of production of natural or synthetic commodities has usually taken place without any consideration of the overall economic and ecological advantages possessed by potential developing country suppliers, for example, for sugar or oilseed production.

Some developing countries have such an advantage in beef production. Once certain constraints have been overcome (for example, lack of effective disease control, and no marketing infrastructure), they could produce large quantities of grassfed beef for export. The developed countries would have to (1) provide financial and technical assistance to the developing countries to overcome their production constraints, (2) restrict their own beef production to that resulting from the dairy sector, and (3) open up their markets to the beef from the developing countries.

Overview

The food problem can only be resolved by the people of the developing countries, in that the primary limitations are institutional rather than physical or technological. Land and water resources are not a major constraint to expanding food production, although in some areas inequitable distribution of these resources is an important limitation. The seed-fertilizer technology is in its infancy in the developing countries and together with other components of modern agriculture, it should be able to support greatly increased food production. These possibilities will not be realised unless politicians and bureaucrats quickly introduce reforms and improvements to remove the current institutional and infrastructural constraints.

The role of agriculture in the developing countries is a crucial one. Without dynamic growth in agriculture, sustained economic growth is unlikely and population growth rates will continue to be very high. Governments must acknowledge that in the main their industrial policies will fail if they neglect agriculture. The development theories of the 1960s and early 1970s concerning the trickle of benefits through the social strata during economic growth have in practice turned out to equate more closely with an irregular drip. Only by fostering agricultural development will there be the widespread increase in economic well-being and effective demand essential for the removal of the food problem.

References

Abelson, P. H., *et al.* (1975). Food and nutrition. *Science* **188**(4188).

Adelman, I., and Morris, C. T. (1973). *Economic Growth and Social Equity in Developing Countries*. Stanford University, Stanford, Calif.

Adelman, I., Hopkins, M. S. D., Robinson, S., Rodgers, G. B., and Wery, R. (1976). *The Political Economy of Egalitarian Growth*. ILO, Geneva, Sw.

Bacon, F. (1625). Of seditions and troubles. In *Essays*. London.

Bardach, J. E., Ryther, J. H., and McLarney, W. O. (1972). *Aquaculture: The Farming and Husbandry of Fresh Water and Marine Organisms*. Wiley-Interscience, New York.

Barraclough, S. (1973). *Agrarian Structure in Latin America*. Lexington Books, Lexington, Mass.

Battelle Institute (1973). Interaction of science and technology in the innovative process: Some case studies. NSF. BCL C 667 73.

Biswas, A. K. (1978). Some Policy Implications of Water Development. *J. Water Supply & Management*. **2**, 215–226.

Biswas, A. K., and Golubev, G. (1978). *Interregional Water Transfers: Problems and Prospects*. Pergamon Press, Oxford.

Blaxter, K. L. (1973). Increasing output of animal production; Technical measures for increasing productivity in man, food and nutrition. Chemical Rubber Co. Cleveland, Ohio.

Brandford, S. (1976). Turning the jungle into ranchland. *Financial Times,* London, 16 December.

Breach, I. (1977). The creeping desert. *Financial Times*, London, February 18.

Brown, L. R. (1970). *Seeds of Change: the Green Revolution and Development in the 1970s*. Praeger, New York.

Brown, L. R., and Eckholm, E. P. (1974). *By Bread Alone*. Praeger, New York (for the Overseas Development Council).

Buringh, P., van Heemst, H. D. J., and Staring, G. J. (1975). Computation of the absolute maximum food production of the world. *Afd. Bodemkunde en Geologie*, Pub no. 598.

Carruthers, I. D. (1974). Water control, irrigation and hydrological research, paper to ODM/IDS seminar on Food Problem in South Asia: 1975–1990, mimeo.

Cho, J. H. (1970). Modernization effect upon exports of agricultural produce: South Korea. *Am. J. Agricul. Econ.* **52**, 91–96.

Cooke, G. W. (1971). Soil fertility problems in cereal growing in temperate zones. *Proc. 9th Cong.*, Int. Potash Inst., 123–133.

Coursey, D. G., and Haynes, P. H. (1970). Root crops and their potential as food in the tropics. *World Crops* **22**(4), 261–265.

Dalrymple, D. G. (1971). Survey of multiple cropping in less developed nations. USDA For. Econ. Dev. Service Publ. FEDR-12, Washington, D.C.

David, C. C. (1975). A model of fertilizer demand of Asian rice farms: A micro-macro analysis. Ph.D. dissertation, Stanford University, Calif.

Donde, W. B. (1970). Market and real prices of fertilizers and impact of price changes on fertilizer consumption and production of crops. *Agric. Sit. India* **25**(5), 493–99.

Dyke, G. V. (1968). Field experiments and increases in yields of crops. *J. Nat. Inst. Agric. Bot.* **11**(2), 329–342.

Eckholm, E. P. (1976). *Losing Ground*. Norton, New York.

Edwardson, W. (1968). Fish farming. Unpublished study for the Systems Analysis Research Unit, London.

EEC (1977). Fisheries in the ACP countries. Special report for *The Courier* **41** (January-February), 47–85.

Elliott, C. S. (1962). The importance of variety testing in relation to crop production. *Ij. Nat. Inst. Agric. Bot.* **9**, 199–206.

FAO (1969). Indicative world plan for agricultural development.

FAO (1972). FFHC Fertilizer programme: Physical and economic summary of trial and demonstration results, 1961/62–1968/69.

FAO (1976). *Production Yearbook*, 1975. Rome.

Gallimore, W. W. (1976). Estimated sale and impact of soy-beef blends in grocery stores. USDA, Econ. Res. Service Rept. NFS-155, Washington, D.C.

Gerardi, I. A. (1968). The significance of agro-climatic conditions in planning the utilisation of water and land resources. *Proc. 8th Regional Conference on Water Resource Development in Asia and the Far East*. UN ECAFE Water Resource Series **38**, Bangkok, Thailand, 262–78.

Greenland, D. J. (1975). Bringing the Green Revolution to the shifting cultivator. *Science* **190**(4217), 841–44.

Griliches, Z. (1958). The demand for fertilizer: An economic interpretation of a technical change. *J. Farm. Econ.* **40**, 511–606.

Heady, E. O. (1976). The agriculture of the U.S.A. *Sci. Am.* **235**(3), 107–127.

Herdt, R. W., and Wickham, T. H. (1974). Major constraints to rice production with emphasis on yields in the Philippines. *Proc. Int. Rice Res. Conf, April 1974*.

Howe, C. W., and Easter, K. W. (1971). *Interbasin Transfer of Water: Economic Issues and Impacts*. Johns Hopkins, Baltimore.

Hunter, G. (1974). The implementation of agricultural development: Towards criteria for the choice of tools. *Agr. Administration* **1**(1), 51–72.

IBRD (1969). Performance evaluation of 8 ongoing irrigation projects. Econ. Dept. Working Paper No. 40.

IBRD (1974). *Land Reform*. World Bank Rural Development Series, 70 pp.

ILO (1976). Employment, growth and basic needs—a one world problem. *Rept. of the Director-General to the Tripartite World Conference on Employment, Income Distribution and Social Progress and the International Division of Labour*, ILO, Geneva, June 1976.

Imrie, F. (1975). Single cell protein from agricultural wastes. *New Scientists*, May 22, 458–60.

Jahoda, J. C., and O'Hearn, D. L. (1975). The reluctant Amazon basin. *Environment* **17**(7), 16–30.

Jennings, P. R. (1976). The amplification of agricultural production. *Sci. Am.* **235**(3), 180–194.

Josling, T. (1975). The world food problem: National and international aspects. *Food Policy* **1**(1), 3–14.

Klatzmann, J. (1975). *Nourrir dix milliards d'hommes?* Presses Universitaires de France. 268 pp.

Legner, E. F., Hauser, W. J., Fisher, T. W., and Medved, R. A. (1975). Biological aquatic weed control by fish in the lower Sonoran Desert of California. *Calif. Agricult.* **29**(11), 8–10.

Lipton, M. (1977). *Why Poor People Stay Poor: Urban Bias in World Development.* Temple Smith, London, 467 pp.

Mayer, J. (1975). Management of famine relief. *Science* **188**(4188), 571–577.

Mellanby, K. (1975). *Can Britain Feed Itself?* Merlin Press, London.

Mesarovic, M., and Pestel, E. (1975). *Mankind at Turning Point.* Hutchinson, London.

Mondot, B. J. (1976). Planning food supplies for an expanding population. Unpublished report of the OECD Development Centre, Paris.

Norse, D. (1976). Development strategies and the world food problem. *J. Agric. Econ.* **27**(1), 137–158.

OECD (1975). *Unconventional Foodstuffs for Human Consumption.* Paris.

OECD (1976). *Study of Trends in World Supply and Demand of Major Agricultural Commodities.* Paris.

Paddock, W., and Paddock, P. (1967). *Famine—1975.* Little Brown, Boston.

Pereira, H. C. (1973). *Land Use and Water Resources in Temperate and Tropical Climates.* Cambridge University Press, Cambridge.

Precoda, N. (1975). Russia redistributes river flow. *Civil Engineering* ASCE, February 1975, 72–73.

PSAC (1967). *The world food problem.* Report of the U.S. President's Scientific Advisory Committee, Washington, D.C.

Revelle, R. (1976). The resources available for agriculture. *Sci. Am.* **235**(3), 164–178.

Rehm, S. (1973). Landwirtschaftliche Produktivität in regenreichen Tropenländern. UMSCHAU **73**, 44–48.

Robinson, P., and Glover, J. (1954). The reliability of rainfall within the growing season. *East African Agr. J.* **19**, 137–139.

Rogers, H. (1976). Crop improvement by plant breeding. *Chemistry and Industry*, 3 July, 541–544.

Russel, C., and Russel, W. M. S. (1968). *Violence, Monkeys and Man.* MacMillan, London.

Sanchez, P. A., and Buol, S. W. (1975). Soils of the tropics and the world food crisis. *Science* **188**(4188), 598–603.

Scoville, O. J. (1976). Improving ruminant livestock production on smallholdings. Agric. Dev. Council Seminar Report 11. October 1976.

Shaw, R. (1970). Jobs and agricultural development. Overseas Development Council Monograph No. 3. Washington, D.C.

Sidhu, S. S. (1974). Economics of technical change in wheat production in the Indian Punjab. *Am. J. Agr. Econ.* **56**, 217–22.

Swaminathan, M. C., Visweswara Rao, K., Hanumantha Rao, D. (1967). Food and nutrition in the drought affected areas of Andhra Pradesh. *Ind. J. Med. Res.* **55**(7), 768–778.

Szczepanik, E. F. (1969). The size and efficiency of agricultural investment in selected developing countries. *FAO. Monthly Bull. Agric. Econ. and Statistics* **18**(12), 1–13.

Szczepanik, E. F. (1970). Agricultural capital formation in selected developing countries. FAO. Agric. Planning Study 11, Rome, Italy.

Taylor, C. E. (1973). Nutrition and population. In *Nutrition, National Development and Planning.* MIT Press, Cambridge, Mass.

Tsutsui, H. (1974). World irrigation status and potential. Unpublished FAO study.
UN (1974). Assessment of the world food situation: Present and future. Paper E:CONF.65/3 to World Food Conference, Rome, November 1974.
UNESCO (1974). *FAO/UNESCO Soil maps of the world.* Paris.
USDA (1968). Crop response to fertilizer. USDA Econ. Res. Service Bull. No. 431.
USDA (1974). The world food situation and prospects to 1985. For. Agric. Econ. Rep 98.
Vega, J. (1971). Fertility, the soil condition which is most limiting to agriculture in Latin America. In *Systematic Land and Water Resource Appraisal.* The Proc. FAO/UNDP Latin America Seminar, Mexico, November 1971.
Wortman, S., *et al.* (1976). Food and agriculture. *Sci. Am.* **235**(3), 30–205.
Weber, E. (1977). *The Modernisation of Rural France, 1870–1914.* Chatto and Windus, 596 pp.
Young, V. R., Scrimshaw, N. S., and Milner, M. (1976). Foods from plants. *Chemistry and Industry* **17**(July 1976), 588–598.

3

WATER AND FOOD PRODUCTION

Gunnar Lindh
University of Lund, Sweden

Water is a necessary condition for organic life, and is also essential for sustaining of human life. It supports that part of our social and economic activities which produce goods by which man may survive. Thus water must be regarded as a factor of production and it permits a higher level of economic and community metabolism. Hence one may conclude that the management of water resources must be done in such a way that water provides:

1. The capacity for sustaining life for the existing population and social activities of different scales; and
2. The potential for a farther expansion and growth, thus enabling an improvement of the social wellbeing through an upgrade of the quality of life.

Such expansion and growth is progressively the consequences of activities where water has to play an important role in competition with the use of other natural resources. The natural resources are commonly classified into two categories: renewable and nonrenewable. However this distinction is not quite clear on account of the principles of conservation of matter and energy. Generally water, air, forests, and fisheries are classified as renewable resources whereas minerals and most energy sources currently being used are considered to be nonrenewable. It has been aptly pointed out that certainly the limitations of human activities and numbers set by renewable resources are more critical than those of the nonrenewable resources. To some extent, this is also evident from the cultural development of human society. In the past, abundance of water and fertile agricultural lands were the most important resources for the support of large population. It is known that such expanding population occurred on the eastern, south-eastern, and southern coasts of Asia. At present all production processes depend on the combination of natural resources. Land, water, energy, potash, phosphates, fixed nitrogen and living plants, animals and microorganisms are combined in agricultural processes, the base activity for food production (United Nations World Food Conference, 1974). The limiting factor in this production sphere can often be water.

Development of food production, agriculture, and industrial activities are some of the means by which the expansion and growth mentioned earlier is kept in progress. Analysis made (Vlachos, 1975) on the role of water in modern society emphasizes the social consequences of an evolution based on water, implying that as the water resource system becomes more developed, the more one may expect related subsystem to react sensitively. Since water is a limited resource and its occurrence is constrained in time and space, a continued supply of water may not be available in the long run for future development; one may have to rely on such things as reallocation by market or political mechanisms. Vlachos expresses this concisely by noting that "whether water should be a tool for farther growth or for expansion options; and, whether society or larger political regional bodies should assume the role of using water as an organizing concept and as an instrument for enforcing desired changes."

The above discussion is especially relevant to this chapter on water and food production. To be concise, food production may be defined as the transformation of matter and (solar) energy into a form that can be utilized for the growth and replacement of human tissue and to supply energy for human metabolism. Water is in fact not the sole requirement for producing food in a traditional, agricultural way. Besides land and water, air, energy, (see Chapters 4 and 5) and nourishment in terms of fertilizers are necessary and these components must be skillfully managed to produce usable end products. For reasons to be dealt with later, this is not an easy task. Certainly, during the history of man, food production has never been sufficient to meet the overall demand for one reason or another. The slow growth of food production compared to the increase in global population, has gradually aggravated the situation. The current global food crisis is caused by a series of unfortunate circumstances. In the early seventies, the climatic situation showed an unfavourable development in several regions of the world, including U.S.S.R., China, India, Australia, in the Sahelian zone in Africa and in south east Asia. Consequently, the total production of cereals decreased for the first time in more than 20 years (Biswas and Biswas, 1975).

In fact, it diminished by 33 million tons, as compared to the previous year, instead of increasing by 25 million tons as expected. The severe food problems faced by the world precipitated international action, one of which was the UN World Food Conference, convened in Rome in November 1974. One year after the food crisis, came the energy crisis which made the food crisis even more worse (Biswas and Biswas, 1976a, b; Johnson, 1975). Increasing oil prices further accelerated food production costs, especially for "Green Revolution" type of agriculture, as discussed in Chapter 2. There were several other consequences of the increase in oil prices (Myrdal, 1975). The high-yield varieties, which had been introduced in many parts of the world, could only be cultivated where there was good access to and control of water, and where significant amount of fertilizers was available. Green Revolution increased agricultural yields *per se* but such developments occurred only where cost for fertilizer was relatively cheap (Poleman and Freebairn, 1974).

An Inventory of Global Water Resources

A discussion on water for food production necessitates a survey of the global occurrence of water. As has been pointed out by several scientists (Biswas, 1977; Falkenmark and Lindh, 1974; Lvovich, 1973a), the water available on the continents is determined by the process of hydrologic cycle. In the hydrologic cycle (Figure 3-1), water is moving continually starting from evaporation from water bodies through the influence of the solar energy. Part of this evaporation comes down as precipitation on the oceans and the rest on the land mass. The cycle then continues in the form of surface runoff, evapotranspiration and infiltration. Infiltration increases the soil moisture storage and the percolation process causes the ground

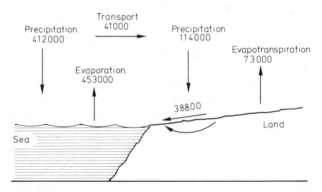

Figure 3-1. Schematic illustration of the hydrologic cycle. Figures according to Lvovich (km³/year).

Table 3-1. Calculated Hydrologic Cycle Coefficients for Continents

Territory	Area (in millions of km²)	Coefficient for the Hydrologic Cycle
Australia	7.96	1.15
Europe	9.68	1.20
South America	17.98	1.30
North America	20.44	1.35
Africa	29.81	1.45
Asia	42.28	1.55
Eurasia	51.95	1.65
Africa and Eurasia	81.76	1.90

water storage to change. Runoff from the surface and the soil moisture storage, the groundwater storage and runoff in the watercourses make up the total runoff. By this process, water is restored to the sea and the cycle is completed. There has been an attempt to define a coefficient for the hydrologic cycle (Kalinin and Bykov, 1969). A portion of the evaporated ocean moisture which falls as rain on land evaporates and the rest conceivably makes its way back to the ocean. Some of this reevaporated moisture falls as rain on the land again. The relative total quantity of rain which then may result from an initial precipitated quantity of ocean moisture before all this moisture gets back to the sea is expressed as the coefficient for the hydrologic cycle. It has been shown that this coefficient depends on the land area (Table 3-1).

One may ask how much water is available for human needs? The answer is that it is not the water in the sea or in the groundwater storage which constitutes the sources for withdrawal. What is mostly used for human activities (mainly for domestic, agricultural and industrial needs) is the flow in movement. Thus fresh water flow in watercourses and the groundwater flow can be used to satisfy man's needs. There are some exceptions to this general statement because there are some lakes, having no outflows, which are used for supplying water to some small regions. A closer study of the occurrence of such lakes reveals that the runoff from such closed areas is about 2.5% of the total runoff. Consequently the amount of water that can in principle be used is equal to the runoff from the continents. The amount of this runoff has been estimated by several scientists. The method of estimating this global runoff is based on the continuum principle which is inherent in the hydrologic cycle. Alternatively the runoff may be determined through direct field measurements.

Table 3-2. Annual River Runoff—in Cubic Kilometers

	Lvovich (1973)	Kalinin and Shiklomanov (1974)
Europe	3,100	3,210
Asia	13,190	14,410
Africa	4,225	4,570
North America	5,960	8,200
South America	10,380	11,760
Australia and Oceania	1,965	2,390
Total (averaged)	38,830	44,540

Two of the most recent studies (Lvovich, 1973b; Kalinin and Shiklomanov, 1974) that calculate annual runoff is shown in Table 3-2.

The figures in Table 3-2 do not include the fresh water reserves contained in Greenland, the Antarctic and the Canadian Archipelago. Lvovich has estimated that the annual flow from this region is 2200 km^3. That means that the world water resources should amount to 41,000 km^3, according to Lvovich, or 47,000 km^3, according to Kalinin and Shiklomanov. The difference between these estimates is about 15%. One may then ask: how accessible are the water quantities given in Table 3-2? Lvovich has considered this problem, and he distinguishes between aggregate stable and nonstable streamflow. The first concept means streamflow of groundwater origin plus the flow regulated by lakes and reservoirs. The fresh water resources available for use are shown in Table 3-3.

Kalinin and Shiklomanov point out that the steady, basic river runoff of the world that changes insignificantly within a year equals about 13,000

Table 3-3. Stable and Nonstable Fresh Water Resources (Lvovich, 1973)

	Runoff (km^3/yr)			Stable Runoff (% of total runoff)
	Total	Stable	Nonstable	
Europe	3,100	1,325	1,775	0.43
Asia	13,190	4,005	9,185	0.30
Africa	4,225	1,905	2,320	0.45
North America	5,960	238	3,580	0.40
South America	10,380	3,900	6,480	0.38
Australia and Oceania	1,965	495	1,470	0.25
Total	38,830	14,010	24,820	0.36

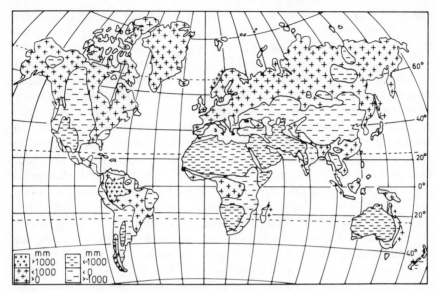

Figure 3-2.   Schematic illustration of regions with water surplus (+) and shortage of water (−) according to Kalinin and Shiklomanov.

km³ per year. Thus the figures produced by the two studies mentioned do not differ significantly, and it may be concluded that only about one-third of the river runoff is available for human activities. The most important fact, however, is that water is unequally distributed in space and time. Distribution of water does not correspond to the intensity of population or its rate of growth. Indeed, greater part of the world shows a water shortage due to the fact that evapotranspiration exceeds precipitation. Figure 3-2 shows the regions of the world having water shortage (minus signs) and regions having water surplus (plus signs). From the figure it is evident that many developing countries are situated in regions having water shortages. Therefore, in such regions, rational water management is of paramount importance. The figure also shows that surplus water exists in tropical regions of the equatorial zone. In these regions there may be too much water, as for example in the tropical rain forests.

Not only the geographical distribution of water but also its variability in time causes great problems. In many parts of the world, river runoff is extremely irregularly distributed within a year. This is a characteristic feature for many countries in less developed areas. The occurrence of heavy rain periods alternating with dry periods is very common (see Chapter 9). Moreover in regions with a dry climate there is an apparent variation in precipitation between different years. Furthermore, dry years may occur several years consecutively. One way of overcoming the effects of this variation of precipitation in space and time is to transfer water from one basin to another. There are several examples of such interbasin and interzonal water transfers at present in many parts of the world (Golubev and Biswas, 1978). Another important factor that must be considered in any discussion of water availability for human consumption, including food production, is the question of the costs to make water available. It is reasonable to assume that if the demand is low, water can be withdrawn from the surface and groundwater at a small cost. In general, however, as water demand increases, greater efforts must be made to make it available, and in all likelihood the costs will increase. This problem has been studied by Balcerski (Szestay, 1970). Balcerski made comprehensive studies as to the economy of water resources management and his results are shown in a condensed form in Table 3-4, which is divided into two columns. The left column shows water use as the percentage of the total runoff and the right column indicates the expected consequences and difficulties when such a withdrawal is made.

If Balcerski calculations are compared with stable runoff given as the percentage of the total runoff, it may be concluded that the situation in Asia and Australia show a stable runoff which is not so far from the 20% that Balcerski considers will cause a series of economic troubles. The situation is alarming because Lvovich's stable water withdrawal refers to fresh water. However, on a global basis, water situation is not whether the fresh water will be sufficient for the world population but rather if there will be enough water of adequate quality when current pollution

Table 3-4. Quantitative Use of Water and the Expected Economic Consequences

Water Use in Percentage of Total Runoff	Consequences and Difficulties to be Expected
Less than 5%	Possibilities for covering water needs are favourable. Interference for increasing natural water availability is required only at places with particularly concentrated requirements.
5–10%	Possibilities of water supply are in general acceptable. The number of districts with temporary water shortage is increasing. The preparation of regional water plans (including several districts) may become necessary.
10–20%	Water resources are inadequate. Comprehensive planning and considerable investments are required for solving water problems.
More than 20%	Water is a decisive factor for the economic development.

trends are considered. In fact, it is not only industrial water which pollute water courses and lakes but also drainage water from agriculture. Another serious problem in this context is that mean values are normally considered in the analysis of global water resources. If the withdrawals are analysed in a more detailed scale than for continents, it may be observed that the Balcerski calculations applied to the GDR and Hungary are about 35% and 65%, respectively. These are figures whose effects on the overall economy should be seriously considered.

Water for Irrigation

Water for food production is needed for both industrial and agricultural uses, and agricultural water needs are primarily discussed in this chapter. Crops require water for two reasons: to support the continuous metabolic activity inside the plant, and to maintain the thermal balance of the plants. The latter demand is the most essential because by this the plant can sustain life, which is achieved by evaporating water by a process generally known as transpiration. There is also evaporation from the ground and the two processes are jointly called evapotranspiration. Loss of water due to evapotranspiration is of great importance for estimating the demand of water for irrigation (Jensen, 1973). Evapotranspiration is affected by climate, availability of water, growth stage of the crop and also by plant characteristics. Food production through agriculture is a highly water consuming process. For example, in industry, it is estimated that roughly 1000 tons of water may be needed to produce one ton of an industrial product. In agriculture, in contrast, more than ten times this amount of water may be used for producing one ton (Horning, 1972).

It is a rather difficult task to estimate how much water is used in agriculture in different countries. Information given in literature seems to be rather contradictory. Kalinin and Shiklomanov (1974) provide estimates of water used for irrigation in some countries which is shown in Table 3-5. They have also calculated the specific withdrawal for irrigation, which can be done if the total withdrawal for irrigation and the area irrigated are known. Specific water withdrawals for irrigation for certain selected countries are shown in Table 3-6. It can be observed from this table that the withdrawal figures are higher for Asian countries and for the U.S.S.R. than for other countries. The reason for this may be explained from the specific climatic conditions, agricultural crops and types of irrigation. The high figure for the U.S.S.R. is due to the fact that in many cases water is transported in big channels for hundreds of kilometers from its source. As to China, there is some information about water withdrawal for rice production which seems to amount to about 4000 to 14,000 m³/ha. For wheat, the withdrawal is estimated to 1800–5500 m³/ha. In Africa,

Table 3-5. Water Withdrawal for Irrigation Use in Some Countries

	Withdrawal (km³/yr)	Percentage of Total Withdrawal
U.S.S.R.	136	57
Comecon countries, excl. U.S.S.R.	13	30
U.S.A.	165	37
France	14	25
India	310	94
Mexico	30	90
China	500	—

Table 3-6. Specific Water Withdrawal for Irrigation—in Thousands of Cubic Meters per Hectare

Italy	5	Iraq	12
France	5.5	India, Indonesia	9–10
Bulgaria	3.5	Pakistan	8
Comecon countries	5.8	Israel	5.5
U.S.A., Mexico	7.5–8.5	U.S.S.R.	12.5

Table 3-7. Total Water Use for Continents (Upper Figure) and Irretrievable Losses (Lower)—in Cubic Kilometers

Continent	1970	1975	1985	2000
Europe	125	150	240	320
	84	100	144	200
Asia	1,400	1,500	1,700	2,400
	1,100	1,170	1,430	1,900
Africa	110	120	140	220
	90	100	120	170
North America	210	230	270	310
	130	140	170	200
South America	55	60	80	120
	45	50	60	100
Australia and Oceania	13	14	18	25
	10	11	14	20

water demands vary significantly over the continent. In the northern zone, the withdrawal appears to be about 12,000–15,000 m³/ha, while in the equatorial zone it is less, that is, about 8–10 million m³/ha. For South America, Australia, and Oceania the withdrawal for irrigation seems to be about 8000 m³/ha.

Up to now, the use of fresh water for irrigation has only been discussed. Several authors, however, mention the possible use of sewerage water for irrigation (Lvovich, 1973b). If sewerage water is to be used, then it must be controlled in a very effective manner in order that river and groundwater pollution can be avoided. According to Lvovich, about 6000 m³ of sewage per hectare is needed for irrigation. One main advantage of using sewerage water is that it is rich in organic fertilizers.

When using water for irrigation, it should be realized that irretrievable losses occur, mainly due to evaporation. Kalinin and Shiklomanov (1974) have tried to compile data on such losses, and Table 3-7 provides some information of expected losses calculated for the year of 1970, and expected losses by the years of 1975, 1985, and 2000 respectively.

Potential Water and Land Resources for Irrigation and Food Production

It is important to recognize that land use, water, and food production are concepts that are very closely interrelated. Prior to the World Population Conference at Bucharest (Biswas and Biswas, 1974), a very crude estimate of a possible world population was made. According to these calculations, the carrying capacity of the earth would be between 38 and 48 billion people—that is nearly ten times the present world population. However, this estimate was made without any consideration of the uneven distribution of the water resources of the world or even the availability of water. Water is a scarce resource, and it is unevenly distributed in time as well as in space. For instance, about a third of the total runoff comes from South America which has less than 15% of the land area of the world. Africa yields only 12% to the runoff, though it contains 23% of the land area of the world.

Nevertheless the documents prepared for the World Population Conference (United Nations World Population Conference, 1974) presented some information about the land used for irrigation. It stressed that as a consequence of the uneven distribution of runoff in the world, only 30% of the land potentially arable with irrigation can actually be irrigated and the potential increase of gross cropped area through irrigation development is limited to 1110 million ha. The total potentially arable land is thereby reduced to 2925 million ha and the potential gross cropped area to 5560 million ha.

Using the data from the World Population Conference documents and based on another report (President's Science Advisory Committee, 1967), it is possible to construct Figure 3-3, where the potential arable land has been divided into two parts. One shows areas that can be cropped without

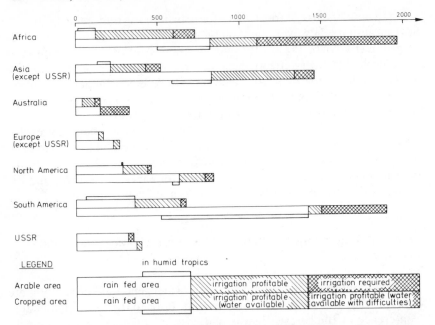

Figure 3-3. **Potentially arable land (million hectares) in different regions. The first column shows arable area with and without irrigation. The latter case shows area profitable to irrigate, as well as area that requires irrigation. The second column shows cropped area (possibly several crops) with and without irrigation. The latter shows area with water available with difficulties.**

irrigation, and the other indicates cropped area which could be added, if irrigation was used. These calculations presume that many crops could be grown where climatic conditions would allow this if water deficit is compensated by irrigation. The figure also indicates those areas for which water is difficult to obtain. Potentially these areas could be added to land available for agricultural production, if water could be transferred for long distances. Moreover, it shows the areas of the humid tropics, where crop conditions are not very favourable for using modern agricultural techniques. This is the consequence of the severe backing of the soils, damages from leaching, insects, etc. (see Chapter 9).

Attempts have been made to estimate the costs for restoring and improving the irrigation systems and also the costs for bringing under cultivation new areas in some parts of the world. Calculations showing these costs were presented in a preliminary report (United Nations World Food Conference, 1974) to the UN World Food Conference in Rome (Biswas and Biswas, 1975). In estimating expected costs it was clearly stated that development of water resources is closely related to the development of land resources, especially in terms of increasing food production. According to the document, one could distinguish between "vertical" and "horizontal" expansions. The first kind of expansion may be exemplified by a study of the functioning of the existing irrigation system and its improvement or when irrigation is brought to hitherto rain-fed arable land. Concerning the horizontal expansion this may deal with efforts to bring virgin or semivirgin land into regular agricultural use with or without irrigation. By such definitions, one can certainly make a distinction between different actions encountered within food production. However, it is also quite evident that there is some difficulty in making a sharp line of demarcation between these two types of expansion. As to the question of costs for development of irrigation facilities up to 1985, these were based upon calculations with the following goals as a prerequisite:

1. To provide the existing world population with sufficient food products.
2. To reduce starvation of the poor of the world by allowing for extra 250 calories per person a day.

It was emphasized that there were apparent difficulties to estimate the capability of the developing nations, even if a maximum degree of external support was assumed. Table 3-8 shows the objective of land and water development to 1985. An important consideration, of course, is the cost of such proposals. These are shown in Table 3-9. The cost figures given in Table 3-9 are quite high. Should such plans be economically feasible, it would require major support from international and bilateral agencies. The report continues: "This will include high level technical

Table 3-8. Objectives of Land and Water Development up to 1985—in Millions of Hectares

Region	Renovation and Improvement of Existing Irrigation Areas	Area to be Covered by New Irrigation	Development of New Land
Far East	28	15	24
Near East	12	3	10
Africa	1	1	34
Latin America	5	4	85
Total	46	23	153

Table 3-9. Estimated Cost of Water and Land Development, 1974–1985—in Millions of Dollars, 1974 Prices

	Renovation and Improvement of Existing Irrigated Area		Equipping New Land for Irrigation		Development of New Arable Land	
	Total Estimated Cost	Foreign Exchange Component	Total Estimated Cost	Foreign Exchange Component	Total Estimated Cost	Foreign Exchange Component
Far East	11,700	3,500	22,000	11,000	9,500	500
Near East	6,700	2,700	7,400	5,000	2,500	250
Africa	500	200	2,400	2,400	1,500	570
Latin America	2,100	100	6,200	2,500	12,800	2,500
Total	21,000	6,500	38,000	20,000	30,000	3,820

advice, massive training courses for local personnel and, of course, investment capital. Some of the countries which have unused land and water potential would be able to undertake the major part of the investment from their own resources and these would contemplate such programmes only if most of the basic investment could be obtained from outside.''

Water Management

It has been emphasized earlier that water, in conjunction with land, is the most essential factor in developing agriculture in an effective manner. For irrigation, surface as well as groundwater can be used. There is a close connection between these two, which is expressed through the process of the hydrologic cycle. Consequently, proper conjunctive use of surface and groundwater is extremely important, especially as groundwater may be used to supplement a scarce surface water supply during dry periods. If not contaminated by salinization (see Chapter 6), groundwater allows the withdrawal of water, having higher quality than could generally be obtained from surface reservoirs. However, groundwater resources are often overlooked and to some extent ignored. Houston (1976) gives the following reasons for such development:

1. The full implications of the hydrologic cycle are a relatively recent discovery.
2. Efficient pumps and low-cost power have only recently been generally available.
3. Hitherto, agriculture has relied on traditional surface sources for water availability.
4. Groundwater science and technology have developed only recently.

Since an integrated use of surface and groundwater must necessarily lead to the most efficient use of water resources in irrigation projects, there is a real need for making an inventory of existing water resources. Surface water supplies are in general well surveyed but normally this is not the case with ground water supplies. Geohydrological studies may give information about quantity and quality. An intelligently integrated use will also help to avoid overexploiting groundwater resources which has often occurred in many countries, leading to serious problems. Assessment of well capacity may now be done by means of different methods. The special problem of the optimal use of groundwater is not solely a problem for developing countries: it is a problem for developed countries as well (Lal, 1972). Solution of such integrated and complex problems may need mathematical techniques for optimization in order to determine the best way of allocating the water resources for irrigation projects (Buras, 1972; O'Loughaire and Himmelblau, 1974; de Neufville and Marks, 1974; Hall and Freedman, 1975; Kisiel and Duckstein, 1976). But it is not the question of allocation between surface and groundwater that is important, equally important and interesting is the problem of multiobjective optimization (Loucks, 1976). A classical example of such a project is that of the Mekong Delta. Another is the Aswan High Dam, which has been under much debate, because of the conflicting situation which often arises when different needs must be satisfied (Biswas, 1978). One of the dilemmas of the allocation process seems to be that water needed for irrigation is unevenly required during the year, which is not the case, say for example for generating hydro power.

However good such sophisticated optimization theories and rules may be, there is still a vast difference between theory and practice concerning use of water for agricultural production. The reason for this is that the success of irrigation in the end inevitably depends on the skill and interests of the farmers and motivation for participating in an irrigation scheme. Thus, theoretical solutions and modern techniques applied to irrigation do not always guarantee the development of an effective water system for food production. One can often witness the contrast between intelligent planning according to modern technical methods on the one hand, and human obstacles arising due to specific socioeconomic situations, climatological and related impediments. What may be the cause for such conflicting situations may often be the fact that planners have not paid due consideration to available physical facilities or socioeconomic conditions. Institutional imperfections may also contribute to the difficulties of solving similar problems. Many of the hitherto unsolved questions of how to combine modern techniques of developed countries with experiences of developing countries, rooted in knowledge acquired through thousands of years, is a problem of major dimension that requires most profound studies of the behaviour of man (Wiener, 1973).

Considered from a more narrow angle of economic viewpoint, comprehensive planning for irrigation development is most important, since otherwise secondary investments are often difficult to guarantee. Such investments may include terrace works, sluices, drainage systems, approach roads, or canals of different kinds, which are not only necessary but also essential, if the main system has to function according to plans. In India and elsewhere, many examples of irrigation projects can be seen wherein the schemes could not be used effectively for decades since adequate secondary investments have not been made. Sometimes such situations have been further aggravated by the fact that some parts of the irrigation system could not be fully used due to political or administrative reasons. Water disputes between neighbouring states is one example.

Such questions naturally lead to a discussion on the transfer of water resources knowledge, with special emphasis on irrigation projects. Much has been written on this topic and it is neither necessary nor possible to review the existing literature in the present context. The fundamental problem is that the transfer of information, know-how and technology is not dependent on the only question of considering water as an isolated resource to be dealt with: it is also a question of transfer of knowledge with appropriate consideration of regional aspects of economic, institutional and political character (Wiener, 1973). The differences of conceptual approach to projects betweens farmers in developed and developing countries is also an important factor. Wiener claims that population in developed countries possesses sufficient adaptive capacity spontaneously to take up appropriate production methods in response to an improved production environment. Contrary to this, the farmers of developing countries rely on tradition and traditional methods, and are disposed to resist changes. Consequently, no spontaneous adaption to new production environment may be expected. The two worlds can be characterized as one that is to a great extent self-regulated as a rural society while the second is not. For the rural society of the developed part, a new challenge will elicit an appropriate response. Thus, this is the fundamental obstacle in all attempts to transfer knowledge from the developed to the developing countries in the water resources field. Wiener mentions that information will be transmitted in five categories:

1. Technology.
2. Agrotechniques.
3. The psychological space of the farmer;
4. Rural and regional institutions; and
5. Considerations relating to the capacity of development agencies.

Such statements indicate a lack of understanding of the farmers of developing countries, and furthermore Wiener's comments on the possibility of carrying out such a transfer of knowledge is not quite correct. This thesis seems to be that only in those cases where the pilot activity has succeeded in creating spontaneously the necessary rural transformation, the problem is solved. He also points out that the transfer of knowledge in water resources during three decades have had three major negative effects:

1. They have led to a high percentage of lop-sided nonsatisfactory projects.
2. They have been instrumental in setting up institutions and political processes for such lop-sided projects and these institutions will resist change.
3. They have failed to create the essential information in relation to the four latter categories of information enumerated above.

When dealing with transfer of water resources knowledge to developing countries, it is of course natural to mention the important efforts made by the Food and Agricultural Organization of the United Nations, commonly known as FAO (Underhill, Thomas and Salomons, 1975). FAO has a very wide experience in the field of transfer of water knowledge from developed to developing countries, especially in the field of irrigation. Their activities include seminars, regional research, meetings of panels of experts, convening of study groups and use of consultants as well as publications. Other activities are mainly field programmes, which means technical assistance, project consultancies and fellowships. The transfer of knowledge is a human-to-human process, and according to FAO, the selection and training of the individuals that are ''donors of knowledge'' as well as those who receive and apply the knowledge are of crucial importance. It should thus be further stressed that transfer of knowledge in the water sciences from developed to developing countries is a problem having sociological, political and cultural aspects (Malassis, 1975). Such an understanding needs worldwide support, and recognition that this is one of the most important activities to implement. In such activities, also all related sciences have to contribute their specific knowledge (United Nations, 1971).

The use of water for food production has been shown to create a series of very serious inadvertent effects on the environment, which have been discussed in Chapter 6. The remedy for many of these inadvertent effects is primarily a problem of information. Transfer of knowledge about the proper use of irrigation as well as drainage, which is equally important as irrigation, is a presumptive measure to be taken. If the soil is already damaged, restoration of the quality of the soil becomes a major problem. Such problems are discussed in Chapters 6, 7 and 9.

Conclusion

It was mentioned earlier that according to some calculations the world should be able to support a population of 38 to 48 billion inhabitants, and that this estimate was made without considering water as a limiting factor for population growth. With this in mind, it may be justified to raise the question whether there will be enough water for food production to sustain the future world population. This is a very difficult question to answer, since available water must be used not only for irrigation, that is, for food production, but also for other purposes like industrial processes, domestic use, etc. However, if it is assumed that 70% of the total runoff could be controlled by man, it would mean that about 27,000 km³/year should be available. If it is further assumed that 1000 m³/year is necessary for each person, then the global water resources should be able to support a world population of 27 billion people. However, this is possible only if water is not seriously polluted by man's other activities.

Some preliminary calculations have been made of the global water situation, based on available population growth statistics and assumed values of industrial, agricultural and domestic use (Lindh, 1975; Falkenmark and Lindh, 1974). From these calculations one may conclude that the stable runoff in Asia will be used by the year 1985. As far as Africa is concerned, the stable runoff will be used by about the year 2100. As for Europe, it will be a long time before the stable part will be fully used. However, as has been pointed out earlier, difficulties in water management will develop well before these stable values are reached. According to Balcerski, a severe economical situation will be encountered when 20% of total runoff is used. Hence, according to the calculation referred to earlier, one can expect that in South and East Asia, the 20% level is already reached. Regarding Africa, the Balcerski number 10 will be reached around 1980, and by the year 2000, the demand percentage will amount to 20. As to Europe, the Balcerski number 10 is already attained, and one could expect to reach 20% in the year 2000. This, of course, is a very serious situation. However, two things should be considered. One is that the figures given refer to mean values for continents, and the second is that reuse and recycling of water are not taken into account in any of these calculations. The use of mean values implies that for some parts of the continent, the situation may perhaps be better than indicated by the mean value, but there will also be areas where the situation will be worse than indicated. The mean values, however, seem to depict the actual situation in Africa and India rather well.

Therefore, it may be concluded that the water situation may become more severe for food production. The situation can be alleviated by:

1. Reducing pollution of surface and groundwater, including pollution of groundwater due to unscientific irrigation practice.
2. Transferring water from surplus locations, which is already practised in many parts of the world.
3. Harvesting excess water by construction of reservoirs (monsoon rain in India).
4. Reusing and recycling of waste water.

There is another phenomenon which plays an important role in this context. This is the competition of water for urban and rural use. Hall (1974) poses a series of questions which show how industrial and agricultural demand interact:

> What is the relationship between the amounts of water used in urban and agricultural sectors in a region and what are the interactions? How much urban water use is directly determined by the use of an acre-foot of water of the farm? There are hundreds of such unanswered questions, almost any one of which could reverse the decision of water reallocation.
>
> Nor are these the only kinds of questions to be answered. Can this nation really produce all the agricultural products it needs for the next thirty years and still reduce irrigation in the west sufficiently to meet growing urban needs?

These are the type of questions that have to be answered in many parts of the world.

References

Biswas, A. K. (1977). Water: A perspective on global issues and politics. Report, Biswas & Associates, Ottawa, Canada, 32 p.

Biswas, A. K. (1978). Environmental implications of water development for developing countries. Key-note Lecture, *Proceedings, International Conference on Water Pollution Control in Developing Countries*, Vol. 2, Pergamon Press, Oxford, UK, 21–32.

Biswas, A. K., and Biswas, M. R. (1976a). State of the environment and its implications to resources policy development. *BioSci.* **26**, No. 1 (Jan.), 19–25.

Biswas, A. K., and Biswas, M. R. (1976b). Energy, environment and international development. *Technos* 5, No. 1 (Jan.-Mar.), 38–65.

Biswas, M. R., and Biswas, A. K. (1974). World population conference: A perspective. *Agric. Environ.* **1**, No. 4 (Dec.), 385–391.

Biswas, M. R., and Biswas, A. K. (1975). World food conference: A perspective. *Agric. Environ.* **2**, No. 1 (June), 15–39.

Biswas, A. K., and Golubev, G. (1978). *Interregional Water Transfers*. Pergamon Press, Oxford.

Buras, N. (1972). *Scientific Allocation of Water Resources*. American Elsevier Publishing Co., New York.

de Neufville, R., and Marks, D. H., Ed. (1974). *Systems Planning and Design*. Prentice-Hall, Englewood Cliffs, N.J.

Falkenmark, M., and Lindh, G. (1974). How Can We Cope With the Water Resources Situation by the Year 2015? *Ambio*, No. 3–4.

Haimes, Y. Y., Hall, W. A., and Freedman, H. T. (1975). *Multi-objective Optimization in Water Resources Systems*. Elsevier Scientific, Amsterdam.

Hall, W. A. (1974). Agriculture and the City. In *Selected Papers from Agricultural and Urban Considerations in Irrigation and Drainage*. Special Conference, Fort Collins, Colorado.

Horning, H. M. (1972). The role of water management in the field. In *Farm Water Management Seminar, Manila*. Irrigation and Drainage Paper 12, FAO, Rome.

Houston, C. E. (1977). Irrigation development in the world. In *Arid Lands Irrigation in Developing Countries*. E. B. Worthington (ed.). Pergamon Press, Oxford, 425–432.

Jensen, M. E. (1973). *Consumptive Use of Water and Irrigation Water Requirements*. American Society of Civil Engineers, New York.

Johnson, D. G. (1975). *World Food Problems and Prospects*. Foreign Affairs Studies, American Enterprise Institute for Policy Research, Washington, D.C.

Kalinin, G. P., and Bykov, V. D. (1969). The world's water resources, present and future. *Impact of Science on Society* **19**, No. 2. UNESCO, Paris.

Kalinin, G. P., and Shiklomanov, J. A. (1974). *World Water Balance and Water Resources of the Earth* (in Russian), U.S.S.R. National Committee for the International Hydrological Decade, Leningrad.

Kisiel, C. C., and Duckstein, L. (1976). Groundwater Models. In *Systems Approach to Water Management*, A. K. Biswas (ed.). McGraw-Hill, New York, 80–155.

Lal, D. (1972). *Wells and Wellfare*. Development Centre Studies, OECD, Paris.

Lindh, G. (1974). *Future Global Water Demand*. University of Lund, Lund, Sweden.

Loucks, D. P., and Haith, D. A. (1976). Multiobjective Water Resources Planning. In *Systems Approach to Water Management*, A. K. Biswas (ed.). McGraw-Hill, New York, 365–397.

Lvovich, M. I. (1973a). The global water balance. *EOS* **54**, No. 1.

Lvovich, M. I. (1973b). *The World's Water: Today and Tomorrow*. Mir, Moscow.

Malassis, L. (1975). *Agriculture and the Development Process*. UNESCO Press, Paris.

Myrdal, G. (1975). The Equality Issue in World Development. Documenta 19, Royal Swedish Academy of Science, Stockholm.

O'Loughaire, D. T., and Himmelblau, D. M. (1974). *Optimal Expansion of a Water Resources System*. Academic Press, New York.

Poleman, T. T., and Freebairn, K. D. (1974). *Food, Population and Employment: The Impact of the Green Revolution*. Praeger, New York.

President's Science Advisory Committee (1967), Water and Land, Chapter 7 of *Report of the Panel on the World Food Supply*. The White House, Washington, D.C., May.

Szesztay, K. (1970). The Hydrosphere and the Human Environment: Results of Research on Representative and Experimental Basins. *Proceedings, Wellington Symposium*, Studies and Reports in Hydrology, No. 12, UNESCO, Paris.

Underhill, H. W., Thomas, R. G., and Salomons, D. (1973). The Role of FAO in the Transfer of Water Resources Knowledge to Developing Regions. *Proc., First Int. Conf. Trans. Water Res. Knowl.* Water Resources Publications, Fort Collins, Colorado.

United Nations (1971). *World Plan of Action for the Application of Science and Technology to Development*. United Nations, New York.

United Nations, World Food Conference (1974). *Assessment of the World Food Situation: Present and Future*, Document E/Conf.63/3; and *The World Food Problem: Proposal for National and International Action*, Document E/CONF.65/4, Rome.

United Nations, World Population Conference (1974). *Population, Resources and the Environment*. United Nations, New York.

Vlachos, E. (1975). The human community. In *Environmental Design for Public Projects*, Water Resources Publications, Fort Collins, Colorado.

Wiener, A. (1972). *The Role of Water in Development*. McGraw-Hill, New York.

Wiener, A. (1973). Water resources development policies and transfer of knowledge from developed to developing countries. *Proc., First Int. Conf. Trans. Water Res. Knowl.* Water Resources Publications, Fort Collins, Colorado.

4

ENERGY AND AGRICULTURE

David Pimentel
Cornell University

The next 25 years are crucial for mankind. Population numbers are currently over 4 billion, and based on projected growth rates world population will reach at least 6 billion by the year 2000 (NAS, 1971) and 16 billion by the year 2135 (UN, 1973).

Food shortages in the world already exist; at least half of the world's population is suffering from protein-calorie malnutrition (PSAC, 1967; Borgstrom, 1973). The United Nations' World Food Conference held in November of 1974 reflected the urgency of the problem (Biswas & Biswas, 1975).

Clearly food production is lagging behind population needs (FAO, 1973a; NAS, 1971). About half of the world population is living on about 2100 kcal/day (PSAC, 1967; Spengler, 1968; Woodham, 1971; Borgstrom, 1973); by comparison, we in the United States are consuming about 3300 kcal/day (USDA, 1973a).

The misery of hunger is only a part of the picture. Children are particularly affected by malnutrition. The extent of child mortality resulting in large measure from malnutrition in developing countries is staggering (FAO, 1970a; Sebrell, 1968, in Berg, 1973). In the United States infant mortality to the age of one is only 25/thousand, whereas in developing countries existing records indicate infant mortality ranges from 100 to nearly 200/1000 live births (PSAC, 1967). A clergyman in Latin America reportedly said he did not bother to register children until they were 2 years old "because so many die [earlier] that it isn't worth it" (Sebrell, 1968, in Berg, 1973). In some parts of Nigeria the mortality rates for children under 5 years are in the order of 50% due to malnutrition and many other factors (Dema, 1965).

Although relatively few people in the United States are malnourished, increased demand for food and exports resulted in a 20% price increase during 1973 (USDA, 1973). The dimensions of the food problem in the U.S., however, seem minor when compared to those of the remainder of the world.

The major question is how to stop uncontrolled human population growth. Without getting bogged down in this significant question no one disagrees that man should try to deal with the impending crises of food, energy, and environment (Huxley, 1964; PSAC, 1967; FAO, 1973a; NAS, 1971; Meadows *et al.*, 1972; and Starr and Rudman, 1973). Man must solve the ultimate problem of population numbers; in the meantime, he must "buy time" while science hurries to develop technology for new energy sources and more effective population controls. These are undisputed ultimate aims. Meanwhile, we must find ways to increase food production on the world's limited arable land resources through the efficient use of fossil energy.

The interrelationship of energy and human numbers can be better appreciated when it is recognized that energy use has been increasing faster than the world population (Figure 4-1). While it took about the past 60 years for the U.S. population to double, the U.S. doubled its energy consumption during the past *20 years*. More alarming is the fact that while the world population doubled its numbers in about the past *30 years*, the world doubled its energy consumption within the past decade.

Energy use in food production also has been increasing faster than many other sectors of the world economy. For example, in the U.S. during the period 1945 to 1970 energy inputs in corn production more than *tripled* (Pimentel, *et al.*, 1973). An estimated 664 liters of gasoline equivalents (6.6 million kcal) currently are utilized to raise a hectare of corn in the U.S. The "Green Revolution" agriculture exported to developing nations is similar to western-type agriculture in that it requires large energy inputs for crop production (see Chapter 2). Black (1971) and Pimentel, *et al.* (1973) have warned that the modern intensive agricultural practices of the western world and those used by "Green Revolution" agriculture will not offer a solution for the world food problem.

Although the energy input in the U.S. food system is relatively small when compared to the total U.S. economy, the energy input is quite large when compared to developing nations. For example, energy input into U.S. agriculture is about 5% of national energy use (Cervinka, *et al.*, 1974). About 5% is expended for food processing and another 5% for distribution and preparation (Hirst, 1974; Steinhart and Steinhart, 1974). Hence, about 15% of the U.S. energy used is by the food system. This is similar to the per capita disposable income spent for food, that is, 16.6% (USDA, 1972a).

Although the total energy (about 15%) involved in the U.S. food system

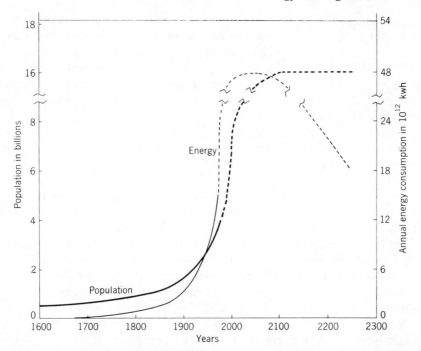

Figure 4-1. Estimated world population numbers (———) from 1600 to 1975 and projected numbers (- - - -) to the year 2250 (Freedman and Berelson, 1974; NAS, 1971; UN, 1973). Estimated fossil fuel consumption (———) from 1650 to 1975 and projected (- - - -) to the year 2250 (Hubbert, 1972).

is relatively small, it is large when compared with the current energy inputs in the less developing countries. World energy resources are too limited for 4 billion humans to be fed utilizing the U.S. food system even assuming that 66% more arable land (needed) was available for crop production purposes. An estimated 1250 liters (330 gallons) of gasoline equivalents of energy are expended in the U.S. food system to feed one person per year. Use of the U.S. food system for production, processing, distribution, and preparation of food for a world population of 4 billion on a U.S. diet for 1 year would require the equivalents of 5000 billion liters of fuel.

To gain an idea of world energy needs for a high protein-calorie diet if U.S. agricultural technology were employed, an estimate is made of how long it would take to deplete known world reserves of petroleum. The known petroleum reserves have been estimated to be 86,912 billion liters (Jiler, 1972). If we assume that 76% of the raw petroleum can be converted into fuel (Jiler, 1972), this would equal a useable reserve of 66,053 billion liters. If petroleum were the only source of energy for food production and if we used all petroleum reserves solely to feed the world population, the 66,053-billion-liter reserve would last a mere 13 years.

The above calculation was made assuming that ample arable land was available. Unfortunately, arable land is also in short supply. To produce the high protein-calorie diet consumed by the average American, about 160 million hectares are utilized for crop production in the U.S. With about 208 million people in the United States, this averages out to be about 0.77 ha per capita planted to crops. Since about 20% of our crops is exported, the estimated arable land is about 0.62 ha (1.5 acres) per capita (USDA, 1973a).

World arable land resources are about 1.5 billion ha (FAO, 1973b). With more than 4 billion humans in the world today, the per capita land available is only 0.38 ha. In the U.S. 0.62 ha of land plus a high-energy agricultural technology are necessary to produce the high protein-calorie diet consumed. Hence, in the world today, arable land is *not sufficient* (even assuming that the energy resources and other technology were also available) to feed the current world population of 4 billion a diet similar to the high protein-calorie diet consumed in the United States.

Suggestions have been made that the world's potential arable land might be doubled with irrigation and other significant alterations of parts of the ecosystem (Kellogg, 1967). Only about 12% of the world's cultivated land is now irrigated (FAO, 1970b). Unfortunately, irrigation and other similar environmental manipulations require enormous amounts of energy. For example, a liter of water weighs 1 kg and about 12.2 million liters (12,200 metric tons) of water are needed to produce 5000 kg of corn/ha in the subtropics (Addison, 1961). The energy cost to pump this water from a depth of a little over 90 m is about 20.6 million kcal (Smerdon, 1974). Using irrigation and this estimate (20.6 million kcal/ha) to double the arable land from 1.5 to 3.0 billion ha would require 3090 billion liters of fuel/yr. This amounts to about 5%/yr of the known usable petroleum reserves or the equivalent of a 20-yr supply if used *solely* for increased irrigation. This appears impractical. In addition, this does not include supplying the machinery (an additional 13% in energy [Pimentel, 1974]) nor does this consider the salination of soil and other problems associated with irrigation (Clark, 1967).

With energy and land shortages, overpopulation, and environmental degradation the world's population is fast losing its capacity to feed itself. The only means available to increase food production on limited arable land to feed a rapidly growing population is to intensify production on this land. This will require greater inputs of energy for fertilizer and other crop production inputs.

To gain a perspective of energy inputs for crop production I will analyze the inputs for several crops produced by different technologies. In addition, various cultural techniques and practices for crops that utilize minimal amounts of energy will also be considered.

Energy Inputs in Crop Production

The three prime resources in crop production are energy (including fertilizers, machinery, fuel, etc.), labor, and land (Figure 4-2). Each of these factors is interrelated and can be substituted (within limits) for the other resource. For example, fossil energy power can be used to reduce the labor-manpower input and vice versa. Increasing the intensity of land management through various energy inputs (fertilizers, tractors, etc.) can reduce the land used and the approach can be reversed.

Although manpower can be substituted for machinery and fuel, it should be pointed out that a "high standard of living" cannot exist if all activities are carried out only by hand labor. For example, raising corn in the U.S. requires only 22 man-hours/ha (Tables 4-1 and 4-2) whereas raising corn by hand in parts of Mexico requires as much as 1144 man-

Table 4-1. Average Energy Inputs per Hectare in U.S. Corn Production

Input	1945	1970
Labor[1]	57 hr	22 hr
Machinery[2]	539,000 kcal	1,078,000 kcal
Fuel[3]	140 liters	206 liters
Nitrogen[4]	8 kg	125 kg
Phosphorus[4]	8 kg	35 kg
Potassium[4]	6 kg	67 kg
Seeds for planting[5]	11 kg	21 kg
Irrigation[6]	103,740 kcal	187,000 kcal
Insecticides[7]	0 kg	1.12 kg
Herbicides[8]	0 kg	1.12 kg
Drying[9]	9880 kcal	296,400 kcal
Electricity[10]	39,500 kcal	380,000 kcal
Transportation[11]	49,400 kcal	172,900 kcal
Corn yields[12]	2132 kg	5080 kg
Protein yield[13]	192 kg	457 kg

Revised after Pimentel, *et al.*, 1973.
For notes see pages 89 to 90.

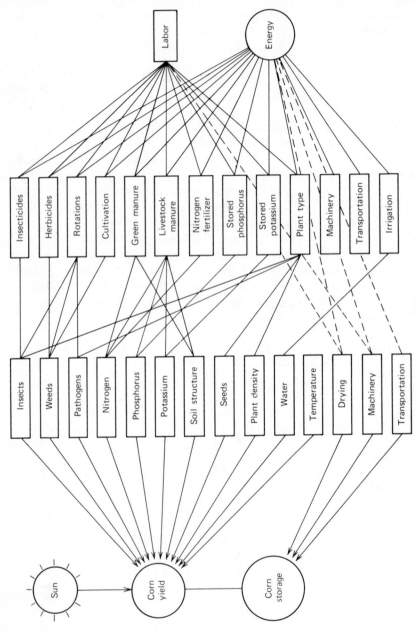

Figure 4-2. Relationships of the inputs in corn production.

Table 4-2. Energy Inputs in U.S. Corn Production—in Kilocalories per Hectare

Input	1945	1970
Machinery[2]	539,000	1,078,000
Fuel[14]	1,400,000	2,060,000
Nitrogen[15]	121,440	1,897,500
Phosphorus[16]	25,600	112,000
Potassium[17]	13,200	147,400
Seeds for planting[18]	77,440	147,840
Irrigation[6]	103,740	187,000
Insecticides[19]	0	82,790
Herbicides[19]	0	82,790
Drying[9]	9,880	296,400
Electricity[10]	39,500	380,000
Transportation[11]	49,400	172,900
Total inputs	2,379,200	6,644,220
Corn yield (output)[20]	7,504,640	17,881,600
kcal return/kcal input	3.15	2.69

Revised after Pimentel, *et al.,* 1973.
For notes see pages 89 to 90.

hours/ha (Table 4-3). Assuming the same profits per hectare in both situations, a U.S. corn grower with current crop production technology can manage more corn, has greater profits, and has a higher standard of living than a farmer who raises corn by hand.

In the production of food for mankind relatively few crops are utilized. The estimate is that 15 crops provide 90% of the world's food for man (Harrar, 1961; Mangelsdorf, 1966; Thurston, 1969). These crops include: rice, wheat, maize, sorghum, millet, rye, barley, cassava, sweet potato, potato, coconut, banana, common bean, soybean, and peanut. These 15 crops also occupy about three-fourths of the total tilled land of the world (FAO, 1973b), The energy inputs, food energy and protein return for several of these crops and a few forage crops will be calculated as a basis of comparison.

Let us consider corn production in Mexico. Producing corn by hand in Mexico using only an "ax and hoe" required, as mentioned, a total of 1144 hr of manpower/ha of corn (Table 4-3). The only energy inputs were the ax, hoe, and seeds. The corn yield was good or about 1944 kg/ha with about 175 kg of protein and 6,842,880 kcal of food energy. By this technology the yield in kcal of corn/input kcal was 128.8. This output/input energy ratio is nearly 50-times the U.S. average of 2.7 (Table 4-2).

Table 4-3. Energy Inputs in Corn Production in Mexico using Only Manpower

Input	Quantity per Hectare	Kilocalories per Hectare
Labor	1,144 hr[21]	
Ax & hoe[22]	16,500 kcal[23]	16,500
Seeds	10.4 kg[24]	36,608[25]
Total		53,108
Corn yield	1,944 kg[21]	6,842,880[25]
Kilocalories return per kilocalories input		128.8
Protein yield	175 kg[13]	

For notes see page 90.

Using draft animals, the number of man-hours necessary to raise a hectare of corn was generally reduced by more than one-half. In Mexico about 198 hr of oxen power reduced the manpower input from 1,144 to 383 hr (Tables 4-3 and 4-4). Assuming that an oxen consumes 20,000 kcal/day, in this case the man-oxen combination required more calories to do the same work. The reason for the difference in yield between 1944 kg (Table 4-3) and 941 kg (Table 4-4) was due to the use of the land. The 1944-kg yield was obtained on newly broken land (cut and burn) where no one could use oxen because of stumps and other obstacles (Lewis, 1951). The 941-kg yield was on bottom land that was cleared and had been in corn for

Table 4-4. Energy Inputs in Corn Production in Mexico using Oxen

Input	Quantity per Hectare	Kilocalories per Hectare
Labor	383 hr[21]	
Oxen	198 hr[21]	693,000[26]
Machinery[27]	41,400 kcal[23]	41,400
Seeds	10.4 kg[24]	36,608[25]
Total		771,008
Corn yield	941 kg[21]	3,312,320[25]
Kilocalories return per kilocalories input		4.3
Protein yield	85 kg[13]	

For notes see page 90.

some time, so the fertility was lower. If leaves and other organic matter had been carried in, the yield would have been greater and, of course, the man and oxen hours would also have been greater.

Before commenting on the energy inputs of other crops, I would like to compare some of the changes that took place in U.S. corn production from 1945 to 1970 (Tables 4-1 and 4-2). Corn yields from 1945 increased from 2132 kg/ha to 5,080 kg/ha by 1970. This is a 2.4-fold increase. However, to accomplish this a 2.8-fold increase in energy input was necessary. The result was a 15% decrease in output/input ratios from 1945 to 1970.

Note that the energy input for nitrogen fertilizer alone in 1970 was about 1.9 million kcal (Table 4-2). This almost equals the total inputs for corn production in 1945 (Table 4-2). The other large inputs for 1970 include machinery, fuel, drying, and electricity.

Several crops from different regions of the world are now evaluated for the fossil energy input and food energy output. It should be emphasized that the energy accounts for these crops are for a particular region and are not to be interpreted as being typical for any particular country. For the U.S. crops for which analyses are made the crop yield and inputs are about average for the U.S. Of course, important differences for each crop exist in different regions of the United States.

Cassava production in a part of Tanga yields about 1164.8 kcal of food energy for every input kcal of fossil fuel (Table 4-5). This is the result of 9 months growth and an input of 1284 man-hours. Furthermore, this crop is noted for its food energy production but is extremely poor in protein; the yield in protein was only 58 kg/ha.

Table 4-5. Energy Inputs in Cassava Production using Manpower in Tanga Region of Africa

Input	Quantity per Hectare	Kilocalories per Hectare
Labor	1,284.4 hr[28]	
Hoe[22]	16,500 kcal[23]	16,500
Stem cuttings	(none)	
Total		16,500
Cassava yield (dry)	5,824 kg[28]	19,219,200[29]
Kilocalories return per kilocalories input		1164.8
Protein yield	58 kg[30]	

For notes see pages 90 to 91.

Table 4-6. Energy Inputs in Sorghum Production in Sudan using Manual Labor

Input	Quantity per Hectare	Kilocalories per Hectare
Labor	240 hr[31]	
Hoe[22]	16,500 kcal[23]	16,500
Seeds	19 kg[31]	62,700[32]
Total		79,200
Sorghum yield	900 kg[31]	2,970,000[32]
Kilocalories return per kilocalories input		37.5
Protein yield	99 kg[33]	

For notes see pages 90 to 91.

The food energy output to energy input ratios for different crops in other nations were much lower than that of cassava. For example, the ratios for some other crops were: sorghum in the Sudan, 37.5 (Table 4-6); wheat in India, 1.08 (Table 4-7); and rice in the Philippines, 3.91 (Table 4-8). Earlier it was mentioned that corn production in Mexico yielded 128.8 (Table 4-3). All of these production systems included large inputs of labor.

Table 4-7. Energy Inputs in Wheat Production in Uttar Pradesh, India, using Bullocks

Input	Quantity per Hectare	Kilocalories per Hectare
Labor	615 hr[34]	
Bullock (pair)	321 hr (each)[34]	2,247,000[26]
Machinery[27]	41,400 kcal[23]	41,400
Manure (included in labor and bullock)		
Irrigation (included in labor and bullock)		
Seeds	65 kg[34]	214,500[35]
Total		2,502,900
Wheat yield	821 kg[34]	2,709,300[35]
Kilocalories return per kilocalories input		1.08
Protein yield	99 kg[36]	

For notes see pages 90 to 91.

Table 4-8. Energy Inputs in Rice Production using Draft Animals in Philippines

Input	Quantity per Hectare	Kilocalories per Hectare
Labor	576 hr[37]	
Equipment[27]	41,400 kcal[23]	41,400
Carabao	272 hr[37]	952,000[26]
Nitrogen	5.6 kg[37]	85,008[15]
Seeds	108 kg[37]	403,920[40]
Irrigation (included in labor and carabao)		
Herbicide	0.6 kg[37]	44,352[19]
Transportation	7410 kcal[38]	7410
Total		1,534,090
Rice yield	1654 kg[37]	6,004,020[41]
Kilocalories return per kilocalories input		3.91
Protein yield	111 kg[39]	

For notes see pages 90 to 91.

Corn production in Mexico (Table 4-3) provided the largest kcal-of-protein output per kcal-of-fossil-energy input, or about 13.2. The other crops mentioned produced significantly poorer yields of protein (from 58 to 111 kg/ha) (Tables 4-5–4-8).

For the food crops analyzed for the U.S., corn produced the best ratio of food energy output to fossil energy input, 2.69 (Table 4-2); this was followed by: potatoes, 2.27 (Table 4-9); oats, 2.49 (Table 4-10); wheat, 2.00 (Table 4-11); soybeans, 1.43 (Table 4-12); rice, 1.35 (Table 4-13); dry beans 1.11 (Table 4-14); and Brussels sprouts, 0.65 (Table 4-15).

In protein yield per hectare, soybeans were the highest with 640 kg/ha (Table 4-12); this was followed by: Brussels sprouts, 604 kg/ha (Table 4-15); potatoes, 524 kg/ha (Table 4-9); corn, 457 kg/ha (Table 4-1); rice, 388 kg/ha (Table 4-13); dry beans, 325 kg/ha (Table 4-14); oats, 276 kg/ha (Table 4-10); and wheat, 274 kg/ha (Table 4-11). Soybeans not only produced the greatest yield of protein per hectare but also required only 2.06 kcal of fossil energy per kcal of protein output.

As a basis of comparison to the above crops used in food energy production, energy accounts for three forage crops—corn silage, alfalfa, and hay—has been included. The food energy yield for these forages is greater than that of the foods that man consumes. Man, of course, cannot make use of forages as cattle, sheep, and goats do.

Table 4-9. Energy Inputs in U.S. Potato Production

Input	Quantity per Hectare	Kilocalories per Hectare
Labor	60 hr[42]	
Machinery	100,000 kcal[43]	1,000,000
Fuel	206 liters[44]	2,060,000[14]
Nitrogen	148 kg[44]	2,246,640[15]
Phosphorus	257 kg[44]	822,400[16]
Potassium	249 kg[44]	547,800[17]
Seeds	350 kg[42]	269,500[48]
Insecticides	6 kg[42]	443,520[19]
Herbicides	6 kg[42]	443,520[19]
Fungicides	6 kg[42]	443,520[19]
Electricity	380,000 kcal[43]	380,000
Transportation	250,000 kcal[45]	250,000
Total		8,906,900
Potato yield	26,208 kg[46]	20,180,160[48]
Kilocalories return per kilocalories input		2.27
Protein yield	524 kg[47]	

For notes see page 91.

Table 4-10. Energy Inputs in U.S. Oat Production

Input	Quantity per Hectare	Kilocalories per Hectare
Labor	6 hr[49]	
Machinery	1,000,000 kcal[43]	1,000,000
Fuel	80 liters[49]	800,000[14]
Nitrogen	15 kg[49]	227,700[15]
Phosphorus	12 kg[49]	38,400[16]
Potassium	21 kg[49]	46,200[17]
Seeds	93 kg[49]	362,700[53]
Herbicides	0.2 kg[49]	14,784[19]
Drying	21,500 kcal[50]	21,500
Electricity	380,000 kcal[43]	380,000
Transportation	86,450 kcal[51]	86,450
Total		2,977,734
Oat yield	1,900 kg[49]	7,410,000[53]
Kilocalories return per kilocalories input		2.49
Protein yield	276 kg[52]	

For notes see page 91.

Table 4-11. Energy Inputs in U.S. Wheat Production

Input	Quantity per Hectare	Kilocalories per Hectare
Labor	7 hr[54]	
Machinery	1,000,000 kcal[43]	1,000,000
Fuel	90 liters[55]	900,000[14]
Nitrogen	50 kg[54]	759,000[15]
Phosphorus	26 kg[54]	83,200[16]
Potassium	30 kg[54]	66,000[17]
Seeds	106 kg[54]	437,250[59]
Herbicides	0.5 kg[54]	36,960[19]
Drying	21,500 kcal[56]	21,500
Electricity	380,000 kcal[43]	380,000
Transportation	86,450 kcal[57]	86,450
Total		3,770,360
Wheat yield	2,284 kg[58]	7,537,200[35]
Kilocalories return per kilocalories input		2.00
Protein yield	274 kg[36]	

For notes see page 91.

Table 4-12. Energy Inputs in U.S. Soybean Production

Input	Quantity per Hectare	Kilocalories per Hectare
Labor	15 hr[60]	
Machinery	1,000,000 kcal[43]	1,000,000
Fuel	178 liters[60]	1,780,000[14]
Nitrogen	16 kg[61]	242,880[15]
Phosphorus	18 kg[61]	57,600[16]
Potassium	47 kg[61]	103,400[17]
Seeds	81 kg[60]	326,430[65]
Insecticides	1.12 kg[43]	82,400[19]
Herbicides	1.12 kg[43]	82,400[19]
Processing	1,057,357 kcal[62]	1,057,357
Electricity	380,000 kcal[43]	380,000
Transportation	172,900 kcal[43]	172,900
Total		5,285,367
Soybean yield	1,882 kg[63]	7,584,460[65]
Kilocalories return per kilocalories input		1.43
Protein yield	640 kg[64]	

For notes see pages 91 to 92.

Table 4-13. Energy Inputs in U.S. Rice Production

Input	Quantity per Hectare		Kilocalories per Hectare
Labor	30	hr[66]	
Machinery	1,000,000	kcal[43]	1,000,000
Fuel	225	liters[66]	2,250,000[14]
Nitrogen	134	kg[66]	2,034,120[15]
Potassium	67	kg[66]	147,400[17]
Seeds	112	kg[66]	813,120[67]
Irrigation	684	liters[66]	6,840,000[14]
Insecticides	5.6	kg[66]	413,952[19]
Herbicides	5.6	kg[66]	413,952[19]
Drying	1,070,597	kcal[66]	1,070,597
Electricity	380,000	kcal[43]	380,000
Transportation	172,900	kcal[43]	172,900
Total			15,536,041
Rice yield	5,796	kg[66]	21,039,480[41]
Kilocalories return per kilocalories input			1.35
Protein yield	388	kg[39]	

For notes see pages 90 to 92.

Table 4-14. Energy Inputs in U.S. Dry Bean Production

Input	Quantity per Hectare		Kilocalories per Hectare
Labor	15	hr[68]	
Machinery	1,000,000	kcal[43]	1,000,000
Fuel	178	liters[68]	1,780,000[14]
Nitrogen	16	kg[68]	242,880[15]
Phosphorus	18	kg[68]	57,600[16]
Potassium	47	kg[68]	103,400[17]
Seeds	81	kg[68]	275,400[71]
Insecticides	1.12	kg[43]	82,790[19]
Herbicides	1.12	kg[43]	82,790[19]
Drying	300,000	kcal[43]	300,000
Electricity	380,000	kcal[43]	380,000
Transportation	172,900	kcal[43]	172,900
Total			4,477,760
Dry bean yield	1,457	kg[69]	4,953,800[71]
Kilocalories return per kilocalories input			1.11
Protein yield	325	kg[70]	

For notes see pages 90 to 92.

Table 4-15. Energy Inputs in U.S. Brussels Sprouts Production

Input	Quantity per Hectare	Kilocalories per Hectare
Labor	60 hr[72]	
Machinery	1,000,000 kcal[43]	1,000,000
Fuel	285 liters[72]	2,850,000[14]
Nitrogen	180 kg[72]	2,732,400[15]
Phosphorus	45 kg[72]	144,000[16]
Potassium	40 kg[73]	88,000[17]
Seeds	4 kg[72]	16,120[76]
Insecticides	5 kg[72]	369,600[19]
Herbicides	10 kg[72]	739,200[19]
Electricity	380,000 kcal[43]	380,000
Transportation	172,900 kcal[43]	172,900
Total		8,492,220
Brussels sprouts yield	12,320 kg[74]	5,544,000[77]
Kilocalories return per kilocalories input		0.65
Protein yield	604 kg[75]	

For notes see pages 90 to 92.

Table 4-16. Energy in U.S. Corn Silage Production

Input	Quantity per Hectare	Kilocalories per Hectare
Labor	25 hr[78]	
Machinery	1,000,000 kcal[43]	1,000,000
Fuel	200 liters[43]	2,000,000[14]
Nitrogen	100 kg[78]	1,518,000[15]
Phosphorus	27 kg[78]	86,400[16]
Potassium	48 kg[78]	105,600[17]
Seeds	21 kg[43]	147,840[18]
Herbicides	1.12 kg[43]	82,400[19]
Electricity	380,000 kcal[43]	380,000
Transportation	172,900 kcal[43]	172,900
Total		5,493,140
Corn silage yield	30,200 kg[78]	24,099,600[80]
Kilocalories return per kilocalories input		4.39
Protein yield	393 kg[79]	

For notes see pages 90 to 92.

Table 4-17. Energy Inputs in U.S. Alfalfa Production

Input	Quantity per Hectare	Kilocalories per Hectare
Labor	9 hr[81]	
Machinery	1,000,000 kcal[43]	1,000,000
Fuel	90 liters[81]	900,000[14]
Phosphorus	22 kg[82]	70,400[16]
Potassium	45 kg[82]	99,000[17]
Seeds	8 kg[83]	12,240[86]
Herbicides	1.12 kg[43]	82,400[19]
Electricity	380,000 kcal[43]	380,000
Transportation	150,000 kcal[43]	150,000
Total		2,694,040
Alfalfa yield	6451 kg[84]	11,426,140[87]
Kilocalories return per kilocalories input		4.24
Protein yield	710 kg[85]	

For notes see pages 90 to 92.

Table 4-18. Energy Inputs in U.S. Tame Hay Production

Input	Quantity per Hectare		Kilocalories per Hectare
Labor	16	hr[88]	
Machinery	1,000,000	kcal[43]	1,000,000
Fuel	129	liters[88]	1,290,000[14]
Nitrogen	7	kg[88]	106,260[15]
Phosphorus	8	kg[88]	25,600[16]
Potassium	16	kg[88]	35,200[17]
Seeds	30	kg[88]	45,000[90]
Herbicides	1.12	kg[43]	82,790[19]
Electricity	380,000	kcal[43]	380,000
Transportation	150,000	kcal[43]	150,000
Total			3,114,850
Tame hay yield	5,000	kg[88]	8,578,680[91]
Kilocalories return per kilocalories input			2.75
Protein yield	200	kg[89]	

For notes see pages 90 to 92.

Notes for Tables 4-1 to 4-18

[1]Mean hours of labor per crop hectare in United States (USDA, 1954 and 1972b).

[2]An estimate of the energy inputs for the construction and repair of tractors, trucks, and other farm machinery was obtained from the data of Berry and Fels (1973), who calculated that about 31,968,000 kcal of energy was necessary to construct an average automobile weighing about 1530 kg. In our calculations we assumed that 244,555,000 kcal (an equivalent of 11,700 kg of machinery) were used for the production of all machinery (tractors, trucks, and miscellaneous) to farm 25 ha of corn. This machinery was assumed to function for 10 yr. Repairs were assumed to be 10% of total machinery production or about 25,000,000 kcal. Hence, a conservative estimate for the production and repair of farm machinery per corn hectare per year for 1970 was 1,078,000 kcal. A high for the number of tractors and other farm machinery on farms was reached in 1964 and continues (USDA, 1953; USBC, 1972). The number of tractors and other types of machinery in 1945 was about half what it is now.

[3]DeGraff and Washbon (1943) reported that corn production required about 140 liters of fuel/ha for tractor use—intermediate between fruit and small grain production. Because corn appeared to be intermediate, the estimated mean fuel (liters) burned in farm machinery per harvested hectare was based on U.S. Department of Agriculture (1953 and 1964) and U.S. Bureau of the Census (1972) data.

[4]Fertilizers (N, P, K) applied to corn are based on USDA (1954, 1957, 1967a, and 1971a) estimates.

[5]During 1970, relatively dense corn planting required about 21 kg of corn (61,750 kernels or 83,980 kcal) per hectare; the less dense plantings in 1945 were estimated to use about 10.5 kg of seed. Because hybrid seed has to be produced with special care, the input for 1970 was estimated to be 147,840 kcal.

[6]Only about 3.8% of the corn grain hectares in the United States were irrigated in 1964 (USBC, 1968), and this is not expected to change much in the near future (Heady, *et al.*, 1972). Although a small percentage, irrigation is costly in terms of energy demand. On the basis of the data of Smerdon (1974), an estimated 4,921,166 kcal is required to irrigate a hectare of corn with 30.48 cm of water for one season. Higher energy costs for irrigation water are given by the Report on the World Food Problem (PSAC, 1967). Since only 3.8% of the corn acres are irrigated (1964–1970), it was estimated that only 187,000 kcal/ha were used for corn irrigation. The percentage of acres irrigated in 1945 was based on trends in irrigated acres in agriculture (USDA, 1970a and USBC, 1968).

[7]Estimates of insecticides applied per hectare of corn are based on the fact that little or no insecticide was used on corn in 1945, and this reached a high in 1964 (USDA, 1968 and 1970b).

[8]Estimates of herbicides applied per hectare of corn are based on the fact that little or no herbicides were used on corn in 1945 and that this use continues to increase (USDA, 1968 and 1970b).

[9]When it is dried for storage to reduce the moisture from about 26.5 to 13%, about

1,008,264 kcal are needed to dry 5,080 kg (CGG, 1968). About 30% of the corn was estimated to have been dried in 1970 as compared to an estimated 10% in 1945.

[10]Agriculture consumed about 2.5% of all electricity produced in 1970 (CAHR, 1971) and an estimated 424.2 trillion British thermal units of fossil fuel were used to produce this power (USBC, 1971); on croplands this divides to 765,700 kcal/ha for 1970 (USDA, 1968 and 1972b). This value was reduced by one-half to account for the electricity used in the farm household independent of growing the crop. The fuel used to produce the electrical energy for 1945 was estimated from data reported in Statistical Abstracts (USBC, 1965).

[11]Estimates of the number of calories burned to transport machinery and supplies to corn hectares and to transport corn to the site of use is based on data from U.S. Department of Commerce (1967), U.S. Bureau of Census (1968, 1971, and 1972), Interstate Commerce Commission (1968a, 1968b, and 1968c), and U.S. Department of Transportation (1970). For 1970 this was estimated to be about 172,900 kcal/ha; it was about 49,400 kcal/ha in 1945.

[12]Corn yield is expressed as a mean of 3 yr, 1 yr previous and 1 yr past (USDA, 1967b, 1970a, and 1972c).

[13]Corn contains an estimated 9% protein (USDA, 1963).

[14]To produce 1 liter of fuel requires 10,000 kcal (Leach and Slesser, 1973).

[15]Nitrogen, 1 kg = 15,180 kcal, including production and processing (Leach and Slesser, 1973; Cervinka, et al., 1974).

[16]Phosphorus, 1 kg = 3200 kcal, including mining and processing (Leach and Slesser, 1973).

[17]Potassium, 1 kg = 2200 kcal, including mining and processing (Leach and Slesser, 1973).

[18]Corn seed, 1 kg = 3,520 kcal (USDA, 1963). This energy input was doubled because of the effort employed in producing hybrid seed corn.

[19]Production of 1 kg of insecticide, herbicide, or fungicide requires a total of 73,920 kcal. This estimate is based on the data of Pimentel, *et al.* (1975b) who reported that the production of 1 kg of insecticide or herbicide requires 24,200 kcal. The insecticide or herbicide is then diluted in approximately 5 liters of kerosene fuel (49,720 kcal) to make a total of 73,920 kcal for the application of 1 kg of insectide or herbicide.

[20]Each kg of corn was assumed to contain 3,520 kcal (USDA, 1963).

[21]Data from Lewis (1951).

[22]Axes and hoes assumed to weigh about 4 kg/ha and last about 5 years.

[23]Energy inputs to produce a kg of equipment were assumed to be 20,712 kcal based on the data of Berry and Fels (1973) in automobile construction which itself includes making, rolling, and casting steel.

[24]Normal quantity of seed for corn planting is 10.4 kg/ha.

[25]Corn contains about 3520 kcal/kg (USDA, 1963).

[26]Draft animal assumed to weigh 300 kg and doing medium work requires about 20,000 kcal of food energy/day (FAO, 1972).

[27]Equipment assumed to weigh 10 kg/ha and last about 5 years.

[28]Data from Ruthenberg (1968).

[29]Cassava dried contains about 3.3 kcal/gram (FAO, 1971).

[30]Cassava dried contains about 1.0% protein (PSAC, 1967).

[31]Data from BDPA (1965).

[32]Sorghum contains about 3.3 kcal/gram (FAO, 1971).

[33]Sorghum contains an estimated 11% protein (USDA, 1963).

[34]Data from MFACDCGI (1966).

[35]Wheat contains about 3.3 kcal/gram (USDA, 1963).

[36]Wheat contains an estimated 12% protein (USDA, 1963).

[37]Data from De Los Reyes, *et al.* (1965).

[38]Transportation inputs assumed to be 7,410 kcal.

[39]Rice contains an estimated 6.7% protein (USDA, 1963).

[40]Rice seed contains about 3.7 kcal/gram (De Los Reyes, *et al.*, 1965).

[41]Rice contains about 3630 kcal/kg (USDA, 1963).

[42]Estimate based on author's knowledge of potato production.

[43]Assumed to be similar to U.S. corn production (see Table 4-1).

[44]Data from Kearl and Snyder (1965).

[45]Estimate based on transportation data for U.S. corn production (Table 4-1). The estimate was increased to 250,000 kcal because the yield (kg) for potato production was considerably greater than that for corn production.

[46]Average U.S. potato yield in 1972 (USDA, 1973a).

[47]Potatoes contain an estimated 2.0% protein (USDA, 1963).

[48]Potatoes contain about 0.77 kcal/gram (FAO, 1971).

[49]Average of data from 8 oat producing regions (USDA, 1971b).

[50]Estimate based on drying data for U.S. corn production (Table 4-1). The estimate was decreased to 21,500 kcal because the yield (kg) for oat production was considerably less than that for corn production.

[51]Estimate based on transportation data for U.S. corn production (Table 4-1). The estimate was decreased to 86,450 kcal because the yield (kg) for oat production was considerably less than that for corn production.

[52]Oats contain an estimated 14.5% protein (Morrison, 1956).

[53]Oats contain about 3.9 kcal/gram (USDA, 1963).

[54]Average of data from 9 wheat producing regions (USDA, 1971b).

[55]Data from USDA (1971b).

[56]Estimate based on drying data for U.S. corn production (Table 4-1). The estimate was decreased to 21,500 kcal because the yield (kg) for wheat production was considerably less than that for corn production.

[57]Estimate based on transportation data for U.S. corn production (Table 4-1). The estimate was decreased to 86,450 kcal because the yield (kg) for wheat production was considerably less than that for corn production.

[58]Average U.S. wheat yield in 1971 (USDA, 1973a).

[59]Wheat contains about 3300 kcal/kg (USDA, 1963). An additional 25% of this amount (825 kcal) was included to cover the cost of producing the seed; thus, the total energy input equaled 4,125 kcal/kg for wheat seed.

[60]Data from Mullins and Grant (1968).

[61]Data from USDA (1971a).

[62]Data from Westoby, et al. (1975).

[63]Average U.S. soybean yield in 1972 (USDA, 1973a).

[64]Soybeans contain an estimated 34% protein (USDA, 1963).

[65]Soybeans contain about 4030 kcal/kg (USDA, 1963).

[66]Data from Grant and Mullins (1963).

[67]Because of the extra effort to produce high grade rice seed, each kg was assumed to cost 7260 kcal for production (Grant and Mullins, 1963).

[68]Assumed to be similar to U.S. soybean production (see Table 4-12).

[69]Average U.S. dry bean yield in 1972 (USDA, 1973a).

[70]Dry beans contain an estimated 22.3% protein (USDA, 1963).

[71]Dry beans contain about 3400 kcal/kg (USDA, 1963).

[72]Estimate based on data from NMSU (1971).

[73]Estimate based on author's knowledge of Brussels sprouts production.

[74]Average U.S. Brussels sprouts yield in 1972 (USDA, 1973a).

[75]Brussels sprouts contain an estimated 4.9% protein (USDA, 1963).

[76]Assumed to be similar to soybean production (see Table 4-12).

[77]Brussels sprouts contain about 450 kcal/kg (USDA, 1963).

[78]Average of data from 10 corn silage producing regions (USDA, 1971b).

[79]Corn silage contains an estimated 1.3% protein (Morrison, 1956).

[80]Corn silage contains about 798 kcal/kg; estimate based on data from Morrison (1956) and Reid (1973).

[81]Average of data from 5 alfalfa producing regions (USDA, 1971c).

[82]Data from Arnold, *et al.* (1974).

[83]Average of data from 6 alfalfa producing regions (USDA, 1973b).

[84]Average U.S. alfalfa yield in 1972 (USDA, 1973a).

[85]Alfalfa contains an estimated 11% protein (Morrison, 1956).

[86]Alfalfa seed estimated to contain 1530 kcal/kg based on data from Morrison (1956).

[87]Alfalfa contains about 1771 kcal/kg; estimate based on data from Morrison (1956) and Reid (1973).

[88]Average of data from 8 hay producing regions (USDA, 1971b).

[89]Tame hay contains an estimated 4% protein (Morrison, 1956).

[90]Tame hay seed estimated to contain 1500 kcal/kg based on data from Morrison (1956).

[91]Tame hay contains about 1716 kcal/kg. Estimate based on data from Morrison (1956) and Reid (1973).

On a per hectare basis, corn silage yielded 24.1 million kcal of livestock feed with an output/input ratio of 4.39 (Table 4-16); alfalfa yielded less than half this amount or 11.4 million kcal (Table 4-17); and hay production yielded 8.6 million kcal/ha (Table 4-18). For protein yield, alfalfa produced 710 kg/ha; corn silage, 393 kg/ha; and hay, 200 kg/ha.

Alternatives for Conserving Energy in Crop Production

With current and future shortages of energy resources, alternatives will be needed to make more effective use of energy resources in agricultural production. Some of the practical alternatives which might be employed in corn and other crop production are reviewed in the following.

Labor is a resource that is in abundant supply (although not always distributed where needed) and becomes more abundant in most of the LDCs as the world population continues to increase. Hence, every effort should be made to make crop production labor intensive within viable economic constraints. Labor input in corn production in the U.S. was estimated to have declined from about 57 hr/ha in 1945 to about 22 hr/ha in 1970 (Pimentel, *et al.*, 1973). To increase the labor inputs requires careful consideration of both the economic and social aspects of the problem.

Manpower, based upon kcal output/input ratios, can do the same farm work using less energy than most machinery. For example, the application of herbicides employing a tractor and sprayer requires about 4.7 liters of petroleum (47,000 kcal/ha) whereas if applied by hand sprayer, the labor input is only about 740 kcal/ha (Pimentel, *et al.*, 1973). Other hand operations also are more efficient than machinery operations. Since there should be abundant manpower available as the human population continues its rapid growth, means must be found to make effective use of this manpower for the total good of society.

Both machinery and gasoline (including diesel fuel) comprise a large energy input in U.S. corn production (Table 4-2). Certainly the use of relatively small minimum powered tractors offers opportunities for increased energy efficiencies in crop production. Also the use of draft animals (water buffalo, carabao, oxen, bullocks, and horses) offers some energy advantage as well as other advantages over tractors. For example, for one hour's work a tractor requires about 90,000 kcal of energy, whereas a water buffalo expends only about 800 kcal/hr.

Buffaloes require daily care (labor), but also produce milk and meat. Also tractors and buffaloes utilize different fuels. Tractors use expensive fossil fuels whereas buffaloes can be fed rice straw and other crop remains. In addition, buffaloes can be fed grass and other vegetation growing along paths, streams, and other noncrop land. The rice straw and other vegetation that passes through the buffalo is still valuable as fertilizer. The milk produced by the buffaloes is extremely valuable as a protein source for people on minimum diets (UN, 1971).

The single largest input in corn production in the United States is fertilizer (N, P, and K). Compared with phosphorus and potassium, nitrogen requires the largest quantity of energy in production (Table 4-2). Thus as energy supplies decrease other potential fertilizer sources such as livestock manure, some agricultural wastes, and other organic wastes (leaves, etc.) can be utilized.

For example, in Table 4-1 note that the fertilizer is applied to an average hectare of corn at a rate of 125 kg of nitrogen, 35 kg of phosphorus, and 67 kg of potassium. About the same amount of nitrogen is available from manure produced during one year by either 3 cows, 22 hogs, or 207 chickens (Benne, *et al.*, 1961; Dyal, 1963; Loehr and Asce, 1969; McEachron, *et al.*, 1969; Surbrook, *et al.*, 1971). Besides adding nutrients to the soil, manure adds organic matter (which increases the number of beneficial bacteria and fungi in the soil), makes plowing easier, improves the water-holding and percolation capacity of soil, reduces soil erosion, and improves the ratio of carbon to nitrogen in the soil (Andrews, 1954; Cook, 1962; Tisdale and Nelson, 1966). These same advantages result from the use of crop and other organic wastes.

The major costs of using manure for cereal production are hauling and spreading. Hauling and spreading manure within a radius of 0.8 to 1.6 km using a tractor and spreader is estimated to require 4.0 liters of gasoline (10,000 kcal/liter) per 900 kg (Linton, 1968). If the average manure application is 22,400 kg (production by 3 buffaloes or 3 dairy cows for 1 year) per hectare, an estimated 1,000,000 kcal (100 liters of gasoline) per hectare is necessary for the application and fertilization of corn with manure. This energy cost could be less if buffaloes were used for hauling the manure and this and other wastes were spread by hand.

In contrast, producing chemical fertilizer (125 kg of nitrogen, 35 kg of phosphorus, 67 kg of potassium) for 1 ha requires about 2,156,000 kcal (Table 4-2). About 9.4 liters of gasoline are used for tractor application per hectare; therefore, about 2,250,000 kcal for chemical fertilizer application is used. Hence if manure or other wastes were substituted for chemical fertilizer, the savings in energy would be a substantial 1,250,000 kcal or more per hectare. The energy savings would be far greater if buffaloes were used and hand labor employed in manure hauling and spreading.

It is possible to plant legumes between corn rows in late August and to plow this green manure under in early spring to add nitrogen to the soil. For example, in the northeastern U.S., Sprague (1936) reports that seeding corn hectares to winter vetch in late August and plowing the vetch under in late April yielded about 150 kg of nitrogen/ha. With rice production, Ghose, *et al.* (1956) reported that both rice and a legume, *Sesbania aculeata*, can be planted at the same time. As the rice crop matures the legume is uprooted and worked into the soil, adding about 96 kg of nitrogen/ha (8 weeks stage).

The energy cost of seeding a legume is estimated to be 222,300 kcal/ha (fuel and seeds [again this would be lower if hand labor were employed]). For the commercial production of 150 kg of chemical nitrogen, 2.28 million kcal are needed; thus the energy saved by planting a legume for green manure in U.S. corn would be substantial or 2.1 million kcal/ha. Hence, green manure offers a significant saving in energy. Also a green manure protects the soil from wind and water erosion during the winter and has the same advantages as manure in adding organic matter to the soil.

An analysis should be made of fertilizer and other alternative inputs to determine the maximum benefits per input in combination with all other inputs in crop production. In an investigation of fertilizer inputs in corn in Iowa, Munson and Doll (1959) reported that with 38 kg of phosphorus/ha and 224 kg of nitrogen/ha, mean corn yields were about 6335 kg/ha with all other inputs held constant (Figure 4-3). Combining most of the energy input data from Table 4-2 with nitrogen, phosphorus, and corn yield data of Munson and Doll, the kcal return per kcal input was calculated (Figure 4-3). Maximum return was 3.0 kcal for 1 kcal input at 134 kg of nitrogen/ha. Similar analyses should be made for the other inputs and for the complex interaction of these inputs.

Rotating crops offers several advantages in controlling pests. Note, over a billion pounds of pesticides are used in the United States annually (Figure 4-4). For example, rotating corn with a legume would effectively control the corn rootworm (Tate and Bare, 1946; Hill, *et al.*, 1948; Metcalf, *et al.*, 1962; Ortman and Fitzgerald, 1964; Robinson, 1966), would reduce corn disease problems (Pearson, 1967), and would reduce weed problems (NAS, 1968).

Weeds can be controlled effectively by mechanical cultivation, herbicides, hoe or combinations of these. On the basis of the energy expenditure, herbicidal weed control requires more energy than mechanical cultivation. For example, the use of 2.2 kg of preemergence, and 2.2 kg of postemergence herbicides, per hectare requires a total energy input of about 419,248 kcal (73,920 kcal/kg of herbicide plus 9.4 liters of gasoline for two applications). The use of three cultivations (rotary hoe twice) would require an estimated 18 liters of gasoline or 180,000 kcal/ha. This is a large saving. However, if the weeding were done by hoe or other hand

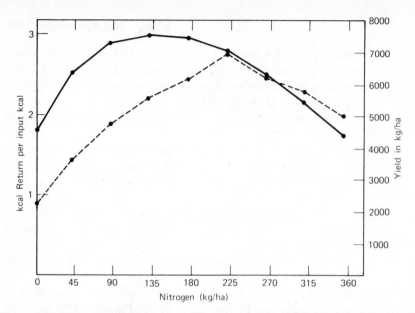

Figure 4-3. Corn yields (kg/ha., ○-----○) with varying amounts of nitrogen (phosphorus = 37 kg/ha.) applied per hectare (Munson and Doll, 1959). Kcal return per input kcal (○———○) was calculated using data of Munson and Doll and data in Pimentel *et al.*, 1973.

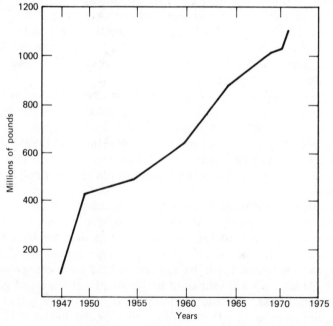

Figure 4-4. Quantities of pesticides produced in the United States (USDA, 1971d, 1973c).

96

implements, the energy input would be only about 12,350 kcal/ha—about 3% of the amount of energy using herbicides.

Minimum tillage may also offer some opportunity to reduce energy inputs in plowing and discing and reduce soil erosion, but this must be balanced against increased pest problems (CAST, 1975). A more complete analysis of this alternative would be necessary to determine the precise costs and benefits relative to energy and the environment.

The protein content of corn has changed little since 1910, averaging about 9% (Sprague, 1955; NAS, 1964 and 1969). However, the protein content of corn might be increased by selection to 12–15% (Harpstead, 1971). The value of increasing the quantity of protein in corn by even 1 percent is clear when it is calculated that this would reduce the need for 1.8×10^9 kg of soybean meal in U.S. mixed feeds (Sprague, 1955). Some increased energy inputs, such as increased nitrogen, would be necessary for cultivars of high protein corn, but the benefits may more than offset the costs.

As important as increasing the protein content of corn and other cereals is improving the quality of protein (Harpstead, 1971). Increasing both the quantity and quality of protein would contribute significantly to the improvement of nutrition for mankind.

Breeding corn and other cereals for insect, disease, and bird resistance would in itself reduce the energy inputs of pesticides. At the same time this would reduce problems from pesticide pollution. Also, less energy would be needed for corn production, if new corn varieties could be developed for faster maturity, reduced moisture content, greater water use efficiency and improved fertilizer response.

Earlier the high-energy cost of irrigation was mentioned and the impracticability of employing irrigation to increase the world's supply of arable land was emphasized. However, under certain circumstances and crops, irrigation may be profitable based on an energy input and return analysis.

A careful analysis of alternatives should suggest strategies for cereal production that would improve yields while minimizing the energy inputs and conserving water and land resources. For example, for U.S. corn production Pimentel *et al.* (1973) estimated that high yields of about 5000 kg of corn might be produced with about one-half of the energy now employed in corn production. Effective utilization of the surplus manpower in many parts of the world might make it possible to produce the same U.S. high yields while using only 20–30% of the energy employed in U.S. corn production. Similar efficiencies are also possible for other crops.

Other means of conserving energy rest with the possibility of altering

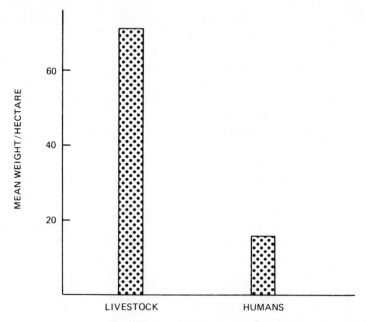

Figure 4-5.   **Livestock biomass significantly outweighs human biomass in the United States.**

eating habits. Per capita meat consumption in the U.S. is about 114 kg (250 lb) annually (USDA, 1975). To produce this animal protein about 69 kg of livestock biomass are maintained per hectare annually in the U.S. (USDA, 1975; USDA, 1973a). Note that human biomass per hectare averages only 15 kg (Figure 4-5). In other words, our livestock outweighs the human population by more than four-fold.

Animal protein is significantly better than vegetable protein in providing the essential amino acids required by man (Burton, 1965). However, because animals have to be fed vegetable protein for animal production, the conversion of vegetable protein to animal protein "costs." The "costs" are primarily the protein-calorie inputs to maintain the livestock during conversion and to maintain the breeding herds. Hence the yield of animal protein resulting from the conversion of vegetable protein is always less than the original quantity of plant protein fed the animals.

The most efficient conversion of vegetable protein into animal protein is milk production using dairy cattle (PSAC, 1967) (Figure 4-6). About 31% of feed protein is converted into milk (Pimentel, *et al.*, 1975a). It should be pointed out that about half of the feed consumed by dairy animals is forage. This points up an important value of cattle in making effective use of pastureland and rangeland that is unsuitable for crop production.

Beef cattle also can make use of forage vegetation, but beef production

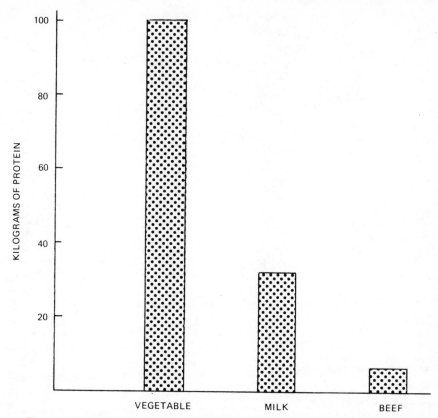

Figure 4-6. The conversion of vegetable protein into edible milk and beef protein.

is not as efficient as milk production (Figure 4-6). For example, it takes about 28 kcal of feed energy to produce 1 kcal of milk protein, but about 123 kcal of feed energy are necessary to produce 1 kcal of beef protein (Reid, 1970).

The high beef consumption of about 53 kg(116 lb)/person/yr accounts for the fact that about 600 kg (1300 lb) of grains are utilized per person in feeding livestock in the United States. In most developing countries where grain is consumed directly, the quantity of grain used per person is about 182 kg (400 lb).

The Energy Crisis and Food Production

Shortages and higher prices for fuel have resulted in increasing prices and shortages of crop production inputs such as fertilizers and pesticides. Re-

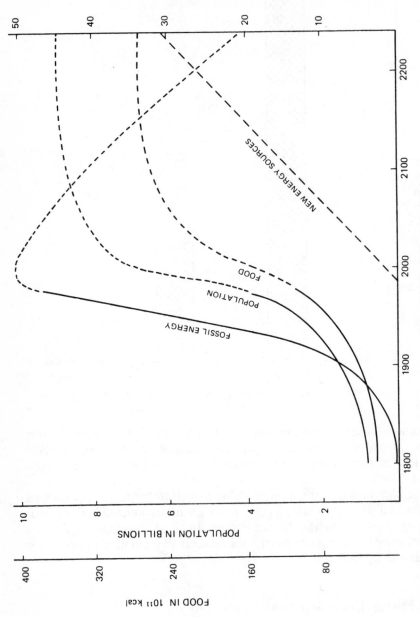

Figure 4-7. Estimated (———) and projected (------) trends in world population numbers, fossil fuel consumption, food production, and new energy sources based on data from Figure 4-1.

100

cently fertilizer prices increased from 3- to 12-fold in various parts of the world and in some cases no fertilizer was to be had at any price. Pesticide prices increased from two- to five-fold and again in some areas none was available. Shortages of these and other agricultural inputs that depend on fossil fuel for their production have had a significant impact upon agricultural production in all parts of the world.

Figure 4-7 shows the overall problem and interrelationships of energy, food, land, and population in perspective. In the introduction we mentioned that the world population is at 4 billion and there is no way to stop it from reaching 6 billion during the next 25 years. Food production has been just staying with human population growth (Figure 4-7). However, food supplies are still inadequate for nearly half the world population.

Earlier I mentioned the shortage of arable land; hence, the only means of increasing food production on the limited arable land will require more intensive crop production technology than in the past. This, of course, will require more fertilizers, hybrid seeds, and other inputs that in turn depend upon fossil energy (Figure 4-7).

According to Hubbert's (1972) estimates, the world's use of fossil fuels should reach a peak shortly after the turn of the century. Then gradually there will be a decline in fossil fuels. To maintain the supply of energy to keep the food system going, hopefully new energy sources will be developed. Obviously, these new energy sources will be far more expensive than our relatively cheap fossil fuels.

The energy used in crop production can be divided into two categories: (1) energy used to increase yields (fertilizers, hybrid seeds, etc.); (2) energy used to reduce manpower inputs (machinery, gasoline, etc.). Food production in the LDCs will have to depend primarily upon energy inputs to increase yields and less upon heavy machinery. A surplus of labor already exists in many parts of the world.

In conclusion, the problem of population control must be reemphasized. The human population cannot continue to increase without a continual decline in living conditions and worse misery than the majority of the world population faces today. The world urgently needs population control in each and every nation. Our efforts in agriculture are toward increasing food supplies and "buying time" to implement population controls.

References

Addison, H. (1961). *Land, Water and Food*. Chapman and Hall, London, 284 pp.
Andrews, N. B. (1954). *The Response of Crops and Soils to Fertilizers and Manures*, 2nd ed. State College, Miss., 463 pp.

Arnold, R. W., *et al.* (1974). *1975 Cornell Recommends for Field Crops.* New York State College of Agriculture and Life Sciences, Cornell University, Ithaca, N.Y., 52 pp.

BDPA (1965). Techniques rurales en Afrique. *Les temps de travaux.* Bureau pour le Développement de la Production Agricole (BDPA). Republique Francaise, Ministere de la Cooperation, 384 pp.

Benne, E. J., *et al.* (1961). Animal manures: What are they worth today? *Mich. Agr. Exp. Sta. Cir. Bull.* **231**, 16 pp.

Berg, A. (1973). *The Nutrition Factor.* The Brookings Inst., Washington, D.C., 290 pp.

Berry, R. S., and Fels, M. F. (1973). *The Production and Consumption of Automobiles: An Energy Analysis of the Manufacture, Discard, and Reuse of the Automobile and its Component Materials.* Dept. Chemistry, Univ. Chicago, Chicago, Ill., 56 pp.

Biswas, M. R., and Biswas, A. K. (1975). World Food Conference: A Perspective. *Agriculture and Environment.* **2**, 15–37.

Black, J. N. (1971). Energy relations in crop production. *Ann. Appl. Biol.* **67**, 272–278.

Borgstrom, G. (1973). *Harvesting the Earth.* Abelard-Schuman, New York, 552 pp.

Burton, B. T. (1965). *The Heinz Handbook of Nutrition.* McGraw-Hill, New York, 462 pp.

CAHR (1971). *Food Costs—Farm Prices.* Comm. on Agr., House of Rep., 92nd Congress, 118 pp.

CAST (1975). *Potential for Energy Conservation in Agricultural Production.* Prepared by a task force of the Council for Agricultural Science and Technology, January 24, 25 pp.

Cervinka, V., *et al.* (1974). *Energy Requirements for Agriculture in California.* Calif. Dept. Food & Agr., Univ. Calif., Davis, 151 pp.

CGG (1968). *Corn Grower's Guide.* P-A-G Div., W. R. Grace & Co., Aurora, Ill., 142 pp.

Clark, C. (1967). *The Economics of Irrigation.* Pergamon, London, 116 pp.

Cook, R. L. (1962). *Soil Management for Conservation and Production.* Wiley, New York, 506 pp.

DeGraff, H. F., and Washbon, W. E. (1943). *Farm-tractor Fuel Requirements.* Cornell University, Agr. Econ. 449, 4 pp.

De Los Reyes, B. N., *et al.* (1965). A case study of the tractor- and carabo-cultivated lowland rice farms in Laguna, crop year 1962–63. *Phil. Agric.* **49**(2), 75–94.

Dema, I. S. (1965). *Nutrition in Relation to Agricultural Production.* FAO, Rome, 123 pp.

Dyal, R. S. (1963). Agricultural value of poultry manure. 15 pp. In *Natl. Symp. on Poultry Ind. Waste Mgt.* Nebr. Ctr. for Continuing Ed., Lincoln, Nebr. (unpaged).

FAO (1970a). *Lives in Peril: Protein and the Child.* FAO, Rome, 52 pp.

FAO (1970b). *Production Yearbook, 1969.* UN Food and Agriculture Organization, Vol. **23**, 825 pp.

FAO (1971). *Food Balance Sheets.* FAO, Rome, 764 pp.

FAO (1972). *Manual on the Employment of Draught Animals in Agriculture.* Centre D'Etudes et D'Experimentation du Machinisme Agricole Tropical, FAO, Rome, 249 pp.

FAO (1973a). *The State of Food and Agriculture, 1973; World Review by Regions.* FAO, Rome

FAO (1973b). *Production Yearbook, 1972.* Vol. **26.** FAO, Rome, 496 pp.

Freedman, R., and Berelson, B. (1974). The human population. *Sci. Am.* **231**(3), 30–39.

Ghose, R. L. M., Ghatge, M. B., and Subrarhmanyan, V. (1956). *Rice in India.* Indian Council of Agr. Res., New Delhi, 507 pp.

Grant, W. R., and Mullins, T. (1963). *Enterprise Costs and Returns on Rice Farms in Grand Prairie, Ark.* Ark. Agr. Exp. Sta. Rep. Series 119, 35 pp.

Harpstead, D. D. (1971). High lysine corn. *Sci. Am.* **225**, 34–42.

Harrar, J. G. (1961). Socio-economic factors that limit needed food production and consumption. *Fed. Proc.* **20**, 381–383.

Heady, E. O., *et al.* (1972). Future water and land use: Effects of selected public agricultural and irrigation policies on water demand and land use. Report of the Center for Agricultural and Rural Development, Iowa State Univ. of Science and Tech. Prepared for the National Water Comm., PB-206-790 (NWC-EES-71-003) NTIS. Springfield, Va.

Hill, R. E., Hixon, E., and Muma, M. H. (1948). Corn rootworm control tests with benzene hexachloride, DDT, nitrogen fertilizers, and crop rotations. *J. Econ. Entomol.* **41**, 392–401.

Hirst, E. (1974). Food-related energy requirements. *Science* **184**, 134–138.

Hubbert, M. K. (1972). Man's conquest for energy: Its ecological and human consequences, pp. 1–50 in *The Environmental and Ecological Forum 1970–1971.* U.S. Atomic Energy Commission Office of Information Services, Oak Ridge, Tennessee, 186 pp.

Huxley, J. S. (1964). The impending crisis. In *The Population Crisis and the Use of World Resources,* S. Mudd (Ed.), pp. 6–11. Junk, the Hague, 562 pp.

ICC (1968a). *Freight Commodity Statistics, Class I Motor Carriers of Property in Intercity Service.* ICC, Govt. Printing Office, Washington, D.C., 97 pp.

ICC (1968b). *Freight Commodity Statistics, Class I Railroads in the U.S.* ICC, Govt. Printing Office, Washington, D.C., 40 pp.

ICC (1968c). *Transportation Statistics, Part 1* (402 pp.), *Part 5* (64 pp.), *Part 7* (165 pp.). ICC, Govt. Printing Office, Washington, D.C.

Jiler, H. (1972). *Commodity Yearbook.* Commodity Res. Bur., New York.

Kearl, C. D., and Snyder, D. P. (1965). Costs and returns in the production of potatoes on upland soils in New York State, 1963. Cornell Univ., Dept. of Agr. Econ. A.E. Res. 160, 31 pp.

Kellogg, C. E. (1967). World food prospects and potentials: A long-run look, pp. 98–111. In *Alternatives for Balancing World Food Production Needs.* E. O. Heady (ed.). Iowa State Univ. Press, Ames, Iowa, 273 pp.

Leach, G., and Slesser, M. (1973). *Energy Equivalents of Network Inputs to Food Producing Processes.* Strathclyde University, Glasgow, 1973, 38 pp.

Lewis, O. (1951). *Life in a Mexican Village: Tepoxtlán revisited.* Univ. of Illinois Pr., Urbana, Ill., 512 pp.

Linton, R. E. (1968). The economics of poultry manure disposal. *Cornell Extension Bull. 1195.* Cornell Univ., Ithaca, N.Y., 23 pp.

Loehr, R. C., and Asce, M. (1969). Animal waste—A natural problem. *J. San. Eng. Div., Proc. Am. Soc. Civil Eng.* **2**, 189–221.

Mangelsdorf, P. C. (1966). Genetic potentials for increasing yields of food crops and animals. In *Prospects of the World Food Supply.* Symp. Proc. Natl. Acad. Sci., Washington, D.C.

McEachron, L. W., *et al.* (1969). Economic return from various land disposal systems for dairy cattle manure, 393–400. In *Cornell Univ. Conf. on Agric. Waste Mgt.* 1969.

Meadows, D. H., *et al.* (1972). *The Limits to Growth.* Universe Books, New York, 205 pp.

Metcalf, C. L., Flint, W. P., and Metcalf, R. L. (1962). *Destructive and Useful Insects.* McGraw-Hill, New York, 1087 pp.

MFACDCGI (1966). *Farm Management in India.* Directorate of Econ. and Stat., Dept. of Agr., Ministry of Food, Agriculture Community Development and Cooperation Government of India (MFACDCGI), 128 pp.

Morrison, F. B. (1956). *Feeds and Feeding: A Handbook for the Student and Stockman.* Morrison, Ithaca, N.Y., 1165 pp.

Mullins, T., and Grant, W. R. (1968). *Enterprise costs and returns on rice farms in the Delta, Ark.* Rep. Ser. Ark. Agric. Exp. Sta. #170. 26 pp.

Munson, R. D., and Doll, J. P. (1959). The economics of fertilizer use in crop production. In A. G. Norman (ed.), *Adv. in Agr. XI*, pp. 133–169.

National Academy of Sciences (1964). *Feed Composition.* Joint Rept. of U.S.A. and Canadian Comm. on Animal Nutrition. Natl. Res. Coun. Pub. 1232, 167 pp.

———— (1968). Weed control. *Principles of Plant and Animal Pest Control, Vol. II.* NAS Pub. 1597, 471 pp.

———— (1969). *United States-Canadian Tables of Feed Composition.* Natl. Res. Council, Comm. on Animal Nutrition, Subcomm. on Feed Composition. NAS. Res. Publ. 1684, 92 pp.

———— (1971). *Rapid Population Growth, Vols. I, II.* Publ. for NAS by Johns Hopkins Press, Baltimore, Md., 105 and 690 pp.

New Mexico State University (1971). *Cost and Return Budgets for Selected Crop Enterprises for 320-, 640-, and 1280-acre Farm Sizes in Northwestern New Mexico.* Agr. Exp. Sta. Research Report 194, 87 pp.

Ortman, E. E., and Fitzgerald, P. J. (1964). Developments in corn rootworm research. *Proc. Ann. Hybrid Corn Industry Res. Conf.* **19**, 38–45.

Pearson, L. C. (1967). *Principles of Agronomy.* Reinhold, New York.

Pimentel, D. (1974). Energy use in world food production. *Environ. Biol.* Cornell University, Ithaca, New York. Report 74-1. 43 pp.

Pimentel, D., *et al.* (1973). Food production and the energy crisis. *Science* **182**, 443–449.

Pimentel, D., *et al.* (1975a). Protein production, energy/land limitations and population pressure. (Manuscript.)

Pimentel, D., Mooney, H., and Stickel, L. (1974b). *Herbicide Report.* Hazardous Materials Advisory Committee, Environmental Protection Agency, Washington, D.C., 196 pp. (issued in 1977).

PSAC (1967). The world food problem. Rept. of Panel on the World Food Supply. Pres. Sci. Adv. Comm., The White House. U.S. Govt. Printing Off. Vols. I, II, III, 127 pp., 772 pp., 332 pp.

Reid, J. T. (1970). Will meat, milk and egg production be possible in the future? *Proc. Cornell Nutr. Conf.*, pp. 50–63.

Reid, J. T. (1973). Potentials for improving production efficiency of dairy and beef cattle. *Proc. 21st Ann. Mtg. Agr. Res. Instit. Natl. Acad. Sci.*, pp. 87–100.

Robinson, R. E. (1966). Sunflower-soybean and grain sorghum-corn rotations versus monoculture. *Agron. J.* **58**, 475–477.

Ruthenberg, H. (ed.) (1968). *Smallholder farming development in Tanzania.* Weltforum Verlag Munchen, Germany, 360 pp.

Sebrell, H. (1968). As reported in interview. In Berg, 1973.

Smerdon, E. T. (1974). Energy conservation practices in irrigated agriculture. Sprinkler Irrigation Assoc. Ann. Tech. Conf., Denver, Colo., Feb. 24, 9 pp.

Spengler, J. J. (1968). World hunger: past, present, prospective "That there should be great famine." *World Rev. of Nutrition and Dietetics* **9**, 1–31.

Sprague, G. F. (1955). *Corn and Corn Improvement.* Academic Press, New York, 699 pp.

Sprague, H. B. (1936). The value of winter green manure crops. New Jersey Agr. Sta. Bull. 609, 19 pp.

Starr, C., and Rudman, R. (1973). Parameters of technological growth. *Science*, **182**, 358–364.

Steinhart, J. S., and Steinhart, C. E. (1974). Energy use in the U.S. food system. *Science* **184**(4134), 307–316.

Surbrook, T. C., *et al.* (1971). Drying poultry waste. In *Proc. Int. Symp. Livestock Wastes.* Amer. Soc. Agr. Eng., St. Joseph, Mich., 360 pp.

Tate, H. D., and Bare, O. S. (1964). Corn rootworms. Neb. Agr. Sta. Bull. 381, 12 pp.

Thurston, H. D. (1969). Tropical agriculture: A key to the world food crises. *Bio. Sci.* **19**, 29–34.

Tisdale, S. L., and Nelson, W. L. (1966). *Soil Fertility and Fertilizers.* 2nd ed. Macmillan, New York, 418 pp.

United Nations (1971). Strategy statement on action to avert the protein crisis in the developing countries. *Report of the Panel of Experts on the Protein Problem Confronting Developing Countries.* U.N. Headquarters, 3–7 May, 1971. UN Publication, 27 pp.

———. (1973). World population prospects as assessed in 1968. Department of Economic and Social Affairs. *Population Studies*, No. 53, 167 pp.

U.S. Bureau of the Census (1965). *Statistical Abstract of the United States.* Washington, D.C., 86th Ed., 1047 pp.

———. (1968). *Census of Agriculture, 1964.* Washington, D.C., Vol. II, pp. 909–955.

———. (1971). *Statistical Abstract of the United States.* Washington, D.C., 92nd Ed, 1008 pp.

———. (1972). *Statistical Abstract of the United States.* Washington, D.C., 93rd Ed, 1017 pp.

U.S. Dept. of Agriculture (1953). *Farm Power and Farm Machines.* Bur. Agr. Econ. Bull. F. M. 101, 35 pp.

———. (1954). Changes in farm production and efficiency. Agric. Research Service, Prod. Econ. Res. Br., 40 pp.

———. (1957). Fertilizer used on crops and pasture in the United States. 1954 estimates. Agric Res. Ser. Stat. Bull. 216, 55 pp.

———. (1963). *Composition of Foods.* Consumer and Food Economics Res. Div., ARS, Agr. Handbook No. 8, 190 pp.

———. (1964). Liquid petroleum fuel used by farmers in 1959 and related data. Econ. Res. Ser. Farm Prod. Econ. Div. Stat. Bull. 344, 20 pp.

———. (1967a). Fertilizer use in the United States: 1964 estimates. Econ. Res. Ser. Stat. Rep. Serv., Stat. Bull. 408, 38 pp.

———. (1967b). *Agricultural Statistics 1967.* U.S. Govt. Printing Office, 758 pp.

———. (1968). Extent of farm pesticide use on crops in 1966. Agric. Econ. Rep. 147. Econ. Res. Ser., 23 pp.

———. (1970a). *Agricultural Statistics 1970*. Govt. Printing Office, 627 pp.

———. (1970b). Quantities of pesticides used by farmers in 1966. Econ. Res. Ser. Agric. Econ. Rep. 179. 61 pp.

———. (1971a). Fertilizer situation. Econ. Res. Ser. FS-1. 42 pp.

———. (1971b). Selected U.S. crop budgets. *Yields, inputs, and variable costs, Vol. II: North Central Region*. Econ. Res. Ser., ERS 458, 217 pp.

———. (1971c). Selected U.S. crop budgets. *Yields, inputs, and variable costs, Vol. III. Great Plains Region*. Econ. Res. Ser., ERS 459, 180 pp.

———. (1971d). The pesticide review 1970. Agr. Stab. and Cons. Ser., 46 pp.

———. (1972a). *Factbook of United States Agriculture*. Office of Information, Misc. Publ. 1063, 87 pp.

———. (1972b). Changes in farm production and efficiency. Econ. Res. Ser. Stat. Bull. 233, 31 pp.

———. (1972c). Crop production. *1971 Annual summary*. Crop Rep. Bd. State Rept. Ser., 82 pp.

———. (1973a). *Agricultural Statistics 1973*. U.S. Govt. Printing Office, Washington, D.C., 617 pp.

———. (1973b). Selected U.S. crop budgets. *Yields, inputs, and variable costs, Vol. VI. Southwest Region*. Econ. Res. Ser., ERS 514, 71 pp.

———. (1973c). The pesticide review, 1972. Agr. Stab. Cons. Ser., 58 pp.

———. (1975). National food situation. Econ. Res. Ser., February, NFS-151, 45 pp.

5

ENERGY AND FOOD PRODUCTION

Margaret R. Biswas, President
Biswas and Associates, Ottawa, Canada, and
International Institute for Applied Systems Analysis
Laxenburg, Austria

The major items that would undoubtedly be in any agenda for immediate world action are population, food, and energy; and their interrelationships. Thus, not surprisingly, a series of world gatherings has been held on these subjects, including the World Population Conference and the World Food Conference under the auspices of the United Nations (Biswas and Biswas, 1974a, 1975a).

Many more similar meetings will undoubtedly be held before mankind can even come close to practical solutions. The problems of population, food, and energy, are not mutually exclusive: in fact they are closely interlinked. These three issues may be highly visible, but they are only three of the many real problems, all closely interrelated, that lie at the heart of the overall global crisis. As the former U.S. Secretary of State, Henry Kissinger (1974), has pointed out: "Each of the problems we face—of combating inflation and stimulating growth, of feeding the hungry and lifting the impoverished, of the scarcity of physical resources and the surplus of despair—is part of the international global problem." Even a cursory analysis of this extremely complex situation will soon convince any sceptic that these problems are multidimensional and that no nation, however rich and powerful, can cope with them individually and unilaterally. Some of the problems indeed go far beyond the capacity of even a small group of the most powerful nations to solve. Also, action taken to combat these types of problems must be well planned and coordinated; otherwise, steps taken to alleviate them in one part of the world could create negative reverberations in another (Biswas and Biswas, 1976a).

Thus, the time has come when politicians and policy-makers must look at these complex problems with a clear understanding of their interrelatedness and synergistic effects and not rely solely on the principle of reductionism to solve individual problems as they surface. Within this context and overall philosophy, the interrelationships between food and energy will be examined herein.

The world demand for food is expanding more rapidly than ever before in history. Increase in population and changes in its spatial distribution have aggravated the food situation during the last 35 years. Many geographical regions, but not Western Europe, were net exporters of grain immediately prior to the Second World War. The situation had changed drastically by 1975: all regions except North America and Australia and New Zealand are now net importers of grains. Beside population growth, rising affluence, agricultural inefficiency and misguided political expediency have contributed to the further aggravation of the problem. Rising affluence is rapidly emerging as a major new claimant on the global food resources. Currently, the agricultural resources necessary to support one inhabitant of a more affluent country can support on an average five citizens of developing countries such as Bangladesh, Uganda or Colombia.

The gravity of the world food situation is illustrated by the fact that demand for food in developing countries is expected to increase at a rate of about 3.6%/yr during the 1972–1985 period compared with an average increase of 2.6% during the preceding 12 years (M. R. Biswas, 1975). If this basic growth-rate is not attained, developing market economy countries will have to import 85 million tons of grain by 1985 in normal years and over 100 million tons in years of bad harvests. The magnitude of the problem becomes self-evident when the costs of such imports are visualized. At the average 1973–1974 cereal price of $200/ton, their import bills in normal years will become $17 billion/year in 1985. These latter figures refer to cereals only: in addition other types of food will also have to be imported (UN, 1974). Comparisons of population and per capita food production for the developed and developing countries and the world as a whole is shown in Figure 5-1.

Faced with this type of a critical situation, some of the world reactions have predictably fallen short of good housekeeping practices. The strategies put forward at the World Food Conference relied heavily on the application of more pesticides, fertilizers, irrigation, and machineries: in other words, the emphasis was to use the North American type of fossil fuel energy-intensive agriculture to increase yield in other parts of the world. Whether such a strategy was desirable in an era of energy crisis, when many of the developing countries were facing serious balance of

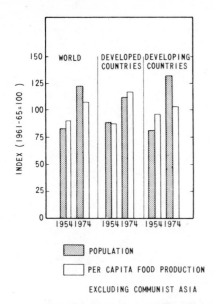

POPULATION

PER CAPITA FOOD PRODUCTION

EXCLUDING COMMUNIST ASIA

Figure 5-1. Comparison between population and per capita food production.

payment deficits even to pay for their existing energy import bills (Biswas and Biswas, 1975b), was not seriously considered. Nor was the question considered whether such a policy was desirable and sustainable on a long-term basis.

The success story of continual increase in agricultural yields in North America is known to every school-boy, but what is not known is the fact that modern agriculture has become increasingly energy intensive during this period. Let us briefly examine some major changes in the agricultural sector during the past four decades. In the United States, the number of operating farms has been reduced from 6.3 million in 1940 to about 2.8 million at present, with nearly one million disappearing since 1961. Consequently average farm size has increased from 167 acres in 1940 to 297 acres in 1960, and close to 400 acres in 1970. The farm population, during the same period, has dwindled drastically—from about 31.9 million (23.2% of the population) in 1940 to 9.4 million (4.8% of the population in 1970 (Perelman, 1972). At the same time, the number of animals used declined from a peak of more than 22 million in 1920 to a very small number at present. Expressed in a different manner, it means that during the last few decades the total agricultural production in the U.S. has increased significantly and at the same time there has been a drastic reduction in the number of farm workers and animals. The general experience has been very similar in other developed nations like Canada or Great Britain (Biswas and Biswas, 1976b; Leach, 1975a, b).

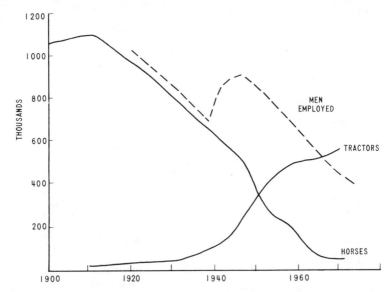

Figure 5-2.   Changing patterns of men, horses and tractors used in the farms, U.K.

One may accordingly ask how such an apparent dichotomy can take place. The answer is fairly simple: it is made possible by vast infusion of energy. In an era of cheap energy prices, such massive and rapid industrialization of the agricultural production practices made economic sense. However, in a different era, when energy prices are high and the point of diminishing return has been reached in many instances, we have to reexamine and perhaps reorient some of our present production practices.

Let us consider the developments in Great Britain as an example. As agricultural workers left for urban centres, they were replaced by a variety of machines. Currently there are more tractors on British farms than employed men, as is shown in Figure 5-2 (after Blaxter, 1973). Another important factor is the fact that the horsepower of the machines has also been increasing continuously. For example, most the tractors used in the 1930s were in the 20-hp range. In contrast, more than 70% of the tractors sold at present are of over 50 hp; the corresponding figure for 50-hp tractors was only 45% as late as 1964.

Paradoxically all these developments can be looked at in a somewhat different light. Blaxter (1973) suggests that the present fuel consumption in British agriculture represents the expenditure of 300 horsepower hours on every acre of crops and grass. If it is assumed that a real horse did 1,500 hp-hr of work/yr, and that all the present agricultural machines have a mean efficiency of 33%, then our present power expenditure is equivalent to the use of 1 horse/5 acres compared with 1 real horse to 25–35 acres in the 1920s and 1930s. Thus, power input to British agriculture has increased by 500–700% within the short period of only four to five decades.

Machines, however, are not the only form of energy input into the agricultural production process that have increased significantly in recent years. We have increased the use of fertilizers, pesticides, herbicides, propionic acid for grain preservation, and a host of other chemicals which all need further energy for their manufacturing processes. For example, 9000 kcal, 1450 kcal, and 1000 kcal, of energy are necessary to manufacture 1 lb of nitrogen, phosphorous, and potassium fertilizers, respectively. Further energy is necessary to apply these and other chemicals to the land and also to manufacture the machines that are used for their application. In addition, modern agriculture has been consuming more and more fertilizers, insecticides, and herbicides. Table 5-1 shows the increase in the number of tractors, combined harvesters and thrashers, and the amount of nitrogenous and phosphatic fertilizers used in some selected countries of the world from 1966 to 1973. The data used in this table have been compiled from various United Nations publications.

According to Revelle (1976), the use of chemical nitrogen fertilizers in world agriculture is estimated to increase 4-fold, from 40 million tons in 1974 to 160 million tons by the year 2000. By 2000, 250–300 million tons of fossil fuels would then be required for fertilizer production—400% of our present consumption. "At 1976 prices of $200 to $250 per ton of fixed nitrogen, the cost of nitrogen fertilizer would be $32 billion to $40 billion, of which the fossil fuel cost would be $15 billion to $20 billion. That would still be a small fraction of the estimated $300 billion value of the crop production that is attributable to the application of fertilizer." Development of grass and cereals possessing the ability to fix nitrogen, or of production systems which increase nitrogen fixation by bacteria and algae in the soil are unlikely to alter fertilizer requirements (Norse, 1977). The additional basic research required makes application of major innovation before 2000 unlikely. Even then, use will be limited for two reasons. Nitrogen fertilizers represent only a small percentage of the retail cost of food, so introduction of biological fixation, would have little effect on food prices. Second, biological nitrogen fixation is inhibited by low soil moisture levels and acid soils, two common conditions.

Energy accounting of crop production can be carried out in several ways. For example, Pimentel in chapter 4 has used process analysis, Hirst (1973) has used input–output analysis and Heichel (1973) used total aggregation on the GNP basis. Process analysis tends to be quite laborious since all inputs and outputs through the entire skein of processes have to

Table 5-1. Selected Examples of Energy Inputs to Agriculture in Different Countries of the World in 1966 and 1973 (Source UN)

| | Tractors | | Combines† | | Fertilizers in Thousand Tons‡ | | | |
| | | | | | Nitrogen | | Phosphate | |
	1966	1973	1966	1973	1966–67	1973–74	1966–67	1973–74
Australia	300,859	342,400	64,744	63,300	108	176	979.7	1,170.6
Brazil	108,900	185,000			71.1	405	91.6	725
Canada	586,905	656,800	165,580	181,500	276.7	530	374	505
China (Mainland)	88,000	170,000			2,010	3,815	538	1,389.7
Egypt	14,500	18,500			243.8	330	43.4	75
Ethiopia	800	3,400	10	130	1.2	9.1	1.5	10.1
France	996,422	1,454,900	102,068	152,700	103	206.4	1,363.8	2,152.4
Germany, West	1,164,113	1,418,056	124,000	171,000	888.6	1,100.8	791.8	916.7
India	48,000	69,600			830.2	1,835	274.6	634
Japan	36,084	283,000	910	1,200	852.7	897.3	613.6	792.9
Kenya	5,729	6,700			11.8	20.4	16.6	20.7
Saudi Arabia	400	860	80	230	5.1	4	3.1	1.2
USSR	1,613,000	2,180,000	519,700	670,000	2,656	6,256	1,664	2,699
UK	475,000	465,000	64,000	64,600	759.8	980	439.1	434.6
United States	4,800,000	4,376,000	895,000	698,000	5,467.7	8,277	3,905.1	4,600
Zaire	850	1,100			1.3	3.2	0.4	1.6

†Combined harvester-thrashers in use.
‡Fertilizer year, 1st July–30th June.

be analysed. Complete analysis is time consuming, and unless such an analysis is complete, it could be misleading. Processes analysed should be the most typical, otherwise errors could be quite significant. The input—output process has the advantage of tracing energy flows between different sectors of the economy by using national input–output tables. However, availability of data, especially latest information, high level of data aggregation that makes it difficult to separate individual products and inputs, and the accuracy of coefficients leave much to be desired. Input–output data for most of the nations of the world are not available, and also when available they are often out of date.

Not much work has been done so far on the energy balance studies of different types of crops. The techniques for such analyses have not yet been properly developed. Blaxter (1973), however, prepared one such analysis for potatoes for Great Britain which is shown in Figure 5-3. The process is self-explanatory. The ratio of energy input to output was shown to be 0.87.

Analysis of the North American agricultural practices show that we have reached the end of an era when increasing energy subsidies will increase food production concomitantly. We have reached the point of diminishing return when further increases in yield are progressively harder to achieve. It is also becoming evident that increasing the energy input is unlikely to bring further reduction of farm labour.

From this discussion it should be quite clear that we cannot feed the world by using the North American system of food production. The dimensions of the problem, and the resource constraints faced, can be gauged from the following calculations. If we assume that the population of India is 600 million, and we feed each Indian the U.S. equivalent of 3000 cal/day, instead of their present 2000 cal, India would need more energy for the food sector alone than she is currently using for all purposes. If we consider the world as a whole on the same basis, we will have to use 80% of the global energy expenditure for the food sector alone. (Pimentel, *et al.*, 1973).

The "Green Revolution" type of high-yielding agriculture in the developing world is somewhat similar to western agriculture in that both are fossil fuel energy-intensive. The new strains of wheat, corn, rice, etc. need more fertilizers and pesticides to provide optimal yields. In addition, careful water-control, or irrigation, is an absolute necessity. This is in contrast to native crops which did not. Irrigation is highly energy intensive.

The present emphasis on monoculture means that even though there are more than 80,000 edible species, only 50 or so are being actively cultivated. Today, most of the people in the world are fed by about 20 crops.

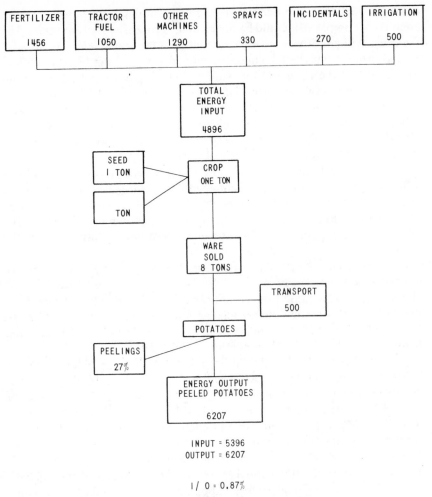

Figure 5-3.   **Energy input-output analysis for potatoes.**

We have been experimenting with the gene-pool to maximize certain features of a few crops and to suppress some "undesirable" features. Often we have sacrificed qualities such as hardiness or resistance to diseases, pests, and adverse climates, for higher yields. Such universal homogenization is fraught with danger, and we must remember that the further we deviate from the original characteristics of plants, the more energy and controlled conditions may generally be necessary to obtain the optimal yield.

This does not mean, however, that we are advocating no use of fertilizers, pesticides and irrigation. In much of the developing world, significant increase in yield can be obtained by further small inputs of energy. This is because a small energy input into low-intensity culture will increase yield much more than an identical energy input into high-intensity production process. For example, application of the first 60 kg of nitrogen/ha to rice in the Philippines increased the yield from 4900 kg to 6150 kg—an improvement of 1250 kg. However, when the fertilizer input was increased once again by 60 kg, from 120 kg to 180 kg/ha, the yield went up from 7050 kg to 7300—an improvement of only 250 kg. Similarly, the first 60 kg of nitrogen fertilizer improved the wheat yield in India from 3844 kg to 4230 kg/ha—an increase of 1386 kg. But if the input was increased from 180 kg to 240 kg, it improved the yield by only 34 kg—from 6651 kg to 6685 kg.

For many of the developing countries, increase in the energy input of the agricultural production processes will significantly increase crop yields. In 1967, the Science Advisory Committee to the U.S. President carried out an analysis of energy inputs and their relation to the average aggregate yield of major crops. The energy input included human, animal, and mechanized power and was expressed in hp/ha. Figure 5-4 is reproduced from that report with some modifications. It shows many of the developing countries to be within a minimal power range, and the Committee, not surprisingly, concluded that "the developing free world is far short of the power required for agricultural efficiency." The efficiency in the report was limited to the consideration of maximization of yield per hectare. In that era of cheap energy, efficiency in energy use was not a major consideration. Pimentel, in Chapter 4, discusses various methods of conserving energy in the agricultural area.

Even though the majority of developing countries can improve yield by increasing energy inputs to agriculture, the motto should not be "more energy" but more "efficient use of energy." We should not try a direct transfer of technology of the Western countries which requires little labour, heavy mechanization and extensive use exhaustible fossil fuels. The American food system requires 15 cal of fossil fuel energy in the form of gasoline, machinery, fertilizer, and pesticides for every calorie of food energy consumed (Steinhart, 1976).

Makhijani (1975) maintains that though fossil fuel energy use in the Third World for agriculture is far lower than in the industrialized nations, farms in developing countries often use more energy per hectare than farms in industrialized nations if all the animal and human labour that goes into farming is considered. It takes more energy to feed the bullocks and mules than to farm with the heavily mechanized methods of U.S.

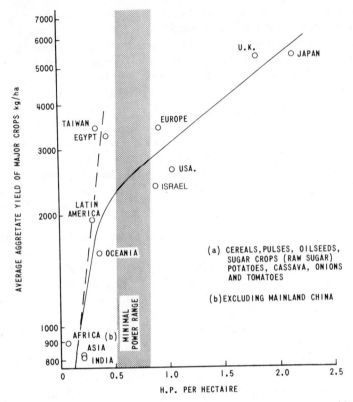

Figure 5-4.   Relation between yield and power for major food crops.[a]

agriculture. Since farms in the United States are generally much more productive per unit of land, energy use per ton of food produced in developing countries is much higher in comparison with mechanized farming, even when irrigation and fertilizers are considered. (Energy use per hectare in rice production is shown in Table 5-2). The source of energy used on subsistence farms is, however, human and animal labour, being wood and vegetation which are plentiful, renewable and cheap. Not only is scarce foreign exchange not required, but almost no money is needed. In addition to working in the fields, the draft animals such as bullocks and water buffaloes provide protein in the form of meat and milk, and transportation.

Presently, mechanized farming uses more nonrenewable energy resources than subsistence farming and wastes the energy value of crop residues, but the crop residues could substitute the petroleum used by machines. Even in the United States potential availability for methane from crop residues and animal dung exceeds energy use for agriculture (Makhijani, 1975). For every ton of cereal grain there are one to two tons of humanly inedible crop residues with an energy content considerably greater than the food energy in the grain (Revelle, 1976). These residues are now being wasted in terms of fuel. The theoretical potential for biomass conversion in the United States is high because its population density is relatively low and solar inputs reasonably high (Leach 1975b). In more densely populated energy intensive societies such as Great Britain, West Germany, and Japan, the potential for agricultural fuel production is much smaller. About 15–20% of the entire land surface of Great Britain or Germany would be needed for fuel crops, grown for entire conversion to provide the energy presently used by the entire food systems.

Biomass conversion is, however, the essential answer to provide adequate energy for developing countries. The basic raw materials for the production of methane and fertilizers in village biogas plants are crop residues and dung. Crop residues increase as agriculture becomes more productive. Biogasification enables the small farmers to use their energy more efficiently by providing the fuel necessary for selective mechanization without destroying the fertilizer potential of the organic wastes. In spite of the abundance of animal and human labour, mechanical power requiring fuels, is necessary for lift irrigation and selective mechanization of agricultural operations which require peak labour; for example, threshing. In general, only operations for which labour is inadequate should be mechanized. Irrigation results in greater yields and allows multiple cropping, thereby increasing employment and production. In spite of the surplus labour, agriculture in the developing world is deficient in the power to maximize production, estimated at 0.5 hp/ha. At present only 0.05 hp/ha is available in Africa, 0.19 hp in Asia, and 0.27 hp in Latin America (FAO, 1970). In Europe about 0.93 hp/ha is used in agriculture.

In all countries, processing, packaging, transporting, distribution, refrigerating, and cooking require more energy than crop production. For every man who works on a farm in the United Kingdom, half a man is employed in the agricultural supply industries and 6½ are in the food distribution industries (Slesser, 1975). At present, one-half of all trucks in the United States haul food and agricultural products (Steinhart, *et al.*, 1976). Although in developing countries distribution and processing is minimal, much more fuel is consumed in cooking food because of inefficient stoves (Makhijani, 1975).

There are many alternatives by which the developed world can drastically reduce energy inputs without sacrificing yields. In the United States

Table 5-2. Energy Use per Hectare in Rice Production in Various Countries (source Makhijani)

Country	Installed Horsepower (hp/ha) Farm Machines and Draft Animals Only	Energy for Farm Operations (million Btu/ha)	Energy for Irrigation and Nitrogen Fertilizers Manufacture (million Btu/ha)	Total Energy Input (million Btu/ha)	Rice Yield (kg/ha)	Energy Intensity (million Btu/ Ton of Rice)
India	0.7	20	6.5	26.5	1,400	19
China	0.7	20	12	32	3,000	10.7
Taiwan	0.5	10	22	32	4,000	8
Japan	1.6	10	25	35	5,600	6.2
U.S.A.	1.5	7	25	32	5,100	6.3

For India and China about 20% of the installed horsepower is in tractors; for Taiwan 50%; for Japan 90%; for the U.S. 100%.

the growth of home gardening and local direct marketing cooperatives in the early 1970s suggest that less centralized and less specialized food production and processing may be beginning (Steinhart, 1976). The United States Department of Agriculture states that in 1976 half of all United States households attempted to grow some food. Equally, there are many alternative agricultural development policies that the developing world can successfully adopt depending on their socioeconomic–cultural conditions. Some of these alternatives have been discussed elsewhere (Biswas and Biswas, 1975c). The basic philosophy must be to develop an agricultural system that produces enough food of adequate quality on a long-term sustaining basis without destroying the ecological basis for production. We must not lose sight of the basic fact that ultimately food is a net product of our ecosystem.

Finally, no discussion of food–energy interrelationships will be complete without consideration of the possibility of using some of the energy-related raw materials as food. One of the possibilities open to mankind at present is the conversion of hydrocarbons to protein. Protein is the basic life substance of the cells, which constitutes the protoplasm, and next to water, is the most important ingredient of the human body. Living organisms, including man, need at least 12% of their calorie intake in the form of protein. This simple fact, however, is often overlooked, for example, when agricultural efficiency is discussed, we consider yield per unit acre. Thus our preoccupation has been with quantity of food and not with its quality. The result of this type of thinking is manifested in the fact that cells of present-day hybrid corns are being filled with carbohydrate at the expense of protein. Hence protein concentrate has to be added to this type of corn to make it fit for hog-feed, whereas, prior to the "agricultural revolution," it was not necessary. (Borgstrom, 1969). Expressed in a different way, "a piece of cheese or ham has to be added to the sandwich to become equivalent in terms of nutritive value to the same sandwich without any additions around the turn of the century." The world is deficient in both protein and calories as shown in Figure 5-5. Thus the war against world starvation can never be won unless we consider calories and proteins simultaneously.

It has been known since 1885 that certain microorganisms can multiply by decomposing petroleum. Champagnat and his co-workers at Compagnie Francaise des Pétroles showed in the early 1960s that vitamins and proteins can be formed by decomposing paraffin with yeast. Yeast is composed of 50% water and 50% dry matter, half of which could be protein (Harada, 1974). Theoretically 1 ton of dry yeast (which would contain 0.5 tons of protein) can be obtained from 1 ton of n-paraffin. Raw petroleum contains 20–30% paraffin and 30% cycloparaffin. The number

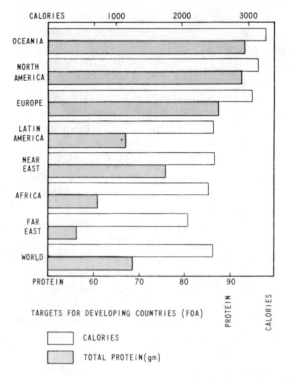

Figure 5-5.   Daily consumption per person of calories and protein.

of hydrocarbons in different kinds of paraffin vary from 6 to 40, and microorganisms generally are effective on paraffins when their number of hydrocarbons range from 12 to 20.

Currently, several U.S. oil companies are building or planning to build small demonstration plants for production of proteins from hydrocarbons. The major effort so far has been on producing animal feed supplement which are currently somewhat more expensive than soymeal products. However, as the price of soybean increases, or for the countries that have to import soybean, the commercial viability of large-scale protein production is a distinct possibility. British Petroleum has two plants selling protein products in the European market. Amoco Foods Co., a subsidiary of Standard Oil Co. (Indiana), claims that it can produce proteins from hydrocarbons for human consumption on a commercial basis. Its plant will produce more than 10 million pounds of tortula yeast per year. The yeast, a natural ingredient used for several years in a variety of foods, contains more than 50% protein as well as other valuable vitamins and minerals. It will be grown on food-grade ethyl alcohol made from petroleum, and according to Standard Oil, will meet all U.S. food regulations.

There are several advantages in producing proteins from hydrocarbons (Ouellette, 1975):

1. The process can be used almost anywhere in the world.
2. The growth rate of microorganisms greatly exceeds that of animals and food crops.
3. The process can produce a large mass of organisms within a relatively small area when compared with ranching or farming.
4. Hydrocarbons are readily transportable to wherever the end product, protein, is most needed.
5. Hydrocarbons are available throughout the year without the risk associated with the growing and harvesting of food crops.
6. The production of animal feed ingredients has relatively modest energy requirements and about half of this is consumed in heat for the spray dryer.

As for the feedstock itself, present technology demands about 1 lb of paraffin per pound of product, the protein content being slightly higher than soybean or other competitive products.

Another possibility for petroleum as a source of energy and protein is the conversion of hydrocarbon oils into edible fats (Pyke, 1971). During World War II this was done on a substantial scale in Germany. Thousands of tons of synthetic fats were manufactured, converted into margarine and eaten. As shown in Table 5-3 the composition of synthetic fat differs from that of natural fat in containing fatty acids with odd numbers of carbon atoms. The only unfavourable physiologic effect, an increased excretion of dicarboxylic acids and a tendency to cause diarrhoea in human beings, due, it was thought, not to the unnatural fatty acids but to the increased concentration of branched-chain fatty acids, though undesirable in human dietetics is probably of only minor significance in animal diets.

The use of synthetic fats as livestock feed should therefore be investigated. The production of edible fats from petroleum is technically feasible, but it may not be economic.

From the previous discussion it is obvious that our petroleum resources can and will play an increasingly important role in alleviating the world malnutrition. And yet, this is one of the significant factors that has not yet been considered by any country in the world in establishing a rational energy policy. In fact some have even short-sightedly argued that we should use up all our hydrocarbon resources as if they are "going out of style." The rationale behind this type of argument seems to be that

Table 5-3. The Chemical Composition of Synthetic Fat Compared with that of Butter Fat and Coconut Oil—in Percentages

Fatty Acid	Synthetic Fat	Butter Fat	Coconut Oil
C_8 and below	0	5.9	6.2
C_{10}	4.2	3.0	4.8
C_{11}	12.0	0	0
C_{12}	10.2	4.1	45.4
C_{13}	10.5	0	0
C_{14}	8.8	13.7	18.0
C_{15}	10.5	0	0
C_{16}	9.5	29.3	11.8
C_{17}	8.0	0	0
C_{18}	9.1	42.4	9.8
C_{19}	17.2	0	0
C_{20}	17.2	1.6	0.4

technologic developments in the energy field will make hydrocarbons obsolete in the next few decades, and hence let us use them up before they become obsolete. What they do not realize is that the same technological developments which they claim will make hydrocarbons obsolete as energy sources, also have the capacity to provide new uses for them, one of them being manufacture of proteins.

Production of proteins from hydrocarbons is a major breakthrough for a protein-short world. Harada (1974) suggests that if 5% of the global annual petroleum consumption (300 million tons) were to be used for conversion to protein, it would yield 7.5 million tons which would be adequate to overcome the protein shortage anticipated by the year 2000. This, certainly, would be no mean achievement.

Many problems, however, remain unsolved, not merely with regard to lack of flavour and digestive disturbances, but major health considerations, such as the carcinogenic nature of some of the micro-organisms produced. It is also important to keep the project in proper perspective. Oil is simply a carbon source and its value should be assessed in comparison with other possible substrates such as molasses, sulphite liquor, straw, sawdust and so on. In some areas it may well be that oil is the cheapest carbon source, and the fraction used appears to be one that the oil companies are glad to get rid of, but any community that already has waste molasses would be well advised to look into its potentialities before thinking about growing microorganisms on oil. In a developing country, the process is much more likely to be feasible if based on molasses than if based on oil. (Pirie, 1975)

References

Biswas, M. R. (1975). Population, resources and environment. Key-note address, Conference on Resources of Southern Africa: Today and Tomorrow, Johannesburg, South Africa, September 22nd–26th, 19 pp.

Biswas, M. R., and Biswas, A. K. (1974a). World population conference: A perspective. *Agric. Environm.* **1**, 385–391.

Biswas, A. K., and Biswas, M. R. (1974b). *Energy and the Environment: Some Further Considerations.* Dept. Environm., Ottawa, Ont., 64 pp.

Biswas, M. R., and Biswas, A. K. (1975a). World food conference: A perspective. *Agric. Environm.* **2**, 15–37.

Biswas, A. K., and Biswas, M. R. (1975b). Energy, environment and world development. *Can. Geogr. J.* **91**, 4–13.

Biswas, A. K., and Biswas, M. R. (1976a). State of the environment and its implications to resource policy formulation. *BioScience* **26**, 19–25.

Biswas, A. K., and Biswas, M. R. (1976b). Energy, environment and international development. *Technos* **5**, No. 1 (Jan.–Mar.), 38–65.

Biswas, A. K., and Biswas, M. R. (1975c). Environmental impacts of increasing world's food production. *Agric. Environm.* **2**, 291–309.

Blaxter, K. L. (1973). The Limits to Agricultural Improvement. Newcastle Agric. Soc., Newcastle-upon-Tyne.

Borgstrom, G. (1969). *Too Many.* Collier, New York, 400 pp.

FAO (1970). *Provisional Indicative World Plan for Agricultural Development.* Vol. 1. Rome.

Harada, T. (1974). The role of micro-organisms in food production. *Impact Sci. Soc.* **24**, 171–177.

Heichel, G. H. (1973). Comparative Efficiency of Energy Use in Crop Productions. Bull. 739, Conn. Agric. Exp. Stn., New Haven, Conn., 26 pp.

Hirst, E. (1973). Energy Use for Food in the United States. Rep. No. ORNL-NSF-EP-57, Oak Ridge Natl. Lab., Oak Ridge, Tenn., 32 pp.

Kissinger, H. (1974). Statement made at Sixth Special Session of the UN General Assembly on Raw Materials and Development. Document A/PV. 2209, United Nations, New York, April 5th, 16–40.

Leach, G. (1975a). *Energy and Food Production.* Int. Inst. Environm. Dev., London, 151 pp.

Leach, G. (1975b). Energy and food production. *Food Policy* **1**, 62–73.

Makhijani, A., and Poole, A. (1975). *Energy and Agriculture in the Third World.* Ballinger, Cambridge, Mass., 168 pp.

Norse, D. (1977). Food and Agriculture (discussion paper). OECD, Paris, 54 pp.

Ouellette, R. (1975). Private communication.

Pyke, M. (1971). Novel sources of energy and protein. In *Potential Crop Production,* Wareing, P. F., and Cooper, J. P. (eds.) Heinemann Educational Books, London, 202–212.

Perelman, M. J. (1972). Farming with petroleum. *Environment* **14**, 8–13.

Pimentel, D., *et al.* (1973). Food production and the energy crisis. *Science* **182**, 443–449.

Pimentel, D., *et al.* (1974). Workshop on Research Methodologies for Studies of Energy, Food, Man and Environment: Phase 1. Cornell University, Ithaca, N.Y., p. 12.

Pirie, N. W. (1975). Potential Protein Sources of Human Food. In *Man/Food Equation,* edited by Steele, F., and Bourne, A. (eds.) Academic Press, London, 176.

President's Science Advisory Committee (1967). *The World Food Problem*. Vol. II, The White House, Washington, D.C.

Revelle, R. (1976). The Resources Available for Agriculture. *Sci. Am.* **235**, No. 3, 166–178.

Slesser, M. (1975). Energy and food. In *Nutrition and Agricultural Development*, Scrimshaw, N. S., and Béhar, M. (eds.) Plenum, New York, 171–178.

Steinhart, J. S., *et al.* (1977). *A Low Energy Scenario for the United States*, 1975–2050. Institute of Environmental Studies, Report 83, Univ. of Wisconsin, Madison, 41 p.

United Nations (1974). World food problem: proposal for national and international action. United Nations World Food Conference, Rome, November 5th–16th, Document E/CONF. 65/4, United Nations, 1–2.

6

ENVIRONMENT AND FOOD PRODUCTION

Margaret R. Biswas, President
Biswas and Associates, Ottawa, Canada, and
International Institute for Applied Systems Analysis,
Laxenburg, Austria

The urgency of increasing world food production should not be underestimated. It is vitally important, however, to ensure that the strategies adopted to increase food production on a short-term basis can be sustained and effectively integrated with long-term policies. There is a very real danger that, in our efforts to increase food production in the short run on a crisis basis, we may adopt strategies that are self-defeating in the long run. In other words, there is a real possibility that we may find ourselves in a far more precarious situation in the mid- or late 1980s, when the demand for food will be much higher than it is today—due to both higher population and increased levels of affluence. This threat comes from the likelihood that food production will level off, or even start to decline, with our present acceptance of a reliance on short-term, *ad hoc,* and ecologically unenlightened, self-defeating strategies. History is replete with telling examples from all corners of the world. As Dr. M. K. Tolba, Executive Director of the UN Environment Program (1974), pointed out in a far-sighted speech at the World Food Conference, man must realize the importance of maximizing agricultural production without destroying the ecological basis on which our entire food production system rests, and this must be done on a long-term, sustaining basis.

Any strategy to increase food production on a sustained basis that does not consider environmental factors explicitly is doomed to failure. The FAO Conference at its Seventeenth Session (November 10–29, 1973) stressed that "the major environmental problems facing agriculture, forestry, and fisheries were not only the avoidance of environmental pollution but the ensuring, in the development process, of the mainte-

125

nance of the productive capacity of the basic natural resources for food and agriculture through rational management and conservation measures." (FAO, 1974). It also "recognized that agricultural development and world food security depended on the careful husbandry of living resources, on their biological laws and ecological balances, as well as on the adjustments of production, supply and reserves to demands." (FAO, 1974). The productive capacity of the biosphere can be sustained and improved only by adopting strategies that are ecologically and environmentally sound. The aim of these strategies should not be growth at the cost of environmental deterioration or destruction of natural resources, but rather development with due concern for conservation of environment and resources. If these concerns are not explicitly incorporated within the development strategies, growth may be greater in the short or even medium terms but will degrade the environment, which will eventually undermine the development process itself. If we accept that the ultimate aim of both development processes and environmental management is to optimize man's social, economic, and mental conditions, there is no contradiction between development and environment: they are, in a real sense, cut out of the same cloth.

With this background, the major parameters that could improve yield of food grains and at the same time have the potential of deteriorating ecological and environmental conditions, thus ultimately jeopardizing the food production process, are briefly discussed.

Food Loss

A multitude of organisms compete with man for the available food supply. Among these are rodents, different species of birds, locusts, termites, snails, and a variety of other animals, including monkeys, antelopes, elephants, kangaroos, dingos, and flying foxes. Currently, the losses encountered during storage, processing, and handling of the foods produced could easily feed hundreds of millions more people. These losses occur in all countries, irrespective of whether they are developed or developing, and whether they are in temperate or tropical regions.

Man's most important competitors for food are rodents. According to some estimates rodents, on a global basis, eat or destroy an amount equal to the average food consumption of nearly 200 million people. Even in a developed country like the United States the rodent population has been estimated at well over 120 million. The U.S. federal authorities estimate that a rat eats nearly 40 lb of food or feedstuff annually and destroys or contaminates at least twice as much. Their cost to the U.S. economy is well over $1 billion/year. In 1974 the Indian Institute of Socio-Economic Studies estimated the rodent population at 2.4 billion, which means they outnumbered people in 1974 by nearly five to one. Paradoxically, as more land was cultivated, more food was available for the rodents, which contributed to their increase in population. They were also helped by ecological side effects of the clearing of the land, which killed their natural predators, such as snakes. The killing of snakes to support the fashion industry has worsened this situation.

In Africa there can be no development of intensive cultivation over large areas, specifically cleared for that purpose, without a corresponding development of harmful rodents. No matter what crop is planted, it is very probable that one or more species, up to then only modestly represented in the area, will begin to flourish, suddenly finding conditions that best suit their ecological needs. Damage is not confined to zones of intensive agriculture; traditional food crops of African farmers are severely damaged, too. Most (but not all) of the rodents that damage crops belong to the Muridae family (Old World rats and mice), which has an enormous capacity to multiply (Giban, 1976). Much less common but more difficult to combat are the burrowing rodents (Tachyoryctes), squirrels and others. Rodent control methods involve a knowledge of the species and its population dynamics. The African *rattus natalensis* can produce litters, each of 10 to 20, once a month (Palmer, 1972). All over the world, a greater food supply in the field or in the warehouses can produce explosive growth in the rodent population.

There are other major competitors for food. In Africa, where nearly 30% of all crops is lost in storage, the quelea (weaver bird) presents a serious problem. Despite the extermination of more than 1000 million queleas, in one year in its main breeding belt stretching from Senegal and Mauritania to the Sudan, Ethiopia, and Tanzania its numbers were little affected. It still invades in flocks of millions.

Plant diseases are not so serious a problem as pests in normal years, but an outbreak of a disease can be just as devastating as a sudden heavy infestation of pests, while in certain localized areas diseases can be a source of regular, substantial loss of crop. Sheath blight (*Corticium sosakii* and *Corticium solani*) is one of the major rice diseases in South and Southeast Asia, and where fungicides have been applied in some areas yields have risen by 60% (Palmer, 1972).

Insects eat or destroy a significant portion of the world's food production. In the United States, where no commercial crop is produced without the application of pesticides, insects destroy 5% of the wheat crop—an average of more than 1 million tons of wheat/year. In the late 1960s the U.S. Department of Agriculture estimated that losses due to insects accounted for $4–5 billion/year. Food losses from various forms of pests and insects could reach 10% (20% in critical years) in temperate climates and may reach as high as 50% in tropical countries (nearly half of the sorghum crop in tropical Africa is often lost to insects). Drawing together information compiled by the U.S. Department of Agriculture, Pimentel has shown that in the U.S. in 1974 the agricultural losses due to insects were 13%, to diseases 12%, and to weeds 8%, totaling 33% (Pimentel, 1976).

Postharvest losses due to pests are nearly 10% in the U.S. and are estimated at 20% worldwide (Pimentel, 1975), ranging from 40 to 50% in some developing nations in the tropics. Even in most developed countries food losses and wastes are often appallingly high, despite the sophisticated crop handling and storage techniques available. For example, more than 13% of the Canadian wheat harvest in 1968 was badly damaged by damp because commercial driers could not cope with the amount. If this is the situation in most developed countries, the conditions in other countries are bound to be worse. Thus the prevention of losses and wastes during the storage, processing, or handling of food is one of the most important parameters to improve the world food situation.

Pesticides

Pesticides in the context of this chapter include insecticides, herbicides, arboricides, fungicides or any chemical that has biocidal activity affecting rodents, arachnids or any other population. The loss of food due to these latter agents on a global basis has been demonstrated to be quite significant in the previous section, and hence if man could effectively control these "pests," more food would be available for human consumption.

The figures available for the average annual world production and consumption of pesticides in general vary extensively from one year to another (estimated global pesticides use to the year 2000 is shown in Table 6-1), but the order of magnitude of world expenditure for pesticides is several thousands of millions of dollars (U.S.) per year, with more than one-third represented by herbicides, about one-third by insecticides, and one-sixth by fungicides. More than two-thirds of the total production is consumed by a few countries of the temperate zone (UNEP, 1977). In the United States some 1.2 billion pounds of pesticides are used each year, nearly 6 lb per person (Pimentel, 1976). Their success in controlling pests on a short-term basis cannot be denied, but their long-term effectiveness in controlling pests or their overall effects on ecosystems (including human health) and environment has to be seriously questioned on two

Table 6-1. Net Total Emission of Pesticides, 1970–2000 in Millions of Tons

Regions	1970	1980	1990	2000
North America	0.98	2.03	2.41	2.56
Latin America, Medium Income	0.04	0.20	0.54	0.95
Latin America, Low Income	0.11	0.22	0.47	1.20
Western Europe, High Income	0.38	0.52	0.68	0.84
Western Europe, Medium Income	0.21	0.40	0.78	1.05
Soviet Union	0.16	0.38	0.70	0.84
Eastern Europe	0.25	0.44	0.51	0.53
Asia, Centrally Planned	—	0.02	0.21	0.70
Japan	0.12	0.28	0.72	1.25
Asia, Low Income	0.16	0.39	1.95	3.77
Middle East	0.05	0.36	1.57	3.35
Africa, Arid	0.05	0.17	0.59	1.00
Africa	0.02	0.04	0.08	0.42
Africa, Southern	0.01	0.01	0.02	0.05
Oceania	0.02	0.02	0.03	0.04

Source: Leontief, *et al.*, 1977.

major counts: increasing concentration of pesticide residues as they move up the food chain, and rapid evolution of new breeds of pests that are immune to the pesticides applied.

After World War II the use of chlorinated hydrocarbons as pesticides increased tremendously. In contrast to the organophosphate group of pesticides that are biodegradable, the chlorinated hydrocarbons do not easily decompose. Many of the organophosphorus compounds found in the surface drains in San Joaquin Valley, California are not found in the subsurface drains because of their biodegradation during passage through the soils (Hotes and Pearson, 1977). Concentration of pesticides are also higher in the surface drains than in the subsurface drains. Pesticide concentrations in subsurface and surface drain effluents in the valley in 1970 are shown in Tables 6-2 and 6-3. In 1970 some 38 million kg of pesticides were applied in the San Joaquin Valley or over half of the amount used in the entire state of California.

Chlorinated hydrocarbons are not biodegradable and are gradually dispersed to ecosystems other than the one intended by drainage waters, or by evaporation and subsequent precipitation. England, for example, receives nearly 36 metric tons/yr of chlorinated hydrocarbon as fallout (Boughey, 1971). These dispersal mechanisms mean that pesticides can be detected in areas far away from the points of application. Thus significant quantities of pesticides, including DDT and its derivatives, have been

Table 6-2. Pesticide Concentrations in Surface Drain Effluents in San Joaquin Valley, California 1970[a]

Pesticide	Times Sampled	Times Detected	Reported Concentrations (ppt)[b]			
			Max	Min	Avg[c]	Avg[d]
Chlorinated hydro-carbons	18					
BHC		3	10	6	5	9
DDD		3	20	3	5	9
DDT		9	450	1	62	82
Dacthal		4	4,780	13	712	1,246
Kelthane		3	75	4	24	48
Toxaphene		10	4,200	88	866	1,125
Complex chlorinated compounds as DDT		6	132,000	80	15,182	22,746
Unknown as DDT		2	320	3	65	162
Summation of identified chlorinated hydro-carbon pesticides[e]		16	7,265	5	1,415	1,592
Organic phosphorus compounds	18					
Ethion		1	225	—	17	225
Thimet		1	35	—	3	35
Methyl Parathion		3	190	10	13	72
Parathion		1	190	—	15	190
Unknown as Parathion		4	175	15	15	59

Source: Hotes and Pearson, 1977.
[a]California Dept. of Water Resources, 1970.   [b]ppt = parts per trillion.   [c]Average value includes 0 values when chlorinated hydrocarbons were not detected.   [d]Average value includes only the detected chlorinated hydrocarbons.   [e]Does not include complex chlorinated compounds as DDT or unknowns as DDT.

found in Antarctic animals (penguins and their eggs, skua, and fish), where there is no agriculture, no insect life, and no use of pesticides.

The pesticides are most commonly distributed through ecosystems by selective concentration as they pass unchanged through successive levels of food chains and food webs. For example, in Lake Michigan the concentration of DDT in lake sediments was 0.0085 ppm. Invertebrate primary consumers concentrated this to 0.41 ppm, their fish predators to 3–8 ppm, and the herring gulls predatory on the fish had levels of no less than 3177

Table 6-3. Pesticide Concentrations in Subsurface Drain Effluents in San Joaquin Valley, California 1970[a]

	Summation of 17 Stations					
	Times Sampled	Times Detected	Reported Concentration (in ppt)[b]			
Pesticide			Max	Min[c]	Avg[d]	Avg[e]
Chlorinated hydro-carbons	60					
BHC		6	7	2	2	5
DDD		1	2	—	0	2
DDE/Dieldrin		1	7	—	0	7
DDT		19	240	2	21	35
Dacthal		3	4,780	4	302	1,608
Dieldrin		4	43	10	5	21
Heptachlor		2	28	14	3	21
Kelthane		3	45	15	6	32
Lindane		6	2,850	3	157	486
Simazine/Atrazine		11	390	5	31	67
Toxaphane		14	630	70	136	262
Complex chlorinated compounds as DDT		15	1,750	5	130	242
Unknowns as DDT		17	140	4	19	33
Summation of identified chlorinated hydro-carbon pesticides[f]		43	2,850	0[g]	129	180
Organic phosphorus compounds	60					
Parathion, Methyl		8	170	10	29	76
Thimet		1	74	—	0	74
Unknown as parathion		10	215	13	23	47

Source: Hotes and Pearson, 1977.
[a] California Dept of Water Resources, 1970.   [b] ppt = parts per trillion.   [c] Detected minimum concentration.   [d] Average value includes 0 value when chlorinated hydrocarbons were not detected.   [e] Average value includes only the detected chlorinated hydrocarbons.   [f] Does not include Complex chlorinated compounds as DDT or Unknowns as DDT.   [g] Actual minimum concentration possible.

ppm (Hickey, *et al.*, 1966). This means that the level of concentration increased nearly 374,000 times between the lake sediments and the gulls. In Clear Lake, California a plankton–fish–bird chain concentrated DDT by a factor of 100,000. There are several other similar examples of heavy concentration as pesticide residues move up the food chain (Pimentel, 1971).

The effect of this selective concentration means that the toxic effects of pesticides are most readily noticeable in top carnivores. Thus U.S. citizens from 1964 to 1966 had an average daily pesticide intake of 0.08–0.12 mg, of which nearly 75% was DDT. Tests in England made in one locality showed that human milk had 22.5 times more DDT and 36 times more DDE than cows' milk. American and British babies consume about 10 times the recommended maximum level of dieldrin (Egan, *et al.*, 1965).

The continued large-scale use of pesticides has resulted, through natural selection and evolution processes, in the appearance and proliferation of new strains of resistant species that generally turn out to be more vicious than their original counterparts. Some pests like the salt marsh sandfly are reported to have evolved resistant strain after only three pesticide applications (Boughey, 1971). Increasing the dosage merely delays the evolution of resistant races; for example, the resistance of the bollworm to insecticides used in its control increased 30,000 times between 1960 and 1965 in the Rio Grande Valley of Texas (Brubecker, 1972).

Over 300 species of insects and mites are now documented as having developed resistance to one or more pesticides. (WHO, 1976; FAO, 1976). Application of different types of pesticides is gradually contributing to the evolution of "super pests" that are immune to the chemicals. There are several strains of flies, ticks, bedbugs, cockroaches, mosquitoes, moths, and hemiptera that are now resistant to both chlorinated hydrocarbon and organophosphate types of pesticides. Resistance to pesticides has also developed in the case of fungi and is beginning to develop in weed control.

New classes of fungicides and herbicides are, however, now being produced to overcome the problem of resistance (UNEP, 1977).

Other side effects include those on nontarget organisms. Pesticides may destroy parasites and predators of pests that were innocuous prior to the application of pesticides, resulting in outbreaks of these pests. There have been outbreaks of mites all over the world after the use of similar pesticides. Herbicides, while killing weeds, may also depress production of the crop or destroy neighboring crops in adjacent fields more sensitive than weeds. Birds, fish, and other animals have been killed by pesticides.

Information on the effect of pesticides is available for less than 1% of the estimated 200,000 species of plants and animals in the United States

(HEW 1969). Little is known about the effects of low dosages over lengthy periods on plants, animals, or people. It has been observed that some pesticide chemicals at extremely low dosages can interfere with fish courtship behavior and rate of growth, decreasing fish productivity (UNEP, 1977). Furthermore, the synergistic effect of low dosages of pesticides, drugs, and food additives consumed by the public has not been studied (Pimentel, 1973). Handling and application of pesticides can also be hazardous. In 1968, 72 deaths occurred accidentally because of the use of agricultural chemicals (HEW, 1971). Thus research on the long-term and other ecological effects of pesticides is essential. Research should also be undertaken to develop further alternative methods of pest control in order to reduce pesticide use.

Continued heavy reliance on pesticides to protect vast areas of monoculture is ultimately bound to be a self-defeating strategy. Such a practice kills all useful insects that could naturally keep the pest population down, and ensures continual increase in the doses of application and continual development of new forms of pesticide-resistant species. Thus, the number of applications of pesticides to cotton in recent years has risen from 8 to 40 in some Central American countries (FAO, 1974), and evolution of new strains of cotton pests necessitates the use of new forms of pesticides every three years or so in Egypt.

The Canete Valley in Peru is an example of an ecological disaster that could occur due to heavy reliance on pesticides. The area covers some 22,000 ha of irrigated land on which cotton was grown. During the period 1949–1956 the use of pesticides was constantly increased to control the cotton pests. New pests appeared in the crops because of the destruction of predators and parasites, and the pests themselves started to develop resistance to the chemicals used. The cost of greater application of pesticides increased tremendously, and gradually all useful insects were destroyed. By 1956, the situation had become critical and nearly 50% of the crop failed (FAO, 1974).

The use of pesticides as the exclusive form of control was banned in 1957. Synthetic organic insecticides were completely prohibited, and mineral insecticides were used. Enemies of cotton pests were reintroduced and cropping practices were changed, based on a study of the ecology of the cotton fields. The equilibrium of the valley's ecosystem was eventually restored several years later (FAO, 1974).

There are several similar examples of eventual reduction in crop production due to heavy reliance on chemical pesticides. What is necessary is to develop effective new concepts of integrated pest management, which can be broadly defined as an ecological approach to pest control by optimal combinations of biological and chemical control technologies.

This would be based upon information about individual pests, their environment, and their natural enemies. Farming practices are modified to control the pest and aid its natural enemies. Realistic economic injury levels of crops would be used to determine the need for suppressive measures. For example, during the first 30 days and for stages after 100 days after planting, cotton can withstand up to 50% defoliation. During the period of fruit formation (30–100 days) the economic level for defoliation drops to about 20%. Integrated pest management takes advantage of these types of sensitivities, and the measures undertaken might include releasing biological control agents or pest-specific diseases or, when necessary, applying pesticides in limited amounts. The use of biological control against fungi and weeds has so far been little exploited. Release of sterile males or artificially reared natural enemies of the pest have proven successful to control a number of insect pests.

Other methods of intervention include choice of sowing, weeding, and harvesting time; location of fields; crop rotation; destruction of crop remains; selection of more resistant crop varieties; and breeding new varieties of plants that are resistant to pests and diseases. For example, some varieties of apples are more resistant to the codling moth than others (Pimentel, 1973). In the last few years, the International Rice Research Institute has released six varieties of rice with at least moderate resistance to six of the major disease and insect pests, including the green leafhopper, brown planthopper, and stem borers. But, breeding for host resistance continues to be difficult because of the emergence of biotypes of the major pests of rice. At least three new biotypes of the brown planthoppers are now known to exist (Brady, 1976).

Crop rotation continues to be a major control method for many crop diseases and also helps control insect pests and weeds. Cropping systems also influence insect pest buildups. For example, in a corn-peanut intercrop pattern, corn borer infestation was significantly lower than where corn was grown alone. This beneficial effect of the peanuts in the intercrop system is thought to be due to predatory spiders which appear to be encouraged by the peanut crop (Brady, 1976).

Integrated pest management provides better pest control at lower cost, and with significantly fewer environmental problems than exclusive reliance on chemical pesticides. This type of systematic approach has progressively reduced the average number of pesticide applications in the cotton fields of Nicaragua from 28 (range 16–35) during the 1967–1968 season to 22 (range 14–30) in 1970–1971, and to 18 (range 10–25) in 1971–1972. It has also reduced pest control costs by about 40%, and has lowered the pesticide residues in adjacent crops, livestock, and dairy products (FAO, 1974).

One of the major problems of existing modes of application of chemical pesticides is their extremely low efficiency rates. Several studies indicate that nearly 70–75% of pesticides applied by aircraft never reaches the target (Akesson, *et al.*, 1971), and this could damage sensitive nontarget plants in the near vicinity in addition to creating totally unnecessary ecological hazards. Widespread drift effect from aircraft applications has been noted, for example, in California, where in applying propanil to rice acreages, fruit tree damages were observed some 55 miles downwind.

Thus, it is essential that instead of placing unwarranted emphasis on increasing the use of chemical pesticides, we should concentrate on increasing the efficiency of pesticides applied. The objective should not be just "more pesticides" but "more efficient use of pesticides." Such a strategy would improve the effectiveness of the already available pesticides by several orders of magnitude. In addition, the pesticides used should be target-specific and not indiscriminately harm the natural enemies of the pest or other useful insects. In other words, man should work with nature, not against it, as seems to be so much the case at present.

Fertilizers

Fertilizers are indispensible for increasing food production but their excessive use has occasioned much concern as a possible environmental threat. Chief among these concerns are the contributions of phosphate and nitrogen fertilizers to eutrophication, and excessive concentration of nitrogen compounds in water and the atmosphere. The reasons why nitrogen compounds are of concern include: the resultant nitrogenous oxygen demand in receiving waters; ammonia toxicity to fish; increased chlorine demand due to ammonia if the water is chlorinated; and health problems in humans and animals. Excessive concentration of nitrites in water could result in methemoglobinemia in infants.

Laboratory experiments indicate that very small quantities of nutrients (15 parts per billion of phosphorus and 0.3 ppm of nitrogen) are necessary to support algal blooms. Thus, if we consider a field treated with 7.3 kg of phosphate/ha, and only a 1% loss of the fertilizer, the resulting nutrient could support noxious blooms in nearly 1000 m^3 of water (Brubecker, 1972). The crucial link between use of fertilizer and aquatic plant growth is the leaching or erosion of fertilizer from the agricultural fields to watercourses. The evidence at present is circumstantial rather than direct. This is because few experimental studies are available on nutrient balance over a long period. This state of affairs is not surprising because until recently fertilizer was cheap, and it was easy to convince farmers that marginal returns exceeded marginal costs. Thus, no one really looked into what happened to excess fertilizer once it was applied to the field.

On the question of the presence of nitrites in water, however, there is evidence that under certain conditions and for certain crops fertilizers do contribute to it. Studies in the Rheingau of Germany have shown that water from sources beneath vineyards had a nitrate content of over 40 mg/liter compared with 10 and 5 mg/liter respectively for water whose source lay beneath arable land and forest (Jung, 1972). The high nitrate levels in wells in the Moselle Valley of Germany have been attributed mainly to nitrogen fertilization of vineyards. Lysimeter studies have confirmed that vines take up little nutrient and therefore a relatively high leaching rate results (Pfaff, 1963).

One report states that "agricultural runoff is the greatest single contributor to nitrogen and phosphorus in water supplies in the United States" (U.S. AWWA Task Group, 1967). Table 6-4, adapted from that same article, shows that there are many other important contributors to the problem, including rainfall.

Furthermore, recent studies have suggested that increased production and use of nitrogenous fertilizer may result in some destruction of the ozone layer. Some projections suggest that the nitrous oxide produced as a result of agriculture could at least double within the next 50 years. If an appreciable fraction of this entered the stratosphere, the ozone layer could eventually be depleted by as much as 15% (McElroy, 1975).

Table 6-4. Estimate of Nutrient Contributions from Various Sources—U.S.A.

	Nitrogen		Phosphorus	
Source	10^6 kg/yr	Usual Concentration mg/l	10^6 kg/yr	Usual Concentration mg/l
Domestic waste	500–750	18–20	90–230	3.5–9
Industrial waste	450	0–10^4	ID	ID
Agricultural land	680–6800	1–70	55–550	0.05–1.1
Rural nonagricultural	180–860	0.1–0.5	68–340	0.04–0.2
Farm animal wastes	450	ID	ID	ID
Urban runoff	50–500	1–10	5–77	0.1–1.5
Rainfall on water surface	14–270	0.1–2.0	1.4–4	0.01–0.03

ID—Insufficient data.

Basically there is no difference between the objectives of farmers and environmentalists, since both would like to maximize food production consistent with minimum environmental disruptions. Both of these objectives can be achieved if fertilizers are used with the maximum efficiency on the farm, for this will reduce the tendency of their overuse. If the right fertilizer is chosen for the crop, correctly formulated and applied in the right quantities at the appropriate times, it would minimize the amount of nutrients that are liable to be leached into the drainage water.

For example, in the case of rice, splitting the nitrogen fertilizer applications, placing part at planting time and part at panicle initiation, has resulted in more efficient use of the fertilizer than if only the initial basal application is made. Similarly, concentrating the nitrogen in a mudball to be placed in the root zone of the rice plants at transplanting time has doubled the efficiency of the applied nitrogen.

What is necessary is to develop new types of fertilizers that can be held in an insoluble form in the soil but can release their nitrogen as nitrate into the soil solution during the growing season at a rate comparable to the crop's need for nitrates. Technically this can be done, but currently there is still no satisfactory slow-release fertilizer available for general agricultural use. The cultural practice that would significantly reduce chemical fertilizer requirements in the tropics is nutrient recycling such as composting, common in Japan, China, and Taiwan. In the Western World, composting is not a widely used process because only a few large-scale composting operations have been successful. It is unlikely that farmers will use high-quality compost for field crop production, but there is some interest in its use for commercial gardens, around home, and in vineyards. Composted manure from dairy corrals in Chino, California, is shipped through the Panama Canal and applied to vineyards along the Rhine (Taiganides, 1977).

Another problem that is rapidly becoming quite serious in several countries is the disposal of animal manures from feedlots. The volume of wastes is growing faster than disposal technology. In earlier times, animal manure was largely returned to the land as valuable nutrients, but in the existing economic climate to collect and spread feedlot manure is more expensive than mechanized application of chemical fertilizers. In terms of waste production, a cow is equivalent to 15–16 men, and a pig or sheep to 2–2.5 men. In large feedlots, cattle may be allowed only 50 sq ft of space per animal. Even if this space is increased ten-fold, annual excretion of nitrogen per animal will amount to nearly 20 tons/acre of feedlot. The best disposal method of animal manure would be to return it to the soil, where it would provide necessary nutrients and would also improve soil structure. However, when the density of animals exceeds a certain threshold value, such disposal becomes economically unattractive, and it becomes very difficult to prevent contamination of local water resources by soluble inorganic and organic constituents.

Furthermore, in recent years environmental health problems have been greatly aggravated in areas of intensive animal production due to negligence in appropriate disposal of large quantities of waste. Odour control is another problem. Animal wastes can be processed to kill disease and odours and to provide fertilizer, animal feed, and fuels.

Irrigation

Man has practiced irrigation to increase crop production for several thousand years, but the real momentum in large-scale use of irrigation started in the nineteenth century with several major undertakings in India (Biswas, 1965), Egypt, and other countries. The irrigated acreages of the world increased by nearly 5.5 times during the nineteenth century, from 8.1 to 45.5 million ha. In 1975, 223 million ha were under irrigation (FAO 1977), the main crop on two-thirds of this land being rice, followed by cotton, oil-bearing crops, fruit trees, cereals, and other crops.

The high-yielding variety of crops currently used requires more moisture (often 2–3 times) than previously. Generally, the amount of water consumed is proportional to the biomass produced, but the actual water requirements vary with crop, climate, soil, and other factors. Thus, rice in the tropics requires 1000 kg of water for each pound of organic matter produced, and wheat in the United States requires 160 kg of water per pound of organic substance, as compared with water requirements of 390 kg in Australia.

Irrigation increases crop yields by improving water availability for intensive agriculture, but it also creates severe ecological and environmental problems (Biswas, 1971b). One of the main problems of irrigated agriculture is secondary salinization and alkalinization, which has turned millions of hectares of productive land into saline barren deserts through the absence of proper drainage systems. Groundwater resources of many areas have been steadily depleted because water was constantly extracted for irrigation without considering the natural replenishment rates. This has happened in Saudi Arabia, Israel, and South Africa, in Texas, Arizona, and Southern California, and in India and many other regions. The history of most of these regions is similar. After a short period of increased food production, the yields were significantly reduced, and in some cases farming had to be abandoned.

Adverse effects of irrigation on water quality include increased salinity, turbidity, color, taste, temperature, nematodes, bacteria and viruses, pesticides, and nutrients. Irrigation return-flows usually show an increase in salinity and hardness, but the relative importance of these changes varies, as illustrated by Hotes and Pearson (1977). The increase in total salts due to irrigation normally has the effect of increasing the hardness of downstream river water. Salinity affects taste. Nitrogen and phosphorus content and pesticides in irrigation return flows have been discussed in previous sections.

The most serious effect of irrigation, however, is the spreading of water-borne diseases and the consequent suffering of millions of human beings and animals. In the tropical and semi-tropical regions of the world, irrigation schemes have enhanced and often created favourable ecological environments for such parasitic and water-borne diseases as schistosomiasis, liver fluke infections, filariasis, and malaria to flourish. These diseases are not new; for example, schistosomiasis was known during the Pharaonic times. But our unprecedented expansion of perennial irrigation systems has introduced such diseases into previously uncontaminated areas (Biswas, 1971a). Table 6-5 shows some of the water-borne diseases that affect man.

Schistosomiasis is currently endemic in over 70 countries, and affects over 200 million people. Prior to the development of the present extensive irrigation networks, and when agriculture depended primarily on seasonal rainfall, the relationship between snail host, schistosome parasite and human host was somewhat stabilized, and infection rates were low. Snail populations increased during the rainy season, when agriculture was possible, which provided the contact between man and parasites. During dry periods, however, there was a lull in infection. With the stabilization of water resource systems through the development of reservoirs and perennial irrigation schemes, the habitats for snails were vastly extended, and they also had a prolonged breeding phase which substantially increased their population. Furthermore, it provided more human contacts with parasites, which not only raised infection rates but also greatly increased worm load per man. The incidence and extension of these diseases can be directly related to the proliferation of irrigation schemes, the stabilization of the aquatic biotope and subsequent ecological changes.

The characteristics of snail habitats, as described by Malek (1972) are the following: "They breed in many different sites, the essential conditions being the presence of water, relatively solid surfaces for egg deposition, and some source of food. These conditions are met by a large variety of habitats: streams, irrigation canals, ponds, borrow-pits, flooded areas, lakes, water-cress fields, and rice fields. Thus in general they inhabit shallow waters with organic content, moderate light penetration, little

Table 6-5. Water-borne diseases, selected examples

Parasites	Diseases Transmitted	Intermediate Host	Infection Route
Nematoda:			
Onchocerca volvulus	River blindness (onchocerciasis)	Black fly (Simulium)	Bite
Wuchereira bancrofti	Elephantiasis (filariasis)	Several mosquitoes	Bite
Protozoa:			
Plasmodium spp.	Malaria	Anopheles mosquito	Bite
Trypanosoma gambiense	African sleeping sickness	Tsetse fly (Glossina p.)	Bite
Trematoda:			
Schistosoma haematobium	Urinary schistosomiasis (bilharziasis)	Aquatic snail (Bulinus)	Percutaneous
Schistosoma mansoni	Intestinal schistosomiasis	Aquatic snails (Biompholaria; Australorbis)	Percutaneous
Schistosoma japonicum	Visceral schistosomiasis	Amphibious snail (Oncomelania)	Percutaneous
Viruses:			
Over 30 mosquito-borne viruses are associated with human infections	Encephalities; dengue	Several mosquitoes	Bite

turbidity, a muddy substratum rich in organic matter, submergent or emergent aquatic vegetation, and abundant microflora.'' Thus, water resources developments, especially improvements for hydropower, irrigation or fishing industry, are most likely to favour increased propagation and spread of these snails (World Bank, 1974).

This relationship has been conclusively demonstrated in several countries of the world. In Egypt, the replacement of simple primitive irrigation with perennial irrigation has caused a high incidence of both *S. mansoni* and *S. haematobium*. Where basin irrigation is still practiced, the incidence is much less. Data from the Ministry of Health shows that for the Asyut, Sohag, and Qena Governorates, the overall prevalence rate for areas with perennial irrigation was 63.9% (Asyut 68.1%, Sohag 61.9%, and Qena 62%), whereas it was only 16.2% (Asyut 18.5%, Sohag 10.4%, and Qena 13%) in the basin irrigated areas (World Bank, 1976). In Sudan, with the introduction of perennial irrigation to 900,000 acres under the Gezira Scheme, the incidence of blood flukes rose greatly (Van der Schalie, 1971). It also increased the incidence of flukes in cattle and sheep. In Kenya, the Lake Victoria is hyperendemic for schistosomiasis. *S. mansoni* infection in school children is up to 100% in areas associated with irrigation schemes (Alves, 1958). In Transvaal, South Africa, the *S. mansoni* infection rate in European farms was 68.5% compared with only 33.5% in the reserves, because the former had irrigation (Anneche, 1955). Similarly, in the Far East, irrigation has not only increased schistosomiasis, but also liver fluke infections, eosinophilic meningitis and bancroft filariasis (Bardach, 1972).

Constant availability of large quantities of water in reservoirs and canals is conducive to the breeding of mosquitoes, which act as intermediate host for diseases like malaria, bancroftian filariasis, yellow fever or arbovirus encephalitides. Currently it is estimated that over 200 million people are infected with malaria in the tropics and sub-tropics and another 250 million are infected with bancroftian filariasis (UNEP, 1977). Similarly, plant growths around water bodies provide a suitable habitat for the tsetse fly to transmit trypanosomiasis to human beings and domestic animals.

In contrast to the diseases discussed above, water developments tend to reduce the incidence of onchocerciasis. The intermediate host, simulum fly, tends to breed in fast-flowing waters, and are often drowned by the construction of dams. Thus, the construction of the Volta Dam destroyed the breeding ground of the simulum fly that existed upstream. However, adequate measures should be taken to ensure that new breeding places do not develop, especially in the fast-flowing waters near spillways.

In addition to contributing to health hazards, dams built for irrigation and other purposes have other serious ecological and environmental problems. The Bennett Dam in Canada, until strong counter-measures were taken, created several environmental problems which very quickly contributed to the deterioration of the life-style in the Peace-Athabasca Delta. Ecological effects on the fish and animal populations of the area soon reverberated to the people who lived in that area, primarily Treaty Indians and Metis. Their income was substantially reduced, and the social and economic dislocation effects were considerable.

The Aswan Dam in Egypt has lowered the fertility of the Nile Valley because of a lack of sediments, and artificial fertilizer currently has to be applied in many areas (Biswas, 1978). Before the dam was constructed, large amounts of silt were either deposited on the Nile Valley or carried all the way to the delta and the sea. The sediments are now being trapped in the reservoir created by the dam, and clean water is now flowing downstream, the dam causing erosion to the river bed and banks.

Another effect of the siltation in the reservoir is the erosion of the Nile Delta, some 1000 km away. Prior to the construction of the dam, the Delta used to be built up during the flood season, with the silt carried by the River to the Mediterranean. This situation in the Delta compensated for the erosion that resulted from the winter waves of the preceding year. Without enough siltation, erosion of the Delta has become a major problem, and studies are now being carried out to find a suitable solution.

Loss of silt has further affected the productive capacity of the Nile Valley, which used to get a regular deposit of sediments every year. Currently, studies are being undertaken to assess the actual nutritive value of the silt, and the trace elements present therein, so that this loss can be compensated for by using chemical fertilizers.

Because of lack of sediments downstream the dam has contributed to the significant reduction of planktons and organic carbons. It has also, in turn, reduced the sardine, scombroid and crustacean population of the area. Loss of sardine along the Eastern Mediterranean has created economic problems for the fishermen who used to depend on the catch for their livelihood. Furthermore, there used to be a thriving small-scale industry in making bricks from the silt dredged from the canals. In the absence of such silts, many such industries have now resorted to using the topsoil near the canals to make bricks, thus contributing further to the loss of productive soil in the country. Egyptian researchers have now succeeded in making bricks out of sand, but it will be some time before the local industry can be persuaded to change from using topsoil to using sand. On the positive side, however, lack of silt has reduced the cost of dredging canals.

The construction of the High Dam and Canal system for irrigation has

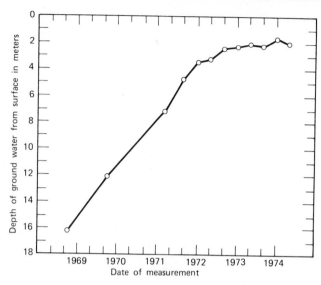

Figure 6-1. Change in ground water level, West Nubariya, October 1969–January 1974.

tended to increase the water table in many parts of Egypt. Such developments, and the tendency to over-irrigate, are contributing to an increase in
the soil salinization problem, requiring expensive and extensive construction of drainage systems. With the disappearance of the annual Nile
floods, the groundwater level has rather stabilized at a higher level. The
salinity in the irrigation canals is increasing, and some of the reclaimed
lands are already facing a salinization problem. For example, on the
mechanized farm, West Nubaria sector, the groundwater level has risen
from 16.2 metres below the surface in October 1969 to 1.3 metres below
the surface in January 1974, an average of 0.94 cm/day (Figure 6-1). The
salinity of the drainage water has risen from 950 ppm in July 1973 to 5050
ppm in October 1975, an average of 4.81 ppm/day (Figure 6-2). The
salinity of the irrigation water has risen from 1150 ppm in July 1973 to 3200
ppm in October 1975, an average of 2.40 ppm/day.

In Egypt about 2 million acres (one-third) of the old land is affected by
salinity, and the newly reclaimed area of one million acres has started to
suffer to varying degrees from waterlogging and salinization (El Gabaly,
1976). Salinity and alkalinity are a common problem in many parts of the
world. Over 50% of the irrigated land in the Euphrates Valley in Syria and
the lower Rafadain Plain of Iraq suffer from salinity and waterlogging. In
Iran, salinity, alkalinity and waterlogging are a problem in over 15% of the
total area of the country. In Pakistan, 27 million acres out of 31 million

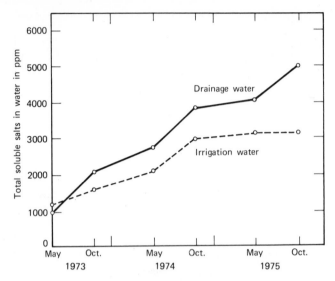

Figure 6-2.   Increase in salinity of drainage and irrigation water, West Nubariya, 1973–75.

acres of irrigated land are affected. (El Gabaly, 1976). At one time, Pakistan was losing 24,300 ha of fertile cropland every year, and currently, nearly 10% of the total Peruvian agriculture is affected by land degradation due to salinization (FAO, 1974). Among other major areas affected by salinization are Helmud Valley in Afghanistan, Imperial Valley and Colorado Basin in the United States, Punjab and Indus Valley in the Indian subcontinent, and Mexicali Valley in Northern Mexico. A study of major modern irrigation schemes in the Punjab shows that seepage from unlined canals has, in the first 10 years of operation, raised the water table 7–9 m above the long-term levels recorded since 1835 (Pereira, 1973). On a global scale, at least 200–300 thousand ha of irrigated land is lost every year due to salinization and waterlogging (Kovda, 1974). Current estimates indicate that 20–25 million ha of land that is saline at present was fertile and productive at one time (Kovda, 1974).

There are many similar cases where man has had to pay heavy prices for irrigation schemes in terms of the overall health of the region, as well as in ecological deterioration. Thus, irrigation does not necessarily bring unmitigated benefits to mankind: it can extract high costs as well. What is necessary is a determined attempt to minimize the costs and maximize the benefits on a long-term basis. This can only be done if we consider ecological and environmental principles in our overall planning.

Loss of Productive Soil

Loss of productive soil is one of the most pressing and difficult problems facing the future of mankind. The problem is not new, but increase in population and attendant need to increase food production have given it an urgency that it lacked before. A historic example is North Africa, which was the fertile granary of the Roman Empire, but is currently a desert or semi-desert which has to import much of its food for basic survival. According to Kovda (1974), the total area of destroyed and degraded soil that was once biologically productive is estimated at 2 billion ha, a figure that is 33% higher than the entire arable area cultivated for agricultural purposes at present, estimated at 1.5 billion ha. The dust bowl experience of the 1930s in the United States was followed by similar examples in the Soviet Union and Africa. Nearly 80% of land in Malagasy Republic is affected by severe erosion. To this must be added worldwide changes in soil property induced by 5,000 million tons of minerals, 32,000 million m^3 of industrial waste water, 250 million tons of dust, 70 million tons of toxic gaseous substances, and grazing and excrements of some 3,000 million head of cattle per year. All these contaminants naturally affect soil fertility (Kovda, 1974). Loss of productive soil should be viewed both in terms of quantity and quality. Quantitatively, soil could be lost physically from agricultural or other land by erosion due to water or wind. In other words, soil is transported from where it is required to another place where it is not necessary, and often contributes to environmental problems. Qualitatively, soil can be considered lost when its fertility declines due to bad management practices. In between is urbanization, where soil is simply taken out of the agricultural production system. While urbanization is physically reversible, it is mostly irreversible due to economic reasons.

There are many reasons for soil loss. These could be the following (Kovda, 1977):

1. Erosion by water and wind.
2. Improvement of the soil, resulting in a disastrous change in its properties unaccompanied by any effort, or at best by inadequate efforts, on the part of man to maintain its level of fertility.
3. Silting of soils with drifts carried by water or wind from the places of erosion activity, resulting in a loss of productive lands.
4. Waterlogging and flooding, resulting in a hazardous change in the water régime.
5. Salinization and alkalinization of soils, resulting from both natural

and man-induced processes, including primary and secondary salinization and alkalinization.

6. Chemical pollution and accumulation of toxic elements and compounds.
7. Soil loss due to widespread mining operations.
8. Soil loss due to building, transport, and communications.
9. Soil loss and degradation due to waste disposal, both domestic and industrial.
10. Soil degradation due to unbalanced and uncontrolled use of fertilizers, herbicides, pesticides and detergents.
11. Soil acidification as a man-induced or natural process connected with sulphur accumulation.
12. Irreversible hazardous change of the physical features of the soil because of its improper utilization in relation to its natural potentialities.

Soil may be considered as a renewable resource, but the time necessary for its formation is much too long to compensate for losses currently taking place for a variety of mismanagement practices. Once soil has been destroyed by natural phenomena, or due to human actions, it may take as long as 7,000 years to reform and to provide an adequate depth of topsoil to sustain the agricultural activities of man. Present estimates indicate that under natural conditions, soil may form at a rate of one cm every 125 to 400 years. The formation process accelerates considerably under normal agricultural practices, when it takes approximately 40 years to form one cm of soil. Even under the most ideal soil management conditions, soil may form at a rate of one cm in about 12 years. Soil formation is thus a lengthy process and thus it is to man's best interest to preserve it as best as possible. Under normal agricultural conditions, approximately 3.75 tons of topsoil is formed/ha/year. In contrast, current average annual loss of topsoil in the United States from agricultural land is estimated to be 30 tons/ha. In other words, agricultural topsoil is being lost in the United States 8 times faster than soil formation.

The magnitude of the loss of productive soil can be best illustrated by considering a specific country, and then analysing losses due to different causes. The country selected in this case is the United States, primarily because good data on soil loss are available. The situation in other countries is somewhat similar, but the magnitude may vary depending on local conditions.

During the last 200 years, at least 30% of the topsoil on U.S. agricultural land has been lost. The Department of Agriculture estimated in 1935 that nearly 100 million acres of land had been ruined for agricultural purposes by soil erosion, and 50 to 100% of topsoil had been lost in another 100 million acres. Thus, by 1935, some 200 million acres of land were either ruined or seriously affected due to soil erosion. The U.S. Soil Conservation Service estimates that more than 3.2 billion metric tons of soil is lost each year through erosion, from approximately two-thirds of the U.S. land which is privately owned (Council on Environmental Quality, 1973). The Service further estimates that soil loss from cropland adequately treated against erosion averages less than 11 metric tons/ha/yr, from pastureland less than 4.5 metric tons/ha/yr, from rangeland about 33 metric tons/ha/yr, and from forest land about 1.1 metric tons/ha/yr (Council on Environmental Quality, 1973).

The dominant form of soil loss in the United States is due to runoff, which carries away fine sediments. Nearly 4 billion tons of sediments are carried every year to the streams in the 48 contiguous states, 3 billion tons of which come from agricultural lands. One-quarter of the water-borne sediments eventually end up in the oceans, and the rest remain in lakes, reservoirs and watercrosses, creating environmental problems. The economic cost of such siltation to the country is quite significant. Some 450 million cubic yards of sediment are dredged every year from water bodies at a cost of about $250 million. Sediments also continually reduce the economic life of man-made lakes, which costs the nation a further $50 million per year (Pimentel, *et al.*, 1976b). These, plus other damages, are estimated at approximately $500 million every year. The total cost obviously is much higher, since the damages estimated do not include the cost of agricultural products that might have been raised had the soil degradation not taken place. Such damages run to about 2% of the total economic value of agricultural products raised every year.

Wind erosion is not as severe as water erosion, but it is still quite significant. Wind erosion is responsible for 850 million tons/year soil loss in the Western United States alone. A very conservative estimate of wind erosion is 1 billion tons every year. Thus, nearly 5 billion tons of soil is lost per year due to combined effects of water and wind. This is equivalent to about 7 inches of soil loss from about 5 million acres of land surface.

In addition to erosion, the United States loses more than 2.5 million acres of arable land every year to urbanization, highways and other special uses. Thus, between 1945 and 1970, the country lost 45 million acres of land, equivalent to the size of the state of Nebraska.

So far some 40 million acres of land have been lost to urbanization, nearly half of which used to be cropland, and another 32 million acres have been lost to roads and highways. In addition, strip mining directly disturbs 153,000 acres of land every year, and affects at least three to five times the exploited area due to acid drainage and accelerated erosion (Pimentel, *et al.*, 1976b).

Studies carried out in Kenya during the period 1948 to 1965 show great variations in erosion and sedimentation in different parts of the country. Highest rates of soil erosion occurred in an area of very steep slopes on the eastern sides of Mount Kenya, where land is cultivated on the steep valley slopes of the upper part of the basin, cultivation and grazing being the dominant form of land use along the gentler but drier hillslopes of the lower parts. Thus, the annual rate of soil loss in the catchment area of the Tana River varied from 1500 tons/km^2, between Kindaruma and Grand-falls (agriculture/grazing), to about 320 tons/km^2 above Kamburu Dam (agriculture/forestry) (Ongweny, 1977). In contrast, soil erosion in undisturbed forest, in areas of steep slopes, is extremely low. For example, in the Sagana Drainage Basin the annual rate of soil loss is approximately 4 tons/km^2. Soil loss tends to increase under agricultural conditions and is much greater in pastoral semi-arid parts of the country.

Currently 46% of the total degradation of the earth's surface due to different hazards can be directly related to water. These hazards can be roughly estimated as follows: water erosion, 22%; waterlogging and flood damage, 8%; salinity and alkalinity, 5%, and frost, 11% (FAO, 1977).

Loss of agricultural land to urbanization is a common but serious problem in all developed and developing countries. Table 6-6 shows the annual loss of cultivated land, not including pastures and meadows, to other uses in Japan during the period 1968 to 1973 (OECD, 1976).

The situation is not much different in a developing country like Egypt, which has continued to lose some of its better agricultural land to urban development. The magnitude of the problem can be best realized by considering the fact that total irrigated land has virtually remained the same in Egypt during the last two decades, in spite of the thousands of hectares of new irrigated land developed in the building of the Aswan Dam. In other words, Egypt has continued to lose good arable land to urbanization as fast as she has brought new land under irrigation, at tremendous investment costs. Closer analysis of these facts indicates that the situation is far worse than normally realized. Overall, better quality agricultural land has been lost to urbanization than that brought under cultivation. Moreover, the agricultural land lost was closer to centres of population, and thus the energy cost of transportation of products to the market and the necessity of developing sophisticated storage systems were minimum. Since the new land is not so conveniently located, more energy has to be expended to transport, store and distribute the products, thus imposing additional costs on the already strained economy.

Table 6-6. Loss of Cultivated Land in Japan—in Hectares

Year	Housing and urban services	Industry and mines	Communication systems	Forests, parks, etc.	Total
1968	23,888	4,502	7,297	5,133	40,820
1969	31,876	7,595	7,067	6,806	53,343
1970	32,228	8,739	7,720	8,447	51,134
1971	29,543	6,958	8,068	15,898	60,468
1972	31,585	6,743	8,780	16,652	63,760
1973	35,941	9,197	9,012	12,625	66,765
1974	23,096	5,385	7,197	9,140	44,818

In a world where the land available per inhabitant is already at a premium, and is being constantly reduced due to increases in population, man can ill afford to lose good soil due to short-sighted management practices. Figure 6-3 shows both total space available and cultivated land area per inhabitant for 1973 for 24 selected countries. Such statistics will continue to be progressively reduced for most countries of the world, at least for the rest of the present century.

There are other reasons that could contribute to soil loss. Waterlogging, salinization, and alkalinization have been discussed in the previous section, and soil degradation due to improper technology transfer is described in the next section. Overgrazing can create serious problems. For example, in the Patagonia region of Latin America (78 million ha in Argentina and 24 million ha in Chile), a vast semi-desert area, sheep were introduced at the beginning of this century. The sheep thrived, and by 1912 their number was well over 25 million. Sheep are highly selective in their grazing habits and started to eat up the best pastures. It gradually reduced the fodder production, which in turn, reduced the sheep population to below 20 million during the last decade. Overgrazing also led to a serious problem of wind erosion, which was further accentuated by the strong wind characteristics of the region (FAO, 1974). Similar problems due to overgrazing have been observed amongst other places in the Sahelian countries and Rajasthan in India. Overgrazing is one of the main reasons for the deterioration of the plant cover and desertification in Iraq and Syria. Although the natural rangelands in the north of Iraq are able to support 250,000 head of sheep, in actual fact they contain around one million. Similarly, the arid and semi-arid natural rangeland zones in Syria contain three times the amount of livestock that they can support (ECWA, 1977).

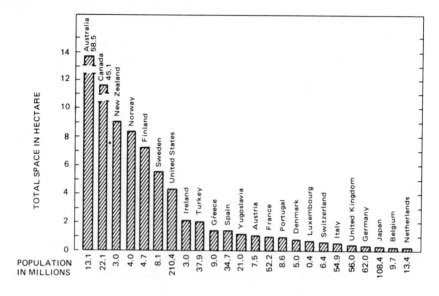

TOTAL SPACE AVAILABLE PER INHABITANT IN 1973

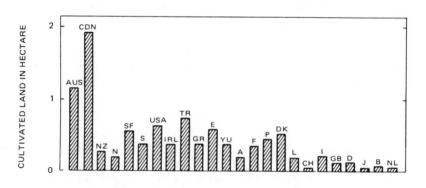

CULTIVATED LAND AREA PER INHABITANT

(The order of countries is the same as in above graph)

Figure 6-3. Total space and cultivated land area available per inhabitant for 1973.

In many developing countries, an expanding population requires more food, and increases pressure to expand the cultivated area. This pressure, coupled with political expediency and lack of expertise, has resulted in more and more utilization of marginal land, for which technology either is not available for farming on a sustained basis, or, if available, has been disregarded for socio-economic reasons. Thus, the expansion of agriculture on steep hillsides has led to serious erosion in Indonesia and Kenya; increasing pressure of slash-and-burn agriculture is destroying tropical forests in the Philippines; deforestation in the Himalayas is contributing to the increase in the frequency and severity of flooding in India, Bangladesh and Pakistan; deforestation to build Transamazonica is accelerating soil erosion in Brazil, and overgrazing and deforestation are contributing to the southward march of the Sahara. These are prime examples of developments that contribute short-term benefits but have long-term costs in terms of soil deterioration, which will eventually negate the increased food production.

Finally, it is important to discuss cost aspects of soil deterioration. According to UN estimates, the degradation of range land, non-irrigated farmland, and the areas destroyed by waterlogging and salinization has held their worldwide annual production of food and animal products $16 billion below their potential. Current estimates of soil erosion data from the United States indicate that more than 50 million tons of plant nutrients are lost each year, and the cost of replacing the nitrogen, phosphorus and one-fourth of the potassium ranges from $6.8 to $7.75 billion. Water and wind erosion further contribute to a 2% annual loss in crop productivity. Currently, soil loss costs most farmers $50/acre—a figure higher than losses from weeds, estimated at $40/acre. Such costs should be compared with the conservation treatment of irrigated land, estimated at $3.10/acre/yr. In the short term, the net farm income will undoubtedly be higher if no soil loss measures are undertaken. Thus, a simulation model of a typical Iowa farm indicates that the maximum net farm revenue obtainable was $4,278 when average annual soil loss was restricted to 6 tons/acre, but it increased to $4,573 when soil loss per acre was increased to 22 tons. The fallacy of such short-term income maximization is that in the long run, the farmer may have no income at all!

Since it is estimated that between 50,000 and 70,000 km² of useful land are going out of production every year (Tolba, 1977), soil management and conservation must be a priority for mankind. Accordingly, the United Nations Conference on Desertification, held in Nairobi in 1977, adopted a Plan of Action that states the principles that guide proper land use and outlines the measures that conform to good practice.

Technology Transfer and Use

The agricultural history of the present century is replete with examples in which straight transfer of technology from developed to developing countries, or from one region to another, has created additional problems. A few select examples are the deep-plowing of the rice paddies in Java by the Dutch, corresponding operations by the British in Burma, failure of the groundnut scheme in Tanzania and broiler production in Gambia, and the folly of cultivating marginal lands which should never have been broken, in Kenya and several Latin American countries.

Probably the most spectacular failure was the British plan to develop large-scale groundnut plantations after the Second World War, in what was then known as Tanganyika. The area selected covered 3.25 million acres, 70% of which was uninhabited, for what later turned out to be good reasons. All sorts of experts were recruited for the ambitious project. Bulldozers were extensively used to remove deep tree roots. The soil, as in several other similar cases in the tropics, could not stand up to the machines, and there were severe losses due to wind and rain. Artificial fertilizers used were not effective because of lack of water, and germination turned out to be difficult in hard-packed soil. The project was eventually abandoned after six years of desperate efforts and capital investment of some $100 million.

Technology transfers have often not been successful because of lack of proper consideration of the social, cultural, educational, economical and ecological conditions of the local regions. But equally dismal has been man's performance to date in failing to use successfully technology that is already available. For example, the effects of soil erosion caused by deforestation and flooding were graphically described by Plato some 23 centuries ago, and the need for terracing for agriculture on sloping land was pointed out by Bernard Palissy of France nearly four centuries ago (Biswas, 1972). And yet, any one who has travelled in Kenya, Indonesia, the Philippines and many other countries cannot help wondering why simple countermeasures like the use of terracing are not taken to prevent soil erosion. The technology has been available for centuries, it is widely known, not expensive to implement, and urgently needed for medium and long-term conservation measures, and yet it is not used.

In order to improve the agricultural yields of developing countries, some form of appropriate technology is necessary (Myrdal, 1974). Appropriate technology in this context may be defined as the latest scientific and technological developments that have been adjusted to suit the local conditions to the highest possible degree. Unfortunately, not only multinational corporations but also certain governments in developed countries are so concerned with protecting markets for their own industrial products that they are opposed to the development and use of appropriate technology in developing countries. This technology, under present conditions, must be highly labour-intensive—in contrast to a high degree of mechanization in developed countries. Otherwise, such developments will solve the problem of increasing agricultural yield at the cost of intensifying another; that is, sending a steady stream of migrants to already overcrowded city slums. However, it should be realized that technological developments by themselves will not be able to solve these complex problems. Simultaneous efforts must be made to change the attitudes and institutions of most of the countries that have significantly contributed to the present stagnant situation.

The "Green Revolution" technology promotes employment, but the use of mechanical power to grow high yielding varieties (HYV) of rice and wheat displaces labour. Fertilizer application, weeding, plant protection, and threshing operations account for the bulk of increased labour utilization when traditional human and animal power is used. For every hectare on which traditional wheat is replaced by HYV wheat in the Hazara district of Pakistan, 205 man-hours of additional employment are generated and 614 kg of additional output is produced (Ahmed, 1975). Although multiple cropping usually requires a degree of mechanization, as it depends to a considerable extent on the timeliness of operations, total labour utilization remains high because of the increased cropping. However, as cultivation methods based on the use of large amounts of energy, fertilizer, pesticides and water cannot be expected to be used by the majority of farmers in developing countries, there is a need for imaginative exploration of untapped local resources, for a better use of plant and animal varieties, of forests and water resources (aquaculture). Unexploited tropical plants, better adapted to the local ecology than temperate zone crops grown in the tropics, present a tremendous potential for increased food production.

Technological innovations can create some problems as well. In the mid-1960s, the Green Revolution spread new strains of high-yielding, miracle rice and wheat strains through vast regions of Asia, Africa, Latin America and the Mediterranean nations. These quickly supplanted the native varieties, many of which have now become extinct. For example, in Greece, in the major wheat growing areas of Thessaly and Macedonia, more than 90–95% of wheat grown is no longer indigenous. Native varieties are so scarce now that the cost of recovering the genetic resources of Greek wheat will be very high, and even then it is highly doubtful that all the strains can be collected (Frankel, 1973).

Genetic erosion is quite serious at present because of the laissez-faire attitudes of most nations. This could have serious repercussions on future world food scenarios. For example, most major high-yielding crops cultivated are already impressively genetically uniform, and consequently are becoming increasingly vulnerable to epidemics. Also, these strains were developed and selected during the era of cheap energy availability and favourable climatic conditions. With rapidly changing energy situations, with attendant shortages of fertilizers and pesticides, and the prospect of more widely fluctuating climates, yields from miracle grains could be significantly lower. New types of strains may have to be developed that are more flexible to available energy inputs. Thus, crop improvement is not static, it is a dynamic process of continually adjusting the genetic substance of the productive system to changing environmental conditions. Development of new strains will depend on the genetic spectrum available, and this means that the present rate of genetic erosion cannot continue indefinitely.

It is vitally necessary to provide better extension services to take available technology to the field level, and also to ensure that the steps taken provide sustained, rather than short-term, benefits. Even in developed countries, farmers' sources of information about the use of pesticides and fertilizers often turn out to be the sales representatives of the respective industries. Thus, not surprisingly, the advice is often to use more fertilizers and pesticides, irrespective of marginal returns to the farmer or total costs to the society. We also need more emphasis to show farmers rational use of water, based on information we already have, rather than further esoteric research in other areas. As a rule, we have not been successful in translating research results into practice, and we have been even less successful in transferring technology from developed to developing countries, with necessary modifications to meet the local needs.

Conclusion

Strategies to solve the world food problem must not be developed in isolation, but in full consideration of the web of interdependence that exists with other major problems facing mankind today—those of population, availability of energy and other raw materials at a reasonable price, and lack of development. It is not in any one of them, but in the interaction amongst them, that the future of mankind will be shaped and decided. Increase in population and provision of basic human necessities to each individual means more food, energy and raw materials; intensifying the supply of food means more land, water, energy and fertilizers; the energy crisis and higher oil prices means less energy available to increase food production and fertilizer shortage; and the common denominator in virtually all responses to these problems is more capital, more technology, more cooperation and less inflation (Biswas and Biswas, 1976). Each affects and is affected by the others. The system of relationships is global in scale. That is not to say that all global problems can be met with global solutions—for there are few global solutions. But they can only be understood and dealt with in a global framework, within which there can be a wide variety of national and regional responses.

The unprecedented nature and magnitude of these problems require unprecedented remedies. The short-term strategies adopted to alleviate the immediate crisis should not foreclose long-term options. Short-term *ad hoc* measures are often deceptive, and could even be diametrically opposed to the long-term development goals of mankind. For example, the history of world agriculture during the period 1951–1966 indicates that a 34% increase in production was made possible by the following increases: 63% in farm machinery, 146% in nitrogenous fertilizers and 300% in pesticides. The empirical proportions of these increases are 1:2:5:10 (1 is the increase in agricultural production) (Meadows, *et al.*, 1973). In other words, if the present trend continues, chemical fertilizers and pesticides will accumulate in the environment at a much faster rate than food production. Continuation of such practices, in addition to being inimical to the long-term objective of increased food production, will also ensure more damages to the environment and the ecosystem, since, for some of these pollutants, damage increases at increasing rates as concentration levels rise.

All ecological systems have experienced traumas and shocks over the period of their existence, and the ones that have survived have explicitly been those that have been able to withstand these changes. They have developed an internal resilience that gives them a domain of stability. So long as the resilience is great, unexpected consequences of an intervention of man can be absorbed without profound effects. With each such intervention, the domain of stability contracts, until an additional incremental change can alter the system to another state. It would generate certain kinds of unexpected consequences—for instance a pesticide that destroys an ecosystem structure and produces new pest species. We now seem to be faced with problems that have emerged simply because we have used up so much of the resilience of the ecosystems. Up to now the resilience of the systems has enabled us to operate on the presumption of knowledge that the consequences of our ignorance are being absorbed by the resilience. As the resilience contracts, traditional approaches to planning might well generate unexpected consequences that are more frequent, more profound and more global. Our future strategies to increase food production must be carefully formulated so that we do not create unnecessary perturbation in the ecological systems.

No strategy to increase food production on a sustaining basis can afford to disregard explicit considerations of environmental and ecological principles. One should also remember the vast number of public service functions rendered by the natural environment. For example, almost all potential plant pests are controlled by natural ecosystems, only those of monoculture being controlled by man. Insects pollinate most of the vegetables, fruits and flowers. Natural vegetation reduces floods, prevents soil erosion and beautifies the landscape. Thus, the strategies developed to increase food production on a sustaining basis must work with nature, and not against it.

References

Ahmed, I. (1975). The Green Revolution, Mechanisation, and Employment. Working Paper WEP 2-22, World Employment Programme Research, International Labour Organisation, Geneva, 49 pp.

Akesson, N. B., Wilce, S. E., and Yates, W. E. (1971). Atomization Control to Confine Spray to Treated Fields. Paper No. 71-662, Annual Meeting, American Society of Agricultural Engineers, Chicago, Illinois.

Alves, W. (1958). The Challenge of Bilharzia in a Developing Africa. *Optima* **8**, 139–146.

Anneche, D. H. S. (1955). Bilharzia in Transvaal. *Public Health* (Johannesburg) **18**, 2–7.

Bardach, J. E. (1972). Some Ecological Implications of Mekong River Development Plans. In *The Careless Technology*, Farvar, M. T., and Milton, J. P. (eds.). Natural History Press, Garden City, N.Y., 236–244.

Biswas, A. K. (1965). Irrigation in India: Past and Present. *J. Irriga. Drain. Div., Am. Soc. Civ. Engineers* **91**, 179–189.

Biswas, A. K. (1971a). Sociological Aspects of Water Development. *Water Res. Bull.* No. 7, 1137–1143.

Biswas, A. K. (1971b). Social and institutional aspects of irrigation and drainage. In *Optimization of Irrigation and Drainage Systems*, American Society of Civil Engineers, New York, 261–264.

Biswas, A. K. (1972). *History of Hydrology*. North-Holland Publishing, Amsterdam, 153–154.

Biswas, A. K. (1978). *Environmental Implications of Water Development for Developing Countries*. J. Wat. Sup. & Manag. **2**, 283–297.

Boughey, A. S. (1971). *Man and the Environment*. Macmillan, New York, 372 pp.

Brady, N. C. (1976). An analysis of food production systems which minimize adverse environmental impact. In *Science for Better Environment*, proceedings of the International Congress on the Human Environment, Kyoto, 1975, Asahi Evening News, Tokyo, 214–220.

Brubecker, S. (1972). *To Live on Earth*. Johns Hopkins Press, Baltimore, Md.

Council on Environmental Quality (1973). *Environmental Quality*. U.S. Govt. Printing Office, Washington, D.C., 317.

Economic Commission for Western Asia (1977). *Some Aspects of Desertification and their Socio-Economic Effects in the ECWA Region*. Report presented to the United Nations Conference on Desertification 1977, No. 77-3211, p. 8.

Egan, H., *et al.* (1965). "Organo-chlorine pesticide residues in human fat and human milk. *British Med. J.* **2**, 66–69.

El Gabaly, M. M. (1977). Problems and effects of irrigation in the near east region. In *Arid Land Irrigation in Developing Countries*, Worthington, E. B. (ed.). Pergamon, Oxford, 239–249.

FAO (1974). *Environment and Development*. 13th FAO Regional Conference for Latin America, Panama City, Panama, 1–11.

FAO (1976). *Report of the 11th session of the FAO Panel of Experts on Resistance of Pesticides*, FAO, Rome.

FAO (1978). Water for Agriculture. In *Water Development and Management*, proceedings of the United Nations Water Conference, Biswas, A. K. (ed.). Pergamon, Oxford, Vol. 3.

Frankel, O. H. (ed.) (1973). *Survey of Crop Genetic Resources in Their Centres of Diversity*. FAO–IBP, Rome, 2–3.

Giban, J. (1976). *Rats*. Development Forum, Vol. 4, No. 4, May 1976, p. 8.

HEW (1969). *Report of the Secretary's Commission on Pesticides and their Relationship to Environmental Health*. U.S. Dept. of Health, Education, and Welfare, U.S. Govt. Printing Off., Washington, D.C., 677 pp.

HEW (1971). *National Clearing House for Poison Control Centers Bull.*, Mar.–Apr. U.S. Dept. of Health, Education and Welfare, Washington, D. C.

Hickey, J. J., Keith, J. A., and Coon, F. B. (1966). *J. Applied Ecology* **3**, 141–154.

Hotes, F. L., and Pearson, E. A. (1977). Effects of irrigation on water quality. In *Arid Land Irrigation in Developing Countries*. Worthington, E. B. (ed.). Pergamon, Oxford, 127–158.

Jung, J. (1972). Factors determining the leaching of nitrogen from soil, including some aspects of water quality. In *Effects of Intensive Fertilizer Use on the Human Environment*. FAO-SIDA, Rome, 101–102.

Kingue, M. D. (1977). *Statement of the United Nations Development Programme to the United Nations Conference on Desertification*. Nairobi, Kenya, 2.

Kovda, V. A. (1974). *Biosphere, Soils and Their Utilization*. Institute of Agro-chemistry and Soil Science, Academy of Sciences of U.S.S.R., Moscow, 35.

Kovda, V. A. (1977). Soil Loss: an Overview. *Agro-Ecosystems* **3**, No. 3, 205–224.

Leontief, W., et al. (1977). *The Future of the World Economy*. Oxford University Press, New York, 54.

Malek, E. A. (1972). Snail Ecology and Man-Made Habitats. In *Schistosomiasis*, Muller, M. J. (ed.). Tulane University, New Orleans, Louisiana, 57–62.

McElroy, M. B. (1975). *Chemical Processes in the Solar System: A Kinetic Perspective*. Centre for Earth and Planetary Physics, Harvard University, Cambridge, Mass.

Myrdal, G. (1974). The transfer of technology of underdeveloped countries. *Sci. Am.* **231**, No. 3, 172–182.

Ongyweny, G. S. (1977). *Problems of Soil Erosion and Sedimentation in Selected Water Catchment Areas in Kenya, with Special Reference to the Tana River*. UN Water Conference, E/CONF. 70/TP23, 23 pp.

Organization for Economic Cooperation and Development (1976). *Land Use Policies and Agriculture*. OECD, Paris, 84 pp.

Palmer, I. (1972). *Science and Agricultural Production*. Report No. 72.8, United Nations Research Institute for Social Development, Geneva, 63–78.

Pereira, H. C. (1973). *Land Use and Water Resources*. Cambridge University Press, London, 186.

Pfaff, C. (1963). Das Verhalten des Stickstoffs in Boden nach Langjahrigen Lysimeter Versuchen. *Z. Acker Pflanzenbau* **117**, 77–99.

Pimentel, D. (1971). *Ecological Effects of Pesticides on Non-Target Species.* Executive Office of the President, Office of Science and Technology, Washington, D.C., 27–28.

Pimentel, D. (1973). Extent of pesticide use, food supply, and pollution. *J. New York Ent. Soc.* **81**, No. 1 (March), 13–33.

Pimentel, D., *et al.* (1975). Energy and land constraints in food protein production. *Science* **190** (November), 754–761.

Pimentel, D. (1976). *Bull. Ent. Soc. Am.*, No. 22, 20.

Pimentel, D., *et al.* (1976b). Land degradation: Effects on food and energy resources. *Science* **194**, No. 4261 (October 8), 149–155.

Taiganides, E. P. (1977). Composting of feedlot wastes. In *Animal Wastes.* Taiganides, E. P. (ed.). Applied Science Publishers, London, 241–251.

Tolba, M. K. (1974). *Address to the World Food Conference.* Rome, 1974.

Tolba, M. K. (1977). *Statement of the Secretary-General to the United Nations Conference on Desertification*, Nairobi, Kenya.

UN Environment Program (1977). *Health of the People and of the Environment.* UNEP Report No. 2, Nairobi, Kenya.

U.S. AWWA Task Group (1967). *Report.* Quoted in Hotes, F. L., and Pearson, E. A. (1977). Effects of irrigation on water quality. In *Arid Land Irrigation in Developing Countries.* Worthington, E. B. (ed.). Pergamon, Oxford, 127–158.

Van der Schalie, H. (1972). World Health Organization project, Egypt 10: A case history of schistosomiasis control project. In *The Careless Technology.* Farvar, M. T., and Milton, J. P. (eds.). Natural History Press, Garden City, N.Y., 116–130.

World Bank (1974). *Environmental Health and Human Ecologic Considerations in Economic Development Projects.* World Bank, Washington, D.C., 50–52.

World Bank (1976). *Appraisal of Upper Egypt Drainage II Project, Arab Republic of Egypt.* Report No. 1111-EGT, Washington, D.C.

WHO (1976). Resistance of vectors and reservoir of diseases to pesticides. 22nd Report of the WHO Expert Committee on Insecticides. WHO Technical Report Series 585, Geneva.

7

SOIL RECLAMATION AND FOOD PRODUCTION

Victor A. Kovda
Moscow State University

The normal functioning and biological productivity of the planet Earth are based on stable and regular interrelations between and among solar energy, organisms, soils, the atmosphere, and the hydrosphere. Until man interferes in it, this system acts as a self-governing mechanism, producing biomass and affecting the composition and properties of the soil, the hydrosphere, and the atmosphere. The organized and scientifically based management of the biosphere and its components (biogeocenoses, water, soil, air, and organisms) is required when man interferes with the biosphere through activities such as agriculture, forestry, industry, and water management. If proper soil management is not provided, the soils deteriorate. As the proportion of soils that become useless to the bioproductivity of the ecological systems of the biosphere grows larger, the volume of production that must be obtained from remaining soils increases, and these soils must play a more important role in the gas, water, and biogeochemical balance of the biosphere. The larger the biomass produced by these soils and removed by man is, the more knowledge man must have about soils and ecological systems in general, so that thoroughly elaborated measures and techniques can be used to manage these systems. Improperly devised measures may lead to grave consequences, whereas drained, irrigated, and terraced lands with fertile soils, high-yielding crops, intensive agriculture, and chemical application, representing the highest level of cultural agrobiogeocenoses management, can lead to the conservation and amelioration of the biosphere. A several-fold increase in soil productivity in cultural landscapes can and must be attained by means of a complex of different measures and on the basis of a profound understanding of the processes and of the effects on soils, ecosystems, and the biosphere.

From a universal point of view, the soil cover of the earth is a global component of environments and the common property of mankind. From the national perspective, soils are the most valuable property of a nation, a sovereign territory in which a national culture and economy have been established and developed. As a natural resource, soils have a number of specific properties, and their importance for man and human society continually increases. Soils are used for growing crops and for varied biological production. The soil cover is also a place for the construction of dwellings and settlements, industrial enterprises and mines, roads and airports, and recreation and rest. Soils and the oceans are the earth's collectors of industrial and other wastes and residues of various kinds. They "clean" the earth, since many organic and organo-mineral compounds are completely decomposed in the soil and in the ocean. If the soil cover is destroyed, there can be no full restoration; even if new soil is formed, it will have new characteristics and often will be less productive. It is almost impossible to restore destroyed soils artificially, because the conditions and history of their formation cannot be reproduced. The creation of new soils is more feasible, but it is a very complex and expensive process that does not always produce the desired effect. Unlike other nonrenewable resources (e.g., oil, gas, coal, metals, ores), the proper utilization of soils not only promotes their conservation but actually improves them and increases their productivity.

The growing knowledge of soil technology provides a basis for augmenting land productivity and for attaining higher living standards. However, man's effect on soils is often inconsistent with the laws governing soil life. These effects may occur either through ignorance or through the desire for cheap production, and they usually result in soil exhaustion, degradation, deterioration, or desertification (erosion, dust storms, soil salinization, compactness, and petrifaction).

Since the soil resources of the earth are limited, the effective utilization of land and its preservation as a component of the biosphere is one of the most important problems of our time. The purity of the atmosphere, an adequate supply of oxygen for living organisms, fresh water, the normal cycling of carbon, nitrogen, phosphorus, sulfur, calcium, iodine, and other elements—all these factors are intimately connected with soil fertility and high biological productivity. To provide these benefits the soil cover should be protected from degradation and preserved for future generations, but the actual state of affairs is quite different. The total area of destroyed and degraded soils that formerly supported biological production is estimated at the colossal figure of about 20 million km^2, more than the entire arable area used for agricultural purposes at the present time (14–15 million km²). For the most part, the loss of fertile lands is due to erosion, desertification, salinization, transport, and construction work that have occurred during comparatively recent times. All forms of land/ soil degradation have negative manifestations and disastrous consequences, particularly for the more fragile arid zones of the earth (Biswas and Biswas, 1978).

Natural and Human Factors of Land Aridization and Soil Degradation. The arid zone covers about 40% of the world's land surface and has about 13% of the world population. Arid and semihumid areas together comprise about 50% of the world's land and 25–30% of its population. The 55– 65 countries located in the arid and semihumid zones are subject to regular or periodic aridity, xerotization, drought, and to the phenomena of wind erosion, soil degradation, salinity, alkalization, and soil compaction. Thus the problem of land degradation is a global one, although it is related first of all to the arid and aridohumid territories of our planet.

The soils of North Africa, central Asia, and Arabia are poor, saline, often eroded, and nonfertile. From Morocco to Somalia and Sudan average wheat yields are not above 0.5–1.0 tons/ha. The same can be said of the soils and grain yields in the no irrigated areas of India, Pakistan, North America, and the arid areas of South America. Severe droughts occurred in the above–mentioned countries in recent years. Even forested areas of Central Europe (1972), Great Britain (1975), Asia (Java, 1961–1967), and Africa (Nigeria, 1972, 1973) were sometimes severely affected by drought.

It is recognized that the last humid pluvial period for the Sahara was between 5500 and 2350 B.C. At that time, the Sahara had rich vegetation and very rich fauna, including gazelles, antelopes, ostriches, elephants, rhinoceroses, hippopotamuses, crocodiles, buffaloes, and giraffes (Lhote, 1959; Clark, 1959). This period was followed by an extremely dry epoch in 2350–800 B.C. Since that time conditions have generally remained at the same level. Some scientists have theorized that there was a moist climate in North Africa during the Greco–Roman culture, but this idea is opposed by Hills (1966) and others.

Historical and archaeological data indicate that some "minor" fluctuations in climate occurred in cycles of 100–300 years. These fluctuations were very influential and resulted in the reduction of land productivity, a decrease in dry farming, the migration of pasturers, and the desertification of the landscape. Then short–term climatic fluctuations in intervals of 10–11 or 30–50 years occurred; the duration of drought periods was 1–2 or 7–10 years.

Unfortunately, modern science is still incapable of predicting the exact time, duration, and alternation of humid and dry periods in arid and semihumid areas, but the prediction of changes in the climate is now attracting the attention of scientists and planners. One persistent question is whether we are living in the dry period of a long climatic cycle with a general trend toward warming, xerotization, and frequent droughts; or whether the climate is becoming colder, with the amount of annual rainfall varying from year to year within very broad limits. The controversy surrounding this question is striking.

On the basis of the personal observation of plains and mountains in Eurasia, Africa, and South America, I believe that a pronounced tendency toward xerotization of steppe, savanna, and prairie land is clearly manifest. The natural factors that are responsible for xerotization (not mentioning rainfall and the water levels of lakes) are (1) a progressive decline in the groundwater table, (2) a slow but measurable upheaval of plains, (3) a cutting down of the base level and an increase in the draining effects of rivers and ravines, and (4) the rise of mountain snowlines and a reduction in the recharge of rivers and groundwater on plains.

The xerotization process has been accelerated by the utilization of groundwater for domestic and industrial needs. Deforestation, a general increase in both evaporation and surface runoff, and the destruction of grass cover have also contributed to the decline of the groundwater table. The lowering of the groundwater level even by 50–75 cm considerably increases the adverse effects of meteorological droughts. Areas of steadily high productivity are usually found on plains with chernozem–meadow soils and shallow fresh groundwater. Overgrazing and wood removal in mountainous, hilly, and plain regions were followed by the destruction of soils in many parts of Indopakistan, North Africa, Trans-Caucasus, and Asia Minor. Every year the great belt of grazing lands in Central and Southeastern Asia, Afghanistan, Iran, Turkey, Arabia, and North Africa loses fertile soils. The same can be said of the semiarid regions of South, Central, and North America, Australia, and the southern part of Europe. Moreover, the process of land degradation here has accelerated during the last 25–20 years.

Desertification of land along the southern Saharian borders probably proceeds at a rate of more than 100,000 ha per year (Le Houerou, 1968, 1970), each year, the Sahara's frontiers move several miles southward. Primitive monoculture and shifting cultivation together with overgrazing now and in the past thousand years are factors in both land degradation and desertification. Some observers are of the opinion that all the deserts of the Middle East are "man made" (Reifenberg, 1953; Emberger, 1957; Pabot, 1960).

Much of the Sonoran Desert of Arizona and much of the desert of New Mexico have been created by overgrazing during the last few hundred years (Cloudsley–Thompson, 1970). The arid lands of central Asia and Asia Minor were once covered with grasses and with a diffused network of trees and shrubs. The same was true in North and South America during the Quaternary period, but bushes, shrubs, and trees disappeared, and grass sod was destroyed and in many places physically eliminated.

Destruction of the vegetation cover in arid and subarid areas was accomplished by grazing, construction, and utilizing plants for food (bulbs, roots, seeds, fruits) and medical purposes. Damage was especially great during periods of drought. Torrential floods following on lands affected by drought could wash away the humus without infiltrating the soils, reinforcing the consequences of the drought. Deforestation of the slopes of hills and mountains was followed by the disappearance of small rivers and streams and the lowering of the groundwater table.

Nomadism and animal husbandry have existed for 3000 or 4000 years. At the present time, the total number of domestic animals is around 3 billion; the number of animals grazing in the arid zones of the world is around 1½ billion. In North Africa, for instance, there are about 30 million cattle, in Australia, about 50 million.

The destruction of land and plant resources due to unwise utilization is much accelerated, but this destructive process has been greatly expanded by modern industrial development and techniques. Deforestation was intensified by cutting wood for charcoal, locomotive fuel, timber chemistry, mines, and various urban needs. Industry and mining, quarry exploitation, shipbuilding, road construction, and petroleum pumping cause the greatest devastation of local landscapes and vegetation cover, as well as soil degradation and destruction (technoerosion). Studies and seminars of the International Society of Soil Science, UNESCO, and FAO have included the following in the process of land degradation in arid and semiarid countries: destruction of forests by fire, barking, or felling and browsing by goats; the uprooting of stumps; charcoal making; the ploughing of forests or pastures for the cultivation of wheat; overgrazing of natural pastures; the disappearance of valuable fodder species; the uprooting of busy or slightly ligneous plants for fuel; trampling and compacting of soils by the numerous animals; the hindering and destruction of grass; the worsening of naked surface microclimate; the increased heating of soil; the intensification of water evaporation and the oxidation of humus; crust formation; and salinity. With the degradation of the vegetation cover, wind erosion, which is particularly destructive to pastures situated on the slopes of deforested hills and mountains and on sand deposits, will increase. Modern mechanization (tractors, lorries) makes possible the clearing of vast areas of arid pasture land and accelerates the land's degradation.

Nonirrigated Farming and Grazing

Xerotization of Land, Droughts, and Moisture Conservation. Adverse changes in the biochemical, physical, and chemical properties of old arable soils make the xerotization tendency of plains and the deterioration of soil moisture regimes more pronounced. In recently cultivated and virgin soils, the humus horizon acts as an important source of energy for the normal cycle of biological and biochemical soil processes. Humus, a soil aggregation factor, optimizes the physical properties of soils (permeability, moisture capacity, decrease in evaporation, etc.). Monocultural farming without grasses, manure, or other organic fertilizers have caused widespread soil dehumification. The humus content in old arable soils in Europe and America has decreased by 25–50%. The thickness of the humus horizon has also decreased, and a pan has been formed (heavy tractors promote its formation). Soil permeability has been reduced, and the wilting coefficient and wasteful evaporation of moisture have become larger.

All modern methods of improving the soil humus state, soil physical properties, and moisture conservation must be given proper attention in a system of the management of soils under drought conditions. The necessity of doubling and tripling crop yields under the same conditions of atmospheric precipitation makes the problem of drought-soil management especially vital. New varieties of crops giving unprecedented high yields require 2–3 times more moisture than the normal requirement (the amount of water consumed is generally proportional to the increment of biomass). Grain yields of 5.0–6.0 and 8.0–9.0 metric tons/ha need 500–550 to 700 mm of annual rainfall, that is, considerably more than the 300–400 mm required by usual crops. Since it is expected that soil moisture deficits and drought situations will be more frequent in the future, all means of soil amelioration management must be used with a view to improving the moisture regime of soils.

About 30–35% of cultivated lands in the arid zone will be irrigated in the future, but other measures of soil amelioration, soil moisture accumulation, and conservation must be taken. The general aim of these measures is the formation of an aggregated, permeable, and sufficiently thick (50–60 cm) cultural horizon rich in humus and capable of absorbing and retaining ample amounts of rain water. The humus content should be increased by grass cultivation, manuring, the sowing of green manure crops, and the utilization of local organic waste–products. Deep loosening, overdeep and multitier tillage, combined with the application of fertilizers, will improve the physical state and moisture regime of structureless compact soils. An interesting experience in this respect is deep (down to 70 cm) soil loosening and tillage of compact structureless soils by new types of rooters, drainers, plows, and chisels in the Federal Republic of Germany. These agricultural implements were successfully demonstrated to participants at the International Conference on Hydromorphic Soils in 1971. It also seems possible to improve the soil moisture regime by artificial aggregation, that is, by the application of synthetic soil conditioners, but this is still very expensive.

Extensive research must be continued on new methods of soil mulching and hydrophobization, methods of changing soil solution surface tension, and the use of porous and spongy plastics for soil moisture condensation control, reducing evaporation and optimizing the soil structure.

The Problem of Solonetzic Soil (Black Alkali) Reclamation. This problem is closely associated with that of drought prevention and moisture control. Even slight alkalinity exerts a harmful effect on the productivity of cultivated lands and pastures. Droughts kill all vegetation in solonetzic soils, takyrs, and vertisols. Solonetzic meadow soils and southern chernozems, chestnut soils, and various solonetzic soil complexes in southern and southeastern Europe, Siberia, Central Asia, Asia Minor, China, Africa, Argentina, Canada, Chile, and Australia produce extremely low crop yields of a poor quality. Takyr-like and solonetzic soils cover hundreds of millions of hectares, but at present their role in agriculture is negligible, and yields undermine crop cultivation and cattle-breeding. The neutralization of alkalinity and the aggregation of dispersed colloidal mass in such soils needs chemical amendments and organic manure. Acid and organic by-products of various industries, mining, and agriculture may be used for solonetz reclamation. Amelioration of solonetzic and takyr soils will not only considerably increase their productivity, but also favorably affect the oxygen and carbon dioxide regime in the atmosphere (the result of the photosynthetic production of phytomass).

Soviet, American, Hungarian, and Rumanian soil specialists have worked out a number of methods for the chemical and physical reclamation of solonetz soils under dry farming conditions. These methods have been tested in field experiments; however, the practical implementation of solonetz amelioration proceeds very slowly. This amelioration technique is not expensive (300–500 roubles/ha), and the cost is returned in 3 or 4 years, from the increased productivity of the improved fields and pastures.

All solonetzic soils of dry savannas, pampas, and steppes could be improved by the application of acid compounds shifting pH towards lower alkalinity, calcium–containing fertilizers, heavy doses of organic manures, a greater proportion of grasses in crop rotation, irrigation, or the retention of snow where possible.

Wind Erosion and Dry Farming. Complete deforestation in semi–humid, semi–arid, and arid regions create conditions for increased wind velocity and soil moisture reduction. The more flat the surface of a field is and the fewer the obstacles (shrubs, trees), the greater is the speed of the wind (30–40% greater than with vegetation) and its destructive effect. Overgrazing and monoculture under these conditions provoke a strong dusting of the soil surface and the hazard of deflation. As a result, soils become overly dry and unprotected. On the Nile delta, eight feet of soil were blown away over 2600 years. In the western U.S. (Hills, 1966), some 850 million tons of soil dust are blown away each year.

Dust storms of increasing force and frequency destroy non–protected soils over vast agricultural territories and grazing lands in Asia, southern Europe, Africa, South and North America, and Australia. Dust storms and wind erosion are becoming a national or regional calamity, adversely affecting local economies. After 5 or 10 days of such a storm, millions of hectares of arable land lose 15–25 cm of top horizon. Coarse grains of dust shift and accumulate as dunes, and the finest particles are blown up to 1000 km away. Fine dust from Mongolia, the Ukraine, Africa, or Iran can be redeposited as far away as Italy, Scandinavia, or England. This erosion of the top soil greatly reduces the fertility of the remaining soil and contributes to crop loss.

One of the most negative consequences of wind erosion is the continuous loss of humus reserves in the upper horizon of the soil. Because of this the nitrogen, phosphorus, potassium, and active microorganisms in the remaining soil are greatly reduced. The structure and hydrophysical properties of the soil are very poor, and very often they are covered with strata of stone (pavement). Areas of North Africa and the Sahel have experienced this phenomenon, especially during recent years.

Dry farming in Africa (wheat, barley) is combined with nomadic grazing, and conducted in an obsolete manner and without the benefit of fertilizers. This results in the depletion, blowing away, and salinization of soils, as well as in low grain yields and the low productivity of animal herds. A similar situation exists in America. In Mexico, dust storms are growing stronger, and deflation has destroyed millions of hectares of land under dry farming.

Measures of wind erosion control consist of proper management and rotation of the land use by season and amount of grazing (Hills, 1966). These measures will lead to the restoration of normal (or at least improved) vegetation cover and to the possibility of wind erosion control. The constant growth of grass is sometimes more effective than forest as a defense against erosion (Messines, 1960). Slopes of 30–40° without vegetation cover are subject to strong water or wind erosion, but slopes of 50–60° with vegetation cover are secure and not affected by degradation (Anderson, 1960).

Experience in the U.S.S.R., the U.S., and Mexico has, however, demonstrated that the most effective wind erosion control measures are windbreaks and crop cultivation in strips rotating with grassland (Xolocotzi, 1970). The protective effect of wind-breaking screens on wind, soils, and yield is proportional to their height: before the screen, 9× height (in meters), behind the screen, 30× height (Nageli, after Tregubov, 1960).

The substantial periodic addition of organic residues, green manure, and farmyard manure is the most desirable way of improving the structure of soils affected by wind erosion and of decreasing evaporation and drying (Farnsworth, 1960). Of course, these additions must be combined with a definite type of crop rotation and controlled grazing.

A very effective method of wind erosion control in arable lands is a gradual creation of the deep permeable structural horizon of the soil, capable of absorbing rain water and preventing the evaporation of soil moisture. This could be achieved by subsoiling compacted soils up to a depth of 30–40 cm and by loosening the soil profile up to 70–80 cm by special rooters (experienced in the U.S.S.R., Algeria, and West Germany).

The close integration of forest and agricultural plant cultivation and forest and animal grazing in proportions adequate for different ecological conditions is an effective principle of soil protection and the profitable and lasting utilization of land.

Summarizing the world's experience in dry farming and in the prevention of wind erosion, the following recommendations can be made:

1. Deep multi–layer loosening without turning the surface humus horizon.
2. Deep subsoiling and loosening of the compacted subhorizon; these two methods will increase infiltration and reduce evaporation.

3. Regular surface cultivation and harrowing for mulching of soils and reducing the capillary movement of water and evaporation.

4. Regular application of muck, dung, and grass and legumes growing in rotation or as a second (after harvest) crop for the green manuring of soils. This will lead to an increase in the humus content of the soils and to the improvement of soil structure and hydrophysical properties.

5. Reasonable limitation of the density of cultivated plants.

6. In very dry climates, limitations on nitrogen fertilizers.

7. A very high level of agricultural knowledge and a scientific understanding of ecology and plant and soil requirements.

8. Introduction of appropriate cultures (drought resistant, fast growing–drought escaping, salt resistant) such as varieties of millet, sorghum, barley, wheat, and some legumes.

9. Creation of windbreaking screens (olive, pistachio, acacia, gledicia, morus, date–palm, tamarix, agava, yucca, opuntia, etc.).

10. Construction of the simplest water basins, ponds, and small–scale reservoirs.

11. Rational combinations of forest, agriculture, and grazing.

The Problem of Shifting Sands. The process of soil and flora degradation is particularly disastrous in territories covered with Tertiary and Quaternary sand deposits. The destruction of psammophytic shrubs and a loose turf of spring ephemeral plants led to a devastating deflation of sandy soils in huge territories of Asia, North America, and Africa. Moving sands, barkhans, and dunes advanced on drinking wells, fields and villages, paths, highways, railroads, and irrigation canals. Even in the temperate climate of Europe, moving dunes and barkhans appeared where man felled woods and shrubbery, plowed sandy soils, and overdrained postglacial marshy sandy areas by deep canals.

The natural overgrowth of sands and their systematic afforestation (phytomelioration), as well as the control of the number of livestock and the establishment of grazing rotations in many regions, gradually helped to stop and fix moving sands (in southern France, Bukhara, and the Baltic and North Sea coasts). However, in many parts of Asia and Africa, where people remain unaware of the serious aftereffects of this process, the problem is still far from being solved. The process of anthropogenic aridization was greatly favored by a general tendency to land evolution in the post-glacial period. The uncontrolled activity of nomadic cattle breeders during the millennia enhanced this process considerably, so that desertification and soil degradation have become disastrous in arid areas.

Sandy areas are very attractive for hunters, shepherds, and nomadic families. "In sand is life," says a Turkoman proverb. In equal climatic conditions, sandy soils will be more productive and more favorable for men than clayey and silty soils. Sandy soils accumulate rain water and preserve moisture better. Sandy soils are usually non–saline or slightly saline, and sandy territories of alluvial origin often have fresh or brackish subsoil water (5–10 m). The native vegetation of sands is much richer than that of clayey and silty soils in the arid zone. Particularly abundant is the ephemeroid vegetation after the rainy season.

For these reasons, sandy areas have attracted nomadic populations for thousands of years. On the other hand, the migratory grazing of livestock is the only reasonable utilization of the scarce bioproduction of typical sand semi–deserts and deserts. "Normal ranching" under such conditions is practically impossible.

Experts consider that the potentials of sandy pastures in Asia and Africa are now near the saturation point. The recommended number of sheep for the deserts of Central Asia is $1\sqrt{5-6}$ ha of pasture; in many regions the number of cattle is much higher. Total deforestation in sandy soils, especially in the areas of drinking wells and springs, has allowed mass mobility and shifting of sands.

Destruction of the native vegetation cover and the cutting of shrubs and trees are followed unavoidably and quickly by the formation of mobile sand dunes, barkhans, and chansets, which provoke disastrous complications in the originally productive area. Fluctuations in rainfall and drought, coupled with overgrazing, reinforce the negative consequences. This has been the case in the last 7 to 10 years in Africa and Asia.

Shifting sands exist in China, India, Pakistan, Iran, Central Asia, Transcaspian areas, the Arabian peninsula, the Sahara, central Africa, South Africa, central Australia, northern Australia, and South America.

Vast territories of sand deserts and sub-deserts were created by the industrial activity of man, the construction of roads, passing automobiles, tractors and bulldozers, mining, oil fields, and gas–oil pipelines. All this, together with overgrazing and tree cutting, have transformed sandy soils into mobile dunes and moving barkhans, occupying roads, fields, canals, and villages.

The initial mobility of sand depends on the size of particles and on the speed of wind (Petrov, 1973; Sokolov, 1884):

Particles, mm	Wind Speed, m/sec
0.1 —0.25	4.5— 6.7
0.25—0.5	6.7— 8.4
0.5 —1.0	9.8—11.4
1.0 —2.0	11.4—13.0

Over a bare surface, the carrying capacity of wind generally increases 2–3 times more than the speed. Vegetation cover, turf, sod, and roots, the structural aggregation of the soil, provide the strongest protection against wind and deflation. The formation of flying sand streams and aerosols is accelerated and reinforced by the dryness of the soil and by high temperatures (often 70–80° C) of the desert surface.

Surface humidity reduces the effect of deflation, and irrigated sands are most resistant to wind erosion. The experiences of Egypt, Uzbekistan, and Turkmenistan demonstrate the great economic effect of sand irrigation. If they are fertilized and manured, sands under irrigation are as productive as other soils. In addition, it was observed in the U.S.S.R., Pakistan, and Egypt that they are much less affected by secondary salinity and alkalinity.

There are a large number of publications in English, French, and Russian that consider recommended sets of plants and types of screens, depending on climate, soils, and economic conditions. The best collection of data is published in a UNESCO book, *Seminar on Soil and Water Conservation* (Teheran, 1960).

From this analysis it is clear that rotational grazing, the restoration of native vegetation, the accumulation of moisture, and the reduction of wind speed would be the main tools in the stabilization of shifting sands. The first step would include cheap hedges, mulching (sprinkling by clay suspension, bitumen, or petrol), and the installation of cheap wind barriers. The next step would be sowing or planting psammophytic vegetation (grass, shrubs, trees), which has both protective and economic importance (Chapman, 1960).

An evaluation of the quality and potential of the arid zone sands depends on:

1. The depth and properties of the underlying (underground) stratum (ancient soil, gypsum crust, limestone, fine earth, etc.).
2. The depth and chemical composition of groundwater (1–2 m, 2–5 m, 5–10 m, > 10 m, fresh, brackish, salty, etc.).
3. The mineralogical composition of sand particles (quartz, feldspar, gypsum, salts, etc.).
4. The degree of stability (mobile or without vegetational cover, with sparse plants, fixed with grass and shrub plants).
5. The degree of aridity of the climate (annual rainfall: less than 100 mm, 100–250 mm, 250–300 mm; annual evaporation: 1000–1500–3000–4000 mm).

Recommendations for the practical utilization of territories with vari-

ous kinds of sands, that is, measures for the preservation, phytoamelioration, and recuperation of shifting sands, will be very different. The ecology of sands and their natural productivity depends on the above listed
peculiarities, but the best and most profitable kind of utilization is still
animal husbandry. Rotational grazing, the preservation of woody plants,
and maintaining the optimal number of animals per hectare result in higher
productive and profitable animal husbandry.

Irrigation, Waterlogging, Secondary Soil Salinity

Irrigation as a Factor of Soil Amelioration in Arid Areas. Irrigation is the
most ancient, complex, and remarkable means of improving arid soils and
increasing land productivity. Irrigation systems illustrate a combined
influence on various components of landscapes with a view to forming
highly productive and controlled agricultural biogeocenoses. Today,
230–240 million ha of the world's land are under irrigation. The main crop
cultivated on irrigated soils is rice, which covers about two-thirds of this
area. After rice comes cotton, oil producing crops, fruit trees, cereals, and
other crops.

By means of irrigation man has created agrobiocenoses with a bioproductivity unheard of in nature, giving 2–3 crop yields annually (or even
6–8 yields; for example, in the river delta near Canton). Drouhin (1970) has
pointed out that the desert soils of the Sahara and Central Asia are
potentially very rich and fertile. They await fresh water for irrigation and
organic manure for revitalization. Irrigation and chemization open new
prospects in the agricultural development of sands. The experience of
Egypt, Uzbekistan, and Turkmenistan shows that irrigated and sufficiently fertilized sandy soils are as productive as loamy and loess
soils. Irrigated sands are less susceptible to salinization, alkalinization,
and the development of a compact structure. Such soils are important
reserves for future agricultural activities.

The irrigation of wheat proves to be profitable when it yields more than
4.0–4.5 tons/ha. Under irrigation and proper soil management, the new
Soviet varieties of wheat (Kavkaz, Aurora) produce as much as 7.0–8.0 or
8.5 tons/ha.

Highly effective systems for paddy field irrigation have been successful
in the previously barren saline soils of the Syr Darya delta, the Manych
valley, the Sivash lowland, the Sarpinsk plain, solonchaks in Daghestan,
and waterlogged lands in the Kuban Valley. These new centers of rice
production obtain 4.0–4.5 and 5.0–6.0 tons of rice/ha, that is, three times
as much as the world average. Rice yields of 6.5–7.0 and even 8.0–10.0

tons/ha have been reported in the U.S., the U.S.S.R., the Philippines, and Japan. With such high yields, rice cultivation becomes one of the most profitable forms of agriculture.

On the other hand, in some cases rice yields decrease after 3–4 years of cultivation, and some rice plants perish. Strong soil salinity, alkalinity, or anaerobic conditions are usually responsible for these phenomena.

Irrigation is very effective for sugar beet, sugar cane, and vegetables: their yields under irrigation increase five or six times. The same applies to orchards and vineyards. The overirrigation of vegetables, however, results in plant disease, soil salinization, and a reduction of the quality of yields (Biswas, 1978).

Particularly profitable is the cultivation of fodder crops on irrigated lands: maize for green feed, grass mixtures, alfalfa. Under irrigation the yields of these crops increase by 7, 8, or 10 times. The physiological susceptibility of vegetables, fruit trees, grape vines, maize, and alfalfa to soil salinity and alkalinity, as well as to nutrient deficiency, is still higher than that of rice or wheat. Therefore the yields of crops decrease considerably on lands subjected to salinization, alkalinization, and waterlogging.

The land resources of the world include hundreds of millions of hectares of low–fertile soils in Asia, Africa, southeastern Europe, and North and South America that can be irrigated in the future. Thorne has said (1970): "Approximately 60% of all potentially arable lands experience 6 months or more of moisture deficit each year." The importance of irrigation for humanity is obvious, and the area under irrigation is expected to grow, since double and triple crop yields are attainable if additional water is supplied to the soil and moisture content is not below 65–75% of field capacity. The area of irrigated lands in India, Pakistan, Iran, Turkey, and the Arab countries will probably increase by 3–5 times in the next 20–40 years. The fulfillment of this program must involve the radical modernization of irrigation systems (closed pipelines, low–intensity sprinkling, automatic water supply according to soil moisture content, heavy fertilization, the use of aerial photographic survey to control the condition of soils and crops, etc.), and new varieties of crops adapted to irrigation will have to be developed. A great number of skilled specialists will be required in irrigated agriculture in order to accomplish these goals.

Problem of Secondary Salinization of Irrigated Land. The main scourge of irrigated agriculture remains the secondary salinization of millions of hectares of soil due to the absence of drainage. Lack of drainage frequently results in the waterlogging, salinization, and alkalinization of soils, the development of soil compactness, and a reduction in crop yields. Irrigation systems must possess a deep ramified horizontal (2–3 m) or vertical drainage network. Solving this problem will not only allow double and triple rice and cotton yields, but also second and third yields of afterstubble crops.

Irrigation exerts a tremendous influence on the natural landscape. It affects the earth's crust a dozen meters down, the lower layers of the atmosphere dozens of meters through, and changes the water and salt regime in a large part of a river basin, including the estuary. Unfortunately, except for a few exceptions, irrigation systems today are built and used almost exactly as they were in ancient Egypt, Khorezm, and Babylon.

The transporting and main irrigation canals are nonlined, and continuous seepage is usually as high as 60–70% of the total volume of water taken at the head of the canals. With seepage (infiltration plus hydrostatic pressure), the level of groundwater rises, sometimes at a speed of 2–3 m/year. As a result, vast territories of land along the canals become waterlogged, swampy, salty, and unfertile. Plantations of palms, citrus, and cotton are ruined, buildings collapse because of the moisture, and malaria is more prevalent. Irrigation practices in India, Iran, Egypt, and Syria provide many examples of the phenomenon of waterlogging followed by salinity. Lining the canals, creating tree plantations, and cultivating wood and alfalfa along the canals are measures which can prevent or decrease seepage and waterlogging. Important additional measures are the periodic closing of canals and the preservation of the canal's silted layers during the annual cleaning. The technical improvement of irrigation systems and the proper utilization of water are the basic prerequisites for preventing secondary salinization and waterlogging. Experience with Soviet and American irrigation systems demonstrates that efficiency may be raised 80–85% by the application of flumes, waterproofing, pipelines, sprinklers, and the controlled distribution of water according to plant requirements and soil properties.

Improved irrigation technology and technical equipment cannot, however, completely prevent salinization and waterlogging, because irrigation radically changes the water and salt balance of the territory. Munn (1974) says: "Recent studies have suggested that in the Great Plains region of North America also, there is reason for concern, with an increase of up to tenfold over the last fifty years in the acreage of saline soils within areas of productive farm land."

Intensive secondary salinization took place in 1920–40 on vast irrigated areas in Soviet Central Asia (Golodnostepskaya, Shaulderskaya, Wakhshskaya irrigation systems, systems on Amu Darya, and in the Khorezm and Tashauz oases). This disastrous phenomenon made it imperative for Soviet scientists to develop preventive measures. Long–term field and laboratory investigations have been conducted by the U.S.S.R.

Academy of Sciences in close cooperation with research institutions of the Central Asian and Caucasian Soviet Republics. It has been found that the soils of naturally poorly drained areas, even in the northern forest–steppe zone, exhibit various forms of soda and soda–sulfate salinity.

Chernozems in the southern part of the U.S.S.R. contain residual soda in subsoils (at the depth of 3–5–20 m.), which becomes active when the soils are irrigated. The greater part of the Aral–Caspian lowland is affected by contemporary accumulations of sulfates and chlorides of sodium. The possibility of secondary salinization in irrigated areas should be taken into account practically in all soil–climatic zones, starting from the forest-steppe to the equatorial belt. Everything depends on the degree and effectiveness of natural or artificial drainage. In the great majority of cases, along with the technical perfection of irrigation systems and methods of irrigation, the water and salt balance of an area must be radically changed by means of deep (2.5–3.5 m) horizontal drainage to remove salts contained in soils, in groundwater, and sometimes in irrigation water.

The initial manifestations of salinization in irrigated soils is the destruction of soil aggregates and the formation of large cemented blocks. The chemical properties of irrigation water (soluble silica, sodium and magnesium carbonates, chlorides and sulfates in low amounts) are to a large degree responsible for these processes. The main factor, however, is shallow saline groundwater (at a depth of 1.5–2.0 m) in drainless irrigation systems. Without artificial drainage, evapotranspiration of groundwater is accompanied by the formation of hydrophilic colloidal substances and an accumulation of soda or chlorides and sulfates in the soil. In the later stages of secondary salinization, toxic salts form a kind of salt crust or salt dust on the surface of soils. Secondary salinization and alkalinization resulting from irrigation without drainage have spoiled millions of hectares of formerly productive lands and turned them into barren saline deserts. The most obvious examples of such lands are found on plains and in river deltas in Iran, India, Pakistan, Iraq, Egypt, Transcaucasus, and Argentina. At least 200–300 thousand ha of irrigated lands are lost annually due to salinization and waterlogging (see also Chapter 6).

In most countries the real proportion of saline soils has not been estimated. According to some indirect estimates, the total area of barren saline lands that have once been fertile is no less than 20–25 million ha. At the same time, large irrigation systems in the U.S.S.R. have demonstrated that desalinization of soils by deep horizontal drainage combined with special leaching and washing is quite effective.

In the Vakhsh valley of Tadjikistan, which was severely affected by secondary salinization in the 1930s and 1940s, all the soils have been desalinized and now produce 3.0–3.5 tons/ha of long-staple cotton. The same is true in the central part of the Ferghana valley of Turkistan, the main cotton growing area in the U.S.S.R. Construction of deep drainage collectors in Khorezm, Tashauz, the Chardzhou oases of the Amu Darya, the Kura–Arax Lowland of Azerbaijan, the Golodnoya steppe, the Syr Darya, the Manych, and the Sivash area of South Russia has significantly increased the yields of rice and cotton. In these areas, deep collectors and horizontal drains were installed, and special leaching and vegetational irrigation were utilized.

The most effective method of reducing water seepage is the construction of irrigation systems equipped with closed pipelines. A second measure is the timely construction of vertical pump drainage in order to prevent the uprise of groundwater where predicted. It is this measure that helped to avoid the rise of groundwater in California and Arizona (U.S.). The third radical measure for salinization prevention and control is deep horizontal drainage maintained in operating condition.

Not every year or every season is totally dry. Irrigation in steppes and savannas supplements precipitation (rainfall, snow). Therefore, irrigation systems must be especially flexible and easy to control and manage. Systems of special sensors and automatic devices must provide an adequate volume of water for plants, depending on the weather, soil properties, and the requirements of plants. Irrigation should be stopped automatically on moist soils during rainy seasons; during dry periods, water must be supplied.

Problem of Soda Salinization. In various publications (1971, 1973), I have expressed my concern about the potential risk to soils of secondary soda salinization in the case of an uprise in alkaline groundwater in irrigated regions. Soda salinization control and the amelioration of soda saline soils (solonchaks) are problems of global importance and subjects of concern to a special subcommission of the ISSS. The general theoretical aspects of the geochemistry of sodium carbonates and bicarbonates in groundwater were discussed in my publications in 1946 and particularly, in 1965 and 1969 (proceedings of the symposia held in Budapest and Yerevan). Many countries of Asia, Africa, Europe, and South and North America have soda-saline soils. These soils are affected by alkaline groundwaters or diluted soda–carrying irrigation waters (the Nile, Indus, and Arax rivers and groundwaters in California, Arizona, Hungary, Pakistan, Chad, and Kenya), or both of these factors.

Soda (sodium carbonate or bicarbonate) is more toxic than sodium chlorides. Soda in irrigation or groundwater causes a number of complicated physical, chemical, and mineralogical changes in soils that adversely affect soil fertility and are in most cases extremely difficult to eliminate. These changes include the following: the soil–absorbing complex becomes saturated with exchangeable sodium up to 50–70% of the cation exchange capacity; pH reaches the level of 9–11; the crumby and granular soil structure degrades, and soils become compact, blocky, and structureless; peptized hydrophyllic organic and mineral colloids are formed; swelling smectite minerals with a mobile crystal lattice appear and become active, promoting soil cementation and development of deep cracks when dry and dispersion of the soil material when wet.

Soils salinized with soda become unproductive. Amelioration of these soils requires not only deep horizontal drainage (combined, if necessary, with vertical drainage), but also the simultaneous application of large amounts of chemical amendments (30–50 tons/ha. of acid, gypsum, etc.), leaching, and high rates of physiologically acid fertilizers. These measures have been proved to be effective by successful research and field experiments conducted in California, Hungary, and Armenia.*

Soils salinized with soda cannot be formed if the parent material contains crystalline gypsum and if gypsum is present in the ground or irrigation water, even in low concentrations. Where the gypsum content in water–bearing horizons and river basins is low, however, waters usually contain some amounts of sodium carbonates and bicarbonates that accumulate in the soils after several years of irrigation.

The principal soda salinization control measures are as follows: a reasonably limited supply of water to soils, a high efficiency of irrigation systems, the prevention of groundwater uprise, the lowering of groundwater levels, and the removal of groundwater containing soda through drainage. If the primary source of soda is river water used for irrigation, as, for example, in the Arax, Indus, and Nile basins, a system is required for the neutralization of irrigation water in canals during its transport to the fields (for example, the addition of gypsum, nitric, sulfuric, or phosphoric acid).

Problem of Irrigation Water Quality. In the previous history of irrigation in the U.S.S.R., the problem of irrigation water quality never arose, because the Angren, Syr Darya, Zeravshan, Amu Darya, Kura, and Volga rivers had very low salt concentrations, 0.2–0.3 grams/liter (g/l) and a favorable composition of salts (a domination of calcium bicarbonate and calcium sulfate). Even if natural drainage were poor, waters of such composition would favorably affect the physical and chemical properties of soils, due to a large amount of suspended particles and the predomi-

---

*Various problems of amelioration of saline and sodasaline soils are considered in detail in the *International Handbook on Irrigation and Drainage,* published by UNESCO and FAO in 1968 (2nd ed., London, 1973).

nance of calcium among cations. In the U.S., Egypt, Algeria, Tunisia, Morocco, Pakistan, and India, water used for irrigation usually exhibits increased salinity (0.5–1.5–5 g/l) and a predominance of sodium among cations. This is why the European, American, Indopakistan, and Egyptian researchers have always paid great attention to the chemical composition of water used for irrigation.

At the present stage of soil amelioration, the quality and chemical composition of irrigation water should be studied more profoundly. Mineralization of water in rivers has gradually increased up to 0.6–0.8–1 g/l during the last decade. The composition of ions changes towards the predominance of sodium over calcium; the concentration of sulfate ion and chlorine ion increases; and a hydrocarbonate ion appears. These changes are brought about by the complete regulation of river flow, an increase in evaporation, larger amounts of drainage water that has passed through the soils and subsoils of irrigated lands into river valleys, and the discharge of urban, mining, and industrial water into rivers.

The planned expansion of drainage network construction in various countries will be accompanied by a higher concentration of sodium salts in the water of the rivers. Due to the shortage of fresh water, mineralized waters will have to be used more extensively for irrigation in the future. Drainage and artesian water, as well as the diluted water of sea bays and river deltas, will be used for irrigation purposes. Brackish water (1–2–3 g/l) can be utilized for irrigation, but this must be done most carefully and on the basis of scientific research and experimentation.

My own investigations demonstrate that it is quite possible to use waters with salt concentrations of 1.5–2–3 and even 5–7 g/l for irrigation. However, with the rise of salt concentration, the whole irrigation system must be modified to increase the outflow in the water–salt balance; in other words, it is necessary to increase the frequency of leaching, the rates of drainage, and the volume of drained and evacuated groundwater. The problems of utilization of highly saline water for irrigation purposes has not yet been sufficiently studied.

A minimum of 10% of water intake must be added for every gram of salts in irrigation water to intensify the drainage outflow. This is why requirements of drainage and leaching when using saline water will grow (see Table 7-1) in proportion to concentration. According to American data, the rates of leaching irrigations and drainage water removal are 30–60% of the total water supplied to an irrigation system if irrigation water mineralization is 2–3 g/l. In the areas of soda salinization and where sodic irrigation waters contain 0.3–0.5–1.5 g/l of salts, drainage outflow in proportion to the irrigation water intake must be about 30–50%. In this case, the chemical amelioration of soils or water is desirable in addition to

Table 7-1. Conditions of Utilization of Saline Waters

Salt Concentration (without soda) in Irrigation Water (g/l)	Frequency of Soil Leachings	Removed Drainage Water (% of total intake)
0.5–1	Once in 1–2 years	10–15
1.0–2	1–2 times annually	20–25
2–3	Several times annually	30–35
4–5	Each watering should be a leaching	50–60

enhanced drainage. Chemical amelioration makes it possible to reduce the amount of drainage water to be removed.

Irrigation water containing a high proportion of sodium is especially harmful, because it causes deterioration of the physical properties of soils and secondary alkalinization, adversely affecting the soil and crop yields. Irrigation with slightly saline–alkaline water and without drainage (or with poor drainage) always gives negative results.

Control of Soil Water-Salt Balance in Land Under Irrigation. It has now been commonly recognized that a study of the water–salt balance of each irrigation system is required and that it is necessary to compute the water–salt balances separately for the initial period, the transitional (ameliorative) period, and for the period of regular (normal) exploitation (after the completion of desalinization) of irrigated land. These three variants of the water–salt balance provide a scientific basis for each irrigation project. The aims of salt–water balance studies are:

1. To show the sources, distribution, chemical composition, and total amounts of various salts, as well as the dynamics of salinization in soil, ground, and irrigation waters in the area to be irrigated.

2. To estimate possible changes in the water–salt balance of the area from the beginning of irrigation through various stages of irrigation and drainage operations. It is desirable to find out whether or not an increase in groundwater is to be expected and to determine the schedule of soil leachings to remove salts, the kinds of temporary and permanent drainage installations to be constructed, and an optimum ameliorative work schedule for the transition period.

3. To determine the point at which a steady water–salt balance is established; the optimum and critical depth of groundwater levels; the most effective irrigation and leaching regimes if required; the

total amounts and proportions of drainage water; and the permanent elements of drainage structures. It will also be necessary to study changes in the water–salt balance in adjacent areas and to determine the size of the area likely to be affected by the new irrigation system.

The scientific elaboration of such water–salt balances by research and design institutes is complex, but important and gratifying, work. The application of a mathematical simulation model, for instance, facilitates the elaboration of water–salt balance. Up to now, most irrigation projects have not taken water–salt balances into account, much less the means of their control. This is why after several years of irrigation, such unexpected and unforeseen phenomena as waterlogging, salinization, or alkalinization may develop. The entire procedure of designing irrigation systems must be changed to avoid such developments. This would require the compilation of detailed soil and lithological maps, an analysis of the physical properties, chemical composition of soils and groundwater, and the distribution of salts in various soil layers.

Determining the water–salt balances of an irrigation system at the design stage requires the analysis and explanation of soil salinization phenomena, a study of the present water–salt characteristics, and the prediction of their future dynamics. Actual water–salt balances of newly irrigated and adjacent areas may differ greatly from those forecasted; therefore, current water–salt balances should be drawn up for reference purposes. Such references (water–salt balances for the whole territory or its part) will enable the managers of irrigation systems to plan and implement all additional measures required to control amelioration processes: expansion of the drainage network, additional land leveling and soil leaching, installation of pumping stations on the collectors, and digging pumping wells of vertical drainage. At present, periodic water–salt balances and information on the desalinization caused by leachings, saline soil dynamics, changes in the level and salinity of groundwater, flow rates and the chemical composition of drainage water, and other necessary data, are very rarely made available to irrigation system managers. Drawing up current water–salt balances for annual modification of amelioration programs requires a knowledge of water intake and distribution data, including the chemical composition of irrigation and drainage water, the actual amount of water applied for soil leaching and removed by a network of drains, the calculated or experimental values of evaporation and transpiration, the level and chemical composition of groundwater for three or four time periods in chart form, the contours and size of saline soil areas, the areas of affected crops (preferably on the basis of aerial photography with ground corrections), the salt content in principal soils in spring and autumn, the flow rates of drainage water in collectors, and, particularly, the amount and composition of salts removed with this water and reliable information on crop yields.

Each irrigation system must have a network of hydrometric and halometric stations and a number of observation holes and plots for studying salt dynamics; it must be provided with materials for aerial photography and must make hydrogeological, pedological, meliorative, and agricultural observations, measurements, and calculations in order to compare and generalize this data. All this requires skilled personnel, adequate research guidance, melioration laboratories, and computing centers. In general, the proper scientific and technical management of irrigation systems and the utilization of reclaimed lands must be based on regularly supplied information that must include the following: every 5–10 years drawing up maps of soils and groundwaters for the entire irrigated territory on a 1:10,000 or 1:25,000 scale and in comparison with actual (not average) crop yields; and annual data on the progress of land leveling, soil leaching, drainage and collector operations, crop yields, and crop loss on irrigated land. All these functions must be the responsibility of a special land reclamation service and of amelioration inspection and forecast centers.

Solutions to these problems require the application of up-to-date technological aids and techniques, such as fast and accurate soil analysis methods, aerial photography and machine interpretation of aerial photos, television cameras, and data recording on punched cards or on magnetic tape with subsequent processing by electronic computers. These techniques would make it possible to obtain reliable information on the extent of salinization, soil moisture content, groundwater, plant growth, and progress in agricultural work, within 2 or 3 weeks.

Necessary and current information on most irrigation systems of the world is either unavailable or incomplete, or is obtained after a 1- or 2-year lag. Land reclamation personnel must have at their disposal adequate means of transport, housing facilities, work rooms, and laboratories. The present level of inspection, forecast, and management in land amelioration cannot be raised, and the drawing up of reliable water–salt balances will be impossible if these facilities are lacking.

In irrigation systems with operational drainage, an ample supply of water, and well–leveled fields, the component of the salt balance that is the easiest to regulate is the removal of salts with drainage water. This becomes obvious from considering the water–versus–salt relationship, which is as follows:

The key to this formula is:

$$J \cdot C = \left[Q \cdot C_1 + Q_{dr} \cdot C_2 \right]$$

where
J = all kinds of irrigation water inflow
C = concentration of salts in irrigation water
C_k = critical salt concentration in groundwaters
Q = natural outflow of groundwaters
C_1 = concentration of salts in naturally drained groundwater
C_2 = the weighted average actual salinity of groundwater in a particular field
Q_{dr} = drainage water outflow.

If drainage is not employed, the functioning of an irrigation system depends upon both J and C, particularly upon Q and C_1. Secondary salinization of land will not take place if $J \cdot C < Q \cdot C_1$ due to adequate natural drainage. If natural drainage is poor ($J \cdot C > Q \cdot C_1$), the decompensation of groundwater, its uprise, salinization, and waterlogging of soils under irrigation are the result.

The introduction of artificial drainage (Q_{dr}) and the removal of groundwater salts (C_2) by leachings and a drainage network (Q_{dr}) turns a positive (accumulative) salt balance into a negative (desalinizing) balance:

$$J \cdot C < \left[Q \cdot C_1 + Q_{dr} \cdot C_2 \right]$$

In the course of successful amelioration, values C_1 and C_2 must decrease considerably and approach the critical groundwater salinity (C_k), which is typical of the territory under consideration. It is evident that the salt balance for an irrigated area is determined by the amount of water removed through artificial drainage and by the concentration of salts in this water. These two factors are significant for groundwater freshing, that is, for the completion of amelioration. In this respect, the water–salt balance index (WSB) suggested by me in 1966–67 is a convenient and simple way of estimating amelioration efficiency. After normal completion of desalinization in the geochemical provinces of chloride and sulfate accumulations, the critical salinity of groundwater (C_k) must be about 3 g/l. If salinity of irrigation water is 0.3 g/l, the ratio $3:0.3 = 10$ is the water–salt balance index (WSB). In this case about 10% of the total volume of water supplied to the fields must be removed by drainage in order to maintain the WSB at the level of 10 after completion of the amelioration period. Irrigation water may be evaporated by not more than 10 times; otherwise the salt concentration in groundwater will be above 3 g/l.

If the WSB is 12–15 rather than 10, it means that salts have accumulated in groundwaters; that is, soil leachings and drainage were ineffective. In this case the amount of drainage water outflow should be increased by 2–5% relative to the total water supply. If salt concentration in groundwater grows to 4–6 g/l, the WSB index increases up to 4/0.3 = 13.33 or 6/0.3 = 20, which necessitates stronger leachings and an increase of groundwater removal to 13.3—20% of the amount of water supplied to the territory.

The degree of permissible evaporation of irrigation water depends on its salt concentration. If salt concentration in irrigation water is higher than 0.3 g/l, 5–8% of the total amount of salt solutions must be removed by drainage outflow per one gram of salts in the waters. A general relationship for the amount of water removed by drainage in the operation of an irrigation system is as follows:

$$X = (5 - 8) \cdot \{C + [(C_2 \cdot 10)/3]\}$$

where X is the percentage of the total water supply to be removed by drainage.

The example given above referred to the area of chloride-sulfate salinization. If pure sulfate salinization occurs, as in the Ferghana and Bukhara areas, critical salt concentration may reach about 6 g/l. In this case, with the same mineralization of irrigation water, the WSB index will be $C_1:C = 6:0.3 = 20$. The permissible degree of irrigation water evaporation is then 20 times. This value can be attained if 1/20 (5%) of the total amount of water supplied to the fields is regularly removed from the irrigation system by drainage as an evaporate. Coefficients in our formula must be changed accordingly; in the case of soda salinization, for instance, the rates of drainage must be much higher. Let us assume that the critical salinity of soda groundwater is about 1 g/l (this value is to be further studied). With an irrigation water salinity of 0.3 g/l and a critical salinity of groundwater of 1 g/l, the WSB index would be 1:0.3 = 3.3, which means that the degree of irrigation water evaporation for soda geochemical provinces (if chemical ameliorations are not applied) may be permitted to increase by 3.3 times only. Thus it may be concluded that the amount of drainage outflow must be about 33% of the total amount of water supplied to the fields if the salinity of soda groundwater is to be maintained at about 1 g/l and the salt concentration in irrigation water at 0.3 g/l. An increase in soda groundwater salinity will immediately require a substantial increase in the amount of drainage water outflow (about 33% per additional gram of salts in soda groundwater). For instance, if the average actual salt concentration of soda groundwater is about 2 g/l, then, according to our formula:

$$X = (2 \cdot 33)/1 = (66\%) + 5 - (8\%) = 71\text{--}74\%$$

In other words, 71–74% of the total amount of irrigation water containing soda must be removed by drainage. This is why soda salinization is so harmful and why regularly repeated (and not one time) chemical ameliorations are required in cases of irrigation and groundwater containing soda. Chemical ameliorations of soda-saline soils by gypsum, sulfuric acid, or sulfur result in the formation of sodium sulfates, and this allows the amount of drainage water to decrease 5–6%.

The basic prerequisites for the accurate estimation of amelioration efficiency are extensive and statistically reliable data on groundwater salinity in each area, a profound knowledge of the salt geochemistry in the area, and reliably determined groundwater concentrations (optimal and critical) recommended for the given irrigation system. In future research, salt balances will have to be established separately for toxic ions (SO_4, Cl, HCO_3, CO_3), but this is another aspect of the problem.

The second conclusion suggested by the above data is that deep drainage plays an extremely important and decisive role in the geochemistry and productivity of irrigation systems. The construction of effective drainage facilities and their proper exploitation in areas affected or endangered by secondary salinization is the most vital and urgent problem of our time. A special emphasis must be placed on these measures in the development of world agriculture. Building irrigation systems is very expensive. Soils salinized to varying degrees, or those prone to salinization, are typical of arid areas. Therefore, the construction of irrigation systems without drainage installations in arid countries leads to a gradual decrease in their efficiency and is a waste of labor and investment.

Urgent Programs and Basic Actions

The arid areas of our planet have extremely great potential. As a basis for the production of grain, food, meat, fat, leather, milk, butter, and wool; as an unlimited land reserve for future irrigation; as a territory rich in mineral deposits, ores, petroleum, and gases; and as a space with exceptionally high sunlight insolation and a healthy climate—the arid zone is not less important than the world ocean.

About one billion people live in the arid zone, most of them in very poor social conditions, suffering from famine and a shortage of water. The rational development of the arid zone's potential by considerably enlarging productivity and the economic effectiveness of husbandry there, by preserving the soils, and by other ecological measures, is now the most acute task for science, technology, politics, and progress.

Desertification processes must be stopped, but the nature, speed, and manifestation of these processes are different, and these differences must be understood.

General Requirements and Programs. The following measures are required in order to achieve the goal of the rational utilization of the arid zone's potential.

1. National, regional, subcontinental, and continental long-term studies, surveys, monitoring, and appraisal.
2. Multi-purpose and long-term planning of national economic and social development and of the utilization of resources in the arid zone.
3. Special studies, evaluation, and elaboration of methods of utilization concerning soils and biological productivity, surface and subterranean waters, and solar and wind energy for local needs.
4. Interdisciplinary research of local endemic illnesses (trypanosomiasis, schistosomiasis, malaria).
5. A network of research field stations, university departments, and applied research institutes for training and conducting appropriate investigations.
6. Empirical pilot studies and research under practical field conditions of such questions as: the phytoamelioration and fixation of shifting sands; the restoration of fertility to eroded, deflated soils; and the reclamation of unfertile, saline, alkaline, waterlogged, compacted, and destroyed soils; modern techniques of irrigation; the scientific principles of dry farming; and the scientific principles of grazing and land preservation.

Network of National Institutions. The effective management, rational utilization, and preservation of land resources must be based on a network of national government institutions and establishments for:

1. The training and education of farmers, skilled workers, technicians, agronomists, botanists, sylviculturists, livestock experts, soil scientists, and irrigation–drainage specialists of different levels and functions.
2. Scientific investigation and research in lithology, geomorphology, hydrology, botany, soil geochemistry, soil amelioration, soil map-

ping, and evaluation. These could be conducted in laboratories, university departments, special institutes, and experimental field stations.

3. Extension services to meet the requirements of individual farmers, cooperatives, and state farms for scientific, technical, or economic advice and to help them adopt modern technology, machinery, fertilizers, irrigation/leaching methods, or a new variety of crops.

4. Conducting integrated predesigned surveys for the collection and analysis of statistical data, for elaboration of the final version of the project (design) before the government has made a decision.

Recommended National–Regional Applied Research Institutes and Stations for Land Resources Utililization.

1. Institute for Tropical Dry Farming and Agriculture, Kenya, Sahelian belt
2. Institute for Livestock Grazing, Ethiopia, Nigeria, Sudan
3. Institute for Amelioration and Development of Sand Deserts, Sahara, Saudi Arabia
4. Institute of Water and Wind Erosion, Iran, Afghanistan, Turkey
5. Institute for Irrigation and Drainage, Egypt, Syria
6. Institute for Reclamation of Saline Soils, Iraq, Pakistan
7. National Centers for Desert Research and Development, Mauritania, Mali, Senegal
8. Soil Survey and Land Evaluation Institute, Brazil, Bolivia, Argentina
9. Institute of Arid Zone Hydrology, Algeria, Tunisia, Morocco
10. Wind and Solar Energy Institute, Kuwait, Peru
11. Water Demineralization Institute, India, Tanzania

References

Biswas, A. K. (1978). Environmental implications of water development for developing countries. *Water Supply & Management* 2(4), 283–297.

Biswas, M. R., and Biswas, A. K. (1978). Loss of Productive Soil. *International Journal of Environmental Studies* 12(3), 189–197.

Dregne, H. E. (ed.) (1970). *Arid Lands in Transition.* Washington, 1970. Articles by H. Dregne, D. F. Peterson, W. Thorne, G. Drouhin, M. Kassas, H. Le Houerou, E. H. Xolocotzi, I. Kanwar, and others.

Hills, E. S. (ed.) (1966). *Arid Lands.* UNESCO, London.

Hollon, W. E. (1966). *The Great American Desert.* Oxford University Press, New York.

Jakubov, T. F. (1946). *Wind Erosion of Soils* (in Russian). Moscow.

Israr-ul-Haq (1974). *Environmental Aspects of Agricultural Development (Africa and Asia).* SCOPE-UNEP, Nairobi (manuscript).

Kane, N. O. (1974). *Environmental Aspects of Land Use in Semi-Arid and Sub-Humid Regions (Africa).* SCOPE-UNEP, Nairobi (manuscript in French).

Kovda, V. A. (1971). *Origin of Saline Soils in Their Regime.* 2 vols. Translated from the Russian edition of 1946, 1947. U.S. Department of Commerce, Springfield, Va.

Kovda, V. A. (ed.) (1973). *Irrigation, Drainage and Salinity: An International Source Book.* FAO/UNESCO, Paris.

Misra, R. (1974). *Environmental Aspects of Land Use in Semi-Arid and Sub-Humid Regions (Asia).* SCOPE-UNEP, Nairobi.

Petrov, M. P. (1973). *The Deserts of Planet Earth* (in Russian). Nauka, Leningrad.

UNESCO (1960). *General Report. Seminar on Soil and Water Conservation. Teheran, May-June, 1960.* Articles by J. Messines, R. B. Farnsworth, H. Pabot, B. H. Anderson, G. W. Chapman, V. Trequbov, N. H. Mossaudi, and others.

United Nations, *World Plan for Asia*, New York.

8

THE EFFECT OF MAN'S ACTIVITIES ON CLIMATE

Helmut E. Landsberg
University of Maryland

The possible influence of man on his atmospheric environment may have seemed largely an academic question only a few short decades ago. Then came voices of doubt, swelling in the mid-1960 decade to a chorus of loud chants presaging immediate disaster. It was well known by then that man had produced small but measurable local climatic alterations, and global climatic impacts by man's activities were feared (Matthews, *et al.*, 1971).

In exploring the validity and extent of man-made effects on climate it is essential to define a few concepts. The totality of weather, that is, all events in the atmosphere, is generally considered to combine into climate. It is thus essentially a statistical concept, with climate made up of individual weather events over a long period of time. As such, climate covers a wide range of conditions in time and space. By long-standing practice climate is expressed by the statistical distributions of discrete, observable elements such as temperature, precipitation, humidity, wind, and other variables. In order to summarize the information, custom has resulted in the use of mean values of these elements to characterize climate. Such means can be formed both for time series of observations at a locality, or in space, to define climatic conditions of areas, regions, or the globe as a whole. Obviously, the use of one measure of central tendency, such as a mean or average, is only a crude approximation. Good practice dictates that measures of dispersion of the individual observations be included, such as standard deviations, and ranges. Further, it is essential to stratify the observations by well-known periodic changes throughout a diurnal or annual cycle.

It is equally essential to understand that all values of climatic elements

Contribution No. 154 of the Graduate Program in Meteorology, University of Maryland.

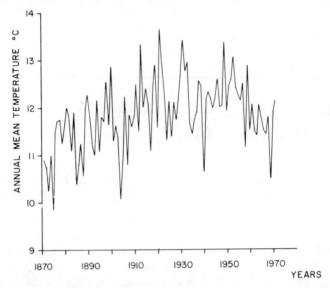

Figure 8-1. Typical climatic time series (100 years of annual temperatures at Woodstock, Maryland—an undisturbed rural site).

fluctuate irregularly with time. They form what has been labelled, in analogy to fluctuating sound in communications engineering, a "noise" pattern (Figure 8-1). Time series of climatic elements may exhibit one-sided trends for a while but these are then reversed after shorter or longer intervals of time. An anthropogenic influence has to be sufficiently sustained to become discernible in the "noise." If that can be done in a statistically, and preferably also physically acceptable fashion, we have a climatic alteration. This term is better usage than the frequently employed term *climatic change*, which has lost much meaning through indiscriminate use. A change implies that the whole frequency distribution of an observational ensemble shifts to a new equilibrium position and stays there for a prolonged period of time. Thus it is best to leave the term climatic change for description of major changes; for example, from a glacial period to an interglacial, or vice versa (Landsberg, 1975).

Just as the time scale is important, the space scale plays a major role in the discussion of human effects on climate. On the smallest scale, in the air layer near the ground, alterations are ubiquitous. This is the layer, often called the biosphere, where man re-arranges the plant cover, constructs homes and buildings, and continuously shapes the landscape. This is the realm of the microclimate (Geiger, 1961; Munn, 1966; Yoshino, 1975). On a space scale the affected area may vary from a few square meters to some square kilometers. The vertical scale of interference rarely exceeds 100 m. Moving to larger dimensions, it is now uncontested that man alters climate on the local scale, especially by urbanization. This may affect a few hundred square kilometers horizontally and layers 500 m vertically. In large conurbations and large-scale irrigation schemes the human interference may reach regional scales, measuring from several hundred to a thousand square kilometers. Occasional effects on tropospheric cloud and rain systems have been made plausible.

Finally we reach the global scale. Pollution effects on the atmosphere by vehicles moving at various levels above the ground have been under scrutiny for some time as possible disturbers of climate. But surface sources of pollution, as well as changes in composition of gas concentrations in the atmosphere, are also potential sources of perturbation of the current climatic equilibrium. These latter effects are still largely conjectural and controversial. It will be our aim here to present the current state of knowledge. For the most part this has to be restricted to the climatic conditions at the surface. Only very limited reference to conditions in the higher levels of the atmosphere can be made because information on the high layers is still very rudimentary.

Controlled Alterations in the Lowest Atmospheric Layer

Man has, for over a century, experimented with methods to improve his farm yields and to protect his crops from weather damage. He has done this by changing physical parameters at the interface between the atmosphere and the soil. There many energy exchanges take place. Shortwave solar radiation is absorbed, some of it is reflected, heat is conducted into the ground, long-wave radiation is emitted. Moisture is absorbed, stored, and evaporated. All these processes can be interfered with to variable degrees. In each case this involves the change of physical characteristics at or near the surface or, in some cases, the artificial augmentation of energy.

A summary of all these controlled alterations is given in Table 8-1.

Albedo effects. One of the most potent procedures for controlled change of the microclimate is a change in albedo, defined as the ratio of absorbed to incoming radiation from the sun and sky. A low albedo indicates large absorption of energy by the surface, a high albedo means considerable reflectivity. The degree of absorption rules the temperature a surface or soil will assume. In nature two forms of water substance are about at the

Table 8-1. Procedures for Microclimatic Control

Process	Property Changed	Changed Element	Results
Dust cover: black white	Albedo of surface (soil, ice, snow)	Soil, air temperature	Daytime increase Daytime reduction
Organic mulch	Conductivity Vapor transfer	Soil and air temperature Evaporation	Range reduction Reduction
Aluminum foil	Albedo Vapor transfer	Soil and air temp. Evaporation	Daytime reduction Reduction
Plastic film	Heat absorption Vapor transfer	Temperature Evaporation	Increase Reduction
Espalier wall (white)	Reflectivity Vapor transfer	Light f. photosynthesis Wind (evaporation)	Increase Reduction
Shelter belt	Roughness	Wind Evaporation	Reduction Reduction
Shade netting	Radiation	Soil & air temperature	Reduction
Wind motor	Air motion	Temperature	Nocturnal increase
Heating elements	Radiation, sensible heat	Temperature	Increase
Fog spray	Radiation	Temperature	Increase
Water spray	Latent heat	Temperature	Increase
Dry ice use on subcooled fog	Nucleation	Fog Visibility	Reduction Increase

extremes of albedo conditions. Liquid water surfaces have low albedos (about 7%), fresh snow and ice surfaces have high albedos (about 90%).

It is easy to change albedos. A light surface, which would ordinarily reflect much energy, can be covered with dark dust and made to absorb more. For example, a snow cover can be dusted in the spring with coal powder to initiate melting and thus make the ground available for cultivation earlier than under natural conditions. In fact, in intense sunshine, snow and ice under a dust layer will begin to melt even at air temperatures somewhat below the freezing point (Landsberg, 1940).

Coal dust is being spread by Siberian farmers in spring on the snow to hasten melting and get the fields ready for planting earlier than would be the case naturally. In the French and Rhenanian vineyards black slate chips are used to keep soil temperatures high, promoting early growth. Conversely, white powders on the soil are being used in countries with intense sunshine to obtain optimal soil temperatures for germination of seeds. Stanhill (1965) reports that a white magnesium carbonate dust layer, only 0.05 mm thick, lowers the maximum soil temperature about 9° C initially. After 10 days of ageing it still produces a temperature reduction of 8° C. But between 20 and 30 days after dusting the effectiveness goes down rapidly. Twice as much incoming energy is reflected by the white dust, and the energy conducted in daytime into the soil is reduced by 85%. Evaporation is also reduced by 20%.

Albedo effects will be encountered again in later sections of this chapter in the discussion of inadvertent climatic changes.

Wind breaks. The use of shelter belts to improve the climate of the surface-near air layer has been practiced since the middle of the last century. Their principal effect is the reduction of wind speed. This, in turn, will reduce wind erosion and conserve soil moisture (Caborn, 1965; van Eimern, 1964). The intent of a shelterbelt is to make the wind speed reduction effective as far downwind as possible. Both in nature and wind tunnel tests it was soon found that neither solid walls nor highly permeable windbreaks are very effective. The former have a notable effect only for a short distance and the latter do not reduce the wind speed adequately. Permeabilities of the shelter belt of 40–60% give optimal results. Figure 8-2 shows the reduction downwind in per cent of the upwind velocity for a shelterbelt of 50% permeability. The maximum reduction is found between 2 and 5 times the distance downwind from the belts in units of shelterbelt height H. From that distance on the speed gradually increases again and the effect vanishes at $30H$ downwind. This has led in some agricultural regions to the echeloning of belts into hedgerow pattern.

Many observations on the microclimatic alterations produced have

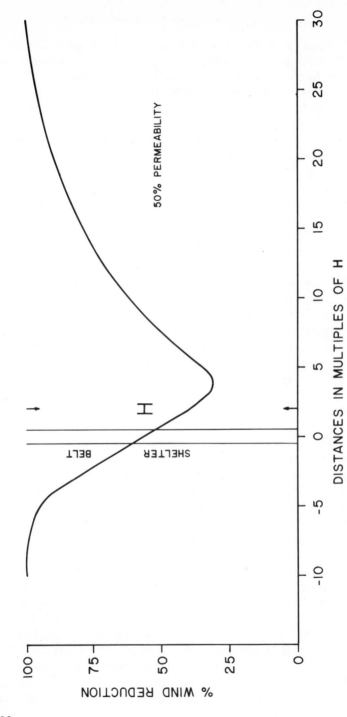

Figure 8-2. Approximate relative wind reduction by shelterbelt of 50% permeability. Distances downwind are given in units of heights of shelterbelt (*H*).

been made (Rosenberg, 1966; Miller *et al.*, 1971). Aside from the wind speed reduction they generally agree that the mean temperature of the sheltered area is higher, although close to the shelter belt daily minimum temperatures are often lower than in the open area. Both absolute and relative humidities are higher in the sheltered area and the area behind the wind break may add to the soil moisture by the increased capture of snow. The aerodynamic drag is increased three to five times by hedges over that in an open field.

In farm operations the shelter effect produces notable increases in crop yields. The same principle is, of course, employed to protect highways in winter from drifting snow. Many models of snow fences have been tested, but ordinary slat fences, 50% permeable, have not only the advantage of simplicity, but are effective if properly placed, about 15 × H upwind from the road that is to be protected (Jensen, 1954).

The problem of wind erosion, that will be encountered again in the context of desert encroachment—which is among the inadvertent climatic results of human activities—has been intensively studied after the "dust bowl" years in the American Great Plains. One of the remedies is creation of increased surface roughness by leaving stubbles from prior years' crops standing and operating on a premise of minimum tillage. On dryland soils this is accomplished by appropriate farm machinery. The left-over stubble also serves as moisture-conserving mulch (Woodruff, *et al.*, 1972).

Frost prevention. Late frosts in spring and early frosts in autumn are in many areas a special hazard to farming. They often occur as isolated events and are preceded and succeeded by two or three weeks with temperatures above freezing. Many of these low nocturnal minimum temperatures are caused by development of intense temperature inversions under clear skies and associated low general wind speeds. Intense outgoing radiation cools the soil and a thin adjacent layer of air. Drainage of cold air from nearby slopes may cause pools with air temperature below freezing in topographic troughs or valleys.

Usually, under these conditions temperatures may go only a degree or two below the freezing point. It is, therefore, tempting to resort to measures for protection of sensitive crops, trying to save blossoms in spring and fruit in autumn. Orchards and vineyards have been the traditional enterprises where protective measures have been practiced (Schultz, 1962).

The simplest devices for achieving temporary temperature rises are orchard heaters, ranging from simple miniature kerosene stoves to electric infrared heat sources. If strategically placed and spaced they can achieve general temperature rises of 2–4° C throughout the orchard. In case of oil heated "smudge pots," damage to fruit from the soot and smoke may vitiate part of the salvage.

Another scheme employs motor-driven propellers, mounted on towers above the orchards. The intense downward-directed turbulent air current is intended to break up the ground inversion of temperature and vent warmer air from aloft into the ground layer. Only limited success, because of the restricted radius of action has been achieved in this fashion. But under suitable conditions temperature rises of 1–2° C are feasible.

A different approach uses a very fine spray of water, taking advantage of the liberation of latent heat of the fluid upon freezing as a thin shell around the fruit. Again, limited success has been achieved with this procedure under suitable conditions.

A more recent process tries to interfere with the radiation process, which creates the temperature inversion and the low air temperatures near the ground in the first place. The process creates an artificial fog by spraying water droplets of approximately 2–50 μm from nozzles placed above the orchard. Most of these droplets, under calm conditions, will stay in suspension for a while and intercept the outgoing radiation. Temperatures in orchards under this protection have stayed from 0.5–4° C above those of unprotected areas (Anonymous, 1974).

Large-scale schemes of climate alterations. There have been numerous proposals for causing major alterations of the macroclimate. In contrast to the preceding, well-tested microclimatic interferences, none of these have gone beyond the discussion stage. Even if a convincing case of feasibility could be established, there exist no cost-benefit analyses. The rigid test of the market place has long since justified the microclimatic procedures (see Table 8-1).

The large-scale modifications all have in common prodigious engineering feats. Some, if successful, might beneficially influence fairly large territories of continental areas. Yet, the analyses carried out by the proponents dwell only on these potential advantages. They do not attempt to predict how the climate of other areas may fare. But it is axiomatic that if a climatic alteration of major scope is produced, global adjustments must take place in order to maintain energy balance, which prescribes that for equilibrium the earth must lose as much energy as it receives from the sun.

Only a few examples of these proposed alterations will be presented. Two of them advocate elimination of the Arctic sea ice. It is likely in the present climatic regime that if the ice is once gone, the Arctic Ocean would stay largely ice free. The first scheme would use the process of changing the albedo of the ice fields by covering them with coal dust dispensed from airplanes and then letting the sun do the job of melting (Fletcher, 1968). The technical feasibility is certain but the estimate of how many times the dusting process would have to be repeated for success is highly uncertain.

The second proposal centers on building a dam to block the Bering Straits (Borisov, 1967). This is intended to lead to radical changes in the circulation of the Arctic Ocean, with the end effect of using the heat of the North Atlantic Drift that enters the polar sea for gradual melting of the sea ice. In this, as well as in the previous scheme, the northern reaches of Eurasia and North America would undoubtedly benefit agriculturally and in reduced energy consumption. But a lowered gradient of temperature between equator and pole would also cause a displacement of the subtropical high pressure belts and reduce rainfall in many places.

Other schemes center around alterations in the Mediterranean space. There is a variety of them but all envisage enormous hydraulic works for the creation of large scale lakes in the arid regions of North Africa and Asia Minor. Several major troughs below present sea level exist, and other geologically created depressions have been suggested as vast inland lakes. Although hydroelectric power incidental to these schemes and the improved agroclimate might seem to support these ideas, no realistic systems assessment exists. And in these, as well as any other similar proposals, one has to face the unpleasant fact that all large-scale improvements of climate in one area are likely to have detrimental effects elsewhere.

Incidental Alterations

Whenever man changes the face of the earth an alteration of the climate automatically follows. The larger the scale of the change, the greater is the alteration in values of climatic elements and the greater on a spatial scale is the atmospheric consequence. In earlier days such alterations were accepted as incidental, but in recent years fairly quantitative estimates of alterations to be expected can be made. It is usually reasoned that the change is so beneficial that the concomitant climatic alteration is too trivial to be a decisive factor. This is true in some cases but not in others, as shall be seen in this section.

Man-made lakes. Water is a precious commodity. Its steady availability is essential for industry, urban areas, and agricultural irrigation. This can, in many places, only be guaranteed by having vast storage basins. In these, runoff from streams as a result of rainfall and snow-melt can be impounded and controlled. Incidental benefits are hydroelectric power, fisheries, and water sports. Thus a large number of dams have been built in various parts of the globe and more are planned.

Some of the man-made lakes approach or even exceed natural lakes in size. For example, Lake Kariba in Africa is 5100 km²; Lake Nasser in Egypt, 4000 km²; Lake Garrison, in North Dakota, 1580 km²; Lake Powell, 850 km²; Lake Meade, 638 km²; as compared with the natural waterbodies of Lake Michigan, 58,000 km²; Great Salt Lake, 5960 km²; Lake Geneva, 583 km²; and Lake Seneca in New York, 173 km².

The effects of natural lakes on the climate of their environment have been extensively studied. The greater the area of a lake the farther its influence reaches. Up to the present all of the man-made lakes have only limited microclimatic influence; none have any measurable effects beyond a kilometer or two from their shore. Most notable is generally the so-called *oasis effect*. This is an increase of a few percentage points in relative humidities downwind from the artificial lake. In dry tropical countries, because of the intense evaporation, this effect is more notable than in moist regions.

There are only a few series of observations available to compare conditions prior to the formation of an artificial lake with subsequent events. The best information has been gathered for the reservoir of the Nysa Klodzka river in Poland (Zych and Dubaniewiez, 1969). The reservoir covers about 30 km²; and a record of climatic data at a town 1 km down-river from the lake is available for 50 years before and 30 years after the flooding. A notable reversal of temperatures has occurred. In the early period climatic stations above the town were warmer than the town because of the frequent temperature inversions, caused by drainage of cold air to lower elevations. Now the situation is reversed. The town below the lake is warmer than the stations above the lake. The lake has mitigated temperature contrasts and the mean annual temperature in the town has risen by 0.7° C. This could only be ascribed to the lake influence in the absence of regional trend. There is an indication of decreased rainfall in the immediate vicinity of the lake, attributable to the stabilizing influence of the large water body.

There is other evidence from artificial lakes in warmer, especially tropical climates, that man-made lakes decrease convective activity and, hence, reduce cloud cover. On the other hand, in seasonally cold regions, during the period prior to freezing, steam fog over the lake and often advective fog over shore lines are common conditions. Only limited experience is as yet available with respect to cooling ponds but calculations, using saturation deficit statistics, show that fog increase in the vicinity is only infrequently to be expected. More on this theme will be presented below.

Measurements of all meteorological elements at the usual 2-m height show that the influence of artificial lakes decreases exponentially from the shore inland. None of the present man-made lakes are sufficiently large to have an appreciable influence on the circulation, even on the meso-scale.

Forest-to-field transformation. The greatest alteration of the Earth's surface has taken place for about the last 6,000 years, since man changed from hunter–gatherer to farmer. In this process vast areas became converted from forest and shrub to fields. Prairies were turned into pastures. Irrigation transformed semiarid areas into crop-producing lands. At the same time many forests were cut down for timber, and before nature could re-establish growth or man became wise enough to replant, erosion denuded the soil to the bare rock.

While these processes were taking place, the physical conditions at the air-atmosphere interface were modified and the atmospheric boundary layer was profoundly affected. All the elements of the radiation balance and the ensuing fluxes assumed new values. It may be useful in this context to look at these fluxes. They can be represented by the equation for the net radiation flux (Q_N):

$$Q_N = Q_I - Q_R + Q_{L\downarrow} - Q_{L\uparrow} = \pm Q_H \pm Q_E \pm Q_S$$

where the symbols represent the following energy fluxes:

Q_I = incoming short-wave radiation from sun and sky.
Q_R = reflected short-wave radiation (function of Albedo A).
$Q_{L\downarrow}$ = long-wave radiation from atmosphere (CO_2, H_2O).
$Q_{L\uparrow}$ = outgoing long-wave surface radiation (Stefan-Boltzmann radiation: $\approx \epsilon\sigma\ T^4$; ϵ emissivity, σ Stefan-Boltzmann constant; T absolute temperature °K).
Q_H = sensible heat, advected (+) or carried away (−).
Q_E = evapotranspiration (−) or condensation (dew +), that is, latent heat.
Q_S = heat conducted into (+) or out of the soil (−).

In changing from forest to field only the two incoming (long- and short-wave) fluxes remain unchanged. All the other components are affected. Forests usually have low albedos (8–12%). The average for a pine forest, for example, is 9% (Stewart; 1971). Fields, if actively growing, may show values as high as 20–25% reflectivity. Straw and stubble after the harvest also may show high values but bare soil may again be low. The outgoing long-wave flux depends on an emissivity, which changes from one soil cover to another, and the absolute temperature of the surface. This again is a function of absorption of energy from sun and sky. The sensible heat flux is usually least affected by surface changes of the type under consideration here but evaporation and condensation can show large differences between a forested and a farmed area.

In forests the energy conduction up from or down into the soil is generally very small because of the shading. In fields it depends on the state of soil preparation. Freshly plowed soil has poor heat conductivity; very wet soil or denuded spots, however, have high conductivity. These conditions have direct bearing on the temperature of the air adjacent to it and are, generally, reflected in the measurements made at conventional 2-m level.

Condensation at the soil surface in form of dew or frost is usually only a very minor contribution in the energy balance. In contrast, evaporation or evapotranspiration (in vegetation cover) is a major energy consumer. Actively growing fields evaporate substantial amounts of water.

Most of this water is drawn from the surficial layers of the soil. When crop growth ceases or drought prevails there is no further water loss and, hence, no energy is used. Trees have mostly deeper root systems, frequently penetrating to the ground water level. They are prodigious evaporators.

From the foregoing it is clear that the microclimatic environment is different in forest and field, principally because of the albedo, shade, and evapotranspiration differences. Thus, as forests yielded to fields, wider ranges of climatic elements in the surface-near layers were a necessary consequence. In addition, the low-level wind field had to change. This is governed by the roughness of the ground. The vertical wind distribution is approximated by a logarithmic rule, with the restriction that the vertical temperature structure is "neurtral" (that is, the adiabatic lapse rate of 1° C/100 meters prevails). On an average one can represent the wind distribution with height by

$$(1) \qquad\qquad \bar{u}_{(z)} = (u_*/k) \ln (z/z_0)$$

where $\bar{u}_{(z)}$ = the mean wind speed at height z.

    z = the vertical length coordinate.

    k = von Kármán's constant (≈ 0.4).

    u_* = friction velocity $\sqrt{\tau/\rho}$ (τ shear stress, ρ air density).

    z_0 = roughness parameter, in length units.

The critical factor is the roughness parameter, z_0, which in fields, depending on the height of the crop stand, is from 10 to 30 cm. Forests, however, are usually considerably "rougher," and z_0 values run around 100 cm, depending on tree type and height.

It is very difficult to assess the total climatic impact of the transformation from forest to farming. It is unlikely to have exceeded the regional scale. The reasons for this are twofold. The total arable land in the world is only about 12% of the land surface or 3½% of the earth's surface. The second reason is that the difference between forest and field, in its effect on atmospheric energy transactions and motions, is considerably smaller than land and sea contrasts, or the effects of mountains or snow and ice fields. Yet local and regional effects must have been substantial and they have led to the artificial control measures discussed to reverse some of these effects.

Irrigation. The topic of whether or not irrigation increases rainfall is highly controversial. It has been pointed out that in the U.S. Great Plains close to 100,000 km² are under irrigation, most of it introduced in the last forty years. Some rainfall statistics indicate a 10% increase in rainfall (Joos, 1969). Considering the high value of the coefficient of variation for the area (Hershfield, 1962), that is not an impressive figure (Figure 8-3). In fact, it would take another 40 years of observations to check if the figure is statistically significant.

Similar claims have been made and contested for the Columbia Basin in Washington. There, 2,000 km² are irrigated. This development took place in the two decades 1950–1970. Irrigation water is supplied only in mid-

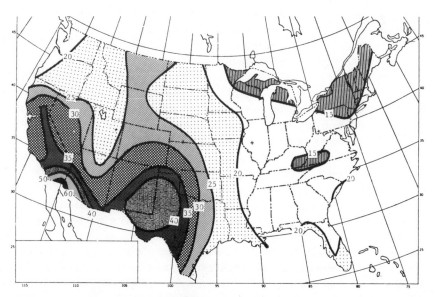

Figure 8-3. Coefficient of variation of precipitation over the contiguous United States (after Hershfield, 1962). The coefficient of variation is $C_v = 100\sigma/\bar{P}$, where $\bar{P}$ is the mean precipitation and σ the standard deviation of the observational series.

summer. Hence an effect, if any, can only be expected in July and August. Different approaches to the statistical evaluation of available rainfall data lead to such divergent opinions as "no significant increase" (Fowler and Helvey, 1974a, 1974b) to increases of 20–35% (Stidd, 1974). The reasons for such discrepant deductions are the inadequacy of the ordinary rain gauge as a sampling device, the already mentioned naturally high variability of rainfall in semiarid areas, and the rather scattered areal distribution of convective showers.

Although the case for effects of even large-scale irrigation on rainfall is still weak, there is little doubt about temperature effects. Usually, the range of the 2-m air temperature is reduced. Daily maxima are lower and minima stay higher. But these effects are small and in average values for the summer months for the daily extreme temperatures they stay around 0.5° C. There are usually increases of a few per cent in relative humidity but there are no records of increases in fog. The fact is that irrigation is only practiced in the warm season when absolute humidities are far from saturation.

Grazing and desert encroachment. Human intrusion into the semiarid fringes of desert regions has been a losing battle for the exploitation of these areas. Here again the problem is the highly variable rainfall. Years of fairly substantial precipitation are followed by intervals of low rainfall to nearly absolute drought (Figure 8-4). These fluctuations are intimately tied to variations of the general atmospheric circulation. Positions of various rain-bringing troughs are decisive for the amounts of rain received.

In the natural stage roots and seeds survive the intervals of drought. Seemingly dead brush and dried stalks of grasses anchor the soil. Small groups of people which try to achieve a symbiosis with this environment are originally nomads. They eke out an existence as subsistence farmers in good years and generally have only few animals competing for the meagre pasturing opportunities. When dry weather strikes they migrate to better sites. Population, by natural controls, is adjusted to what the land can sustain.

Change in governmental policies and overpopulation as a result of disease control have radically altered the natural systems. Nomads and others have been settled in the marginal areas, usually in the periods of ample rainfall. Wells have been drilled to provide a steady water supply. This interpretation of rainfall conditions led to large increases in herds of cattle, sheep and goats. When the drought years return the results are disastrous. The case of the Sahel drought of 1972–73 is a vivid example. From the available weather records this was an entirely foreseeable event, if not precisely predictable on a time scale as to when it would strike (Landsberg, 1975).

DAKAR (SENEGAL)
ALTERNATION OF WET AND DRY YEARS

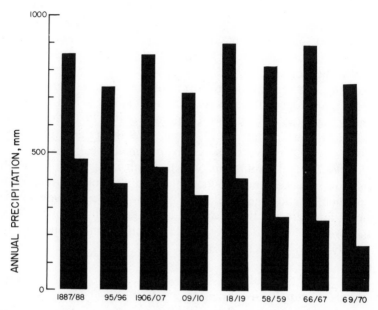

Figure 8-4. Observed alternations of wet and dry years in Dakar, Senegal showing the high variability of rainfall in the area south of the Sahara.

   The sequence of events then takes an inexorable course, which was not unique to the Sahel but had been noted at other times at the northern border of the Sahara (Flohn, 1970) and near other deserts. When the drought starts, the cattle collect near the water holes. What little vegetation is there is rapidly eaten or stampeded down. Sheep and goats will consume everything else growing in the area. They will dig and eat the roots. That will not only prevent resurrection of growth when the rains return but also lay the soil open to wind erosion. The soil is powdery dry and the particle sizes are such that they are readily lifted by the wind. Wind speeds of 4–5 m/sec^{-1} are enough to convert the top soil to dust clouds. This was the condition during the disastrous droughts in the Great Plains of the U.S. in 1934–1936, where native grass land had been converted to wheat fields. These were seasonally bare; drought pulverized the soil and strong winds eroded 10^4 million tons of top soil. Only the most patient measures of soil conservation coupled with the returning rains eventually restored most of the area to productivity (see Chapter 6).
   In areas near the Sahara and similar deserts the ecosystem is exceedingly fragile. Human interference, especially grazing of domestic animals,

can destroy it completely. At the same time land in the same zone that is protected will maintain itself. Fenced-in areas in the Sahel where grazing did not take place during the 1972–73 drought clearly showed up with vegetation intact on satellite pictures. Only such rigid protection will protect against encroachment of the desert. This process is plainly a retreat of the vegetated zone by human interference rather than an active advance of the desert.

Arguments that increased albedo because of decrease of plant cover reinforces the tendency for drought (Charney, *et al.*, 1975) have not been universally accepted (Ripley, 1976; Charney, *et al.*, 1976). Nature seems to have given the answer. In 1974 and 1975 the rainfall in the Sahel increased again. Clearly, such relatively small local changes cannot influence the general circulation, which through migration of the Intertropical Convergence Zone produces the rainfall. But returning rains do not immediately return the vegetation. Although, given enough time without human interference, the biosphere might gradually recover. Man can help this process by wind breaks, rigid restrictions on grazing, and planting suitably hardy grasses.

Alterations Through Urbanization

The most radical surface changes man has brought about is by urbanization. These have caused a series of local climatic alterations. They came early to the attention of meteorologists (Howard, 1818). The documentation of these alterations is quite extensive. It covers many urban areas and many elements. The literature consists of many books, monographs, and papers (Chandler, 1970). There have been a number of recent reviews, which cover all aspects of the subject (Peterson, 1969; Oke, 1973; Landsberg, 1974). Although not all of the discovered alterations are necessarily detrimental or undesirable, there are enough of them to consider measures to minimize them and incorporate effects of possible climatic alterations into urban planning (Chandler, 1976). Although the effects of cities on their atmospheric boundary layer are quantitatively known, it remains to be explored how far downwind some of the effects extend. Also, we have at best speculations as to what the influence of vast conurbations, which begin to shape up, will be. This is by no means a trivial question. United Nations statistical projections indicate that by the year 2000 there will be a number of metropolitan areas with 20 million inhabitants each and 70% of the anticipated world population of 6½ billion persons at that time will live in cities. Hence their local climatic environment must be of great concern to them and considerable climatic effects on a larger scale

Table 8-2. Some Urban Climatic Alterations

Element	Comparison with Rural Environs
Radiation:	
Global	10 to 20% less
Ultraviolet: low sun	30 to 50% less
high sun	5 to 10% less
Temperature:	
Annual mean	1 to 2° C higher
Maximum difference	3 to 10° C higher
Winter minima	1 to 3° C higher
Cloudiness:	
General cloud cover	5 to 10% more
Fog: winter	100% more
summer	20 to 30% more
Precipitation totals: summer	10% more
winter	5% more
Relative humidity: Annual mean	4–6% less
Evapotranspiration: total amount	30 to 60% less
Dew: amounts	50 to 80% less
Wind speed: $\leqslant 3$ m sec^{-1}	40% less
Speeds: 3–6 m sec	20% less
> 6 m sec	10% less
Thunderstorms: Number of days	5 to 10% more

have to be anticipated. These should extend at least to the meteorological mesoscale. Table 8-2 summarizes the urban effects on the atmosphere.

Hydrological cycle and runoff. Urban areas radically change the local hydrological conditions. Rain and snowfall in a city are a nuisance. Except for limited park areas, shade trees and residential yards there is no dire need for precipitation. There are no crops to raise, water supplies are usually imported, and it is often far the most critical task to keep traffic flowing smoothly.

The urban areas are a principal cause for rapid runoff of liquid precipitation. Rain runs off the roofs and from paved areas of streets and parking lots. Special storm sewers are designed to drain this runoff into the stream system. Some of the natural streams of an urban area often have been built over or relocated. Rivers have been channelized, all in the interest of speeding the runoff away. The drainage systems have been often designed for a hypothetical 50-year high intensity rainfall but nature does not always cooperate with that design goal. Intense local cloudbursts and rains in tropical storms passing over an area can bring precipitation far in excess of design values. The ensuing flash floods can be devastating.

An additional problem is the fact that dwellings, industrial and commercial establishments, and roads and railroads have been built in bottomland, close to rivers and streams. That land is flat and construction is easier than on slopes. In some narrow valleys necessity forced development close to the waterway. Flood plains are usually well-marked in the landscape but they too are not invariant. The channelization and the intensified runoff from the urban area may cause considerable changes in the height of sudden floods.

The undisputed effect of the rapid runoff in urban areas is the precipitous rise of the water in the natural channels. Under natural conditions, in every rainfall a large amount of water is intercepted by vegetation which causes a delaying action of the water reaching the ground. Much of the water is stored in the soil and only gradually percolates into the ground-water table and from there reaches the streams. Even in heavy rains surface runoff is usually small unless the soil is frozen or already saturated from a preceding rainfall. Even then there are natural reservoirs in swampland and topographic depressions, most of which are eliminated by the urbanization process. In many of our cities 50–60% of the surface is impermeable.

The results can be startling. For a small stream a typical example is shown in Figure 8-5. This shows rapid rise of the stream as result of a small frontal shower. This stream drained at the time 2 km^2 of residential land in the developing town of Columbia, Maryland (Landsberg, 1975). A rainfall of just under 2 cm in three hours led to immediate stream rise of 30 cm.

The acceleration of the runoff as a function of the area made impermeable by various urban structures is well known. It is shown in Figure 8-6 (Leopold, 1965). The rapidity of runoff jeopardizes many low-lying structures in urban areas. Annual flood damage figures there run into many millions of dollars. In recent years legislative acts have begun to prevent building on flood plains (Arnold, 1975).

The high flood-producing potential of urban areas is only one of the effects of cities on the hydrological cycle. Every other element of the water balance is also affected: Relative humidity, evaporation and condensation, clouds and rain. The details will be related below.

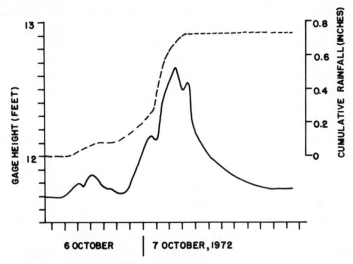

Figure 8-5. Runoff from urbanized area (Columbia, Maryland) during short rain interval and corresponding stream response (solid line: runoff, left scale; dashed line: rainfall, right scale).

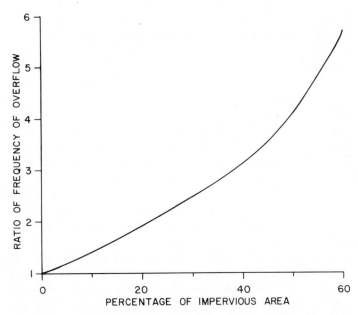

Figure 8-6. Frequency ratio of stream overflow related to impervious area (after Leopold, 1968).

205

Temperature and humidity. The first urban effect on a meteorological element was Howard's (1818) observation that the temperatures in the city of London were often higher than those of the rural surroundings. As other cities grew the same phenomenon was noted elsewhere. Little thought was given to the cause for this temperature rise. A routine explanation was that the surplus heat from furnaces and fireplaces was responsible. In fanciful speculations the heat from metabolism of people and horses was cited as an additional reason. There was also doubt that the effect was actually a result of the urbanization process. It was pointed out that urban areas often owed their location to some topographic feature of the landscape and that the local climate there might well have shown differences of the same magnitude with respect to the environs had there been no city.

Systematic observations of the energy balance have cleared up most of the open questions and in essence have confirmed the reality of the urban temperature rise. The phenomenon is now called the urban heat island. It has been shown to exist in all seasons and in low as well as high latitudes. The fact that it exists in summer in higher latitudes and also in the tropics indicates that furnaces are not the main cause. In fact, there is not a single cause for the heat island. A combination of causes is responsible.

Most important in creating the heat island is the radical change in surface. The soil becomes compacted and covered with dense material—brick, concrete, asphalt with high heat conductivity and capacity. Most of this material also has a low albedo, certainly lower than that of most growing vegetation, except coniferous forests. All this leads to a high absorption of short wave energy received in daytime from sun and sky. Much of this energy is conducted into the ground or into the walls of buildings. These walls and roofs will also absorb more energy than horizontal surfaces from the incoming radiation at low solar elevations.

In daytime this leads to rather high surface temperatures on sunny days. The hot pavements of cities are notorious, often softening macadam or buckling expanding concrete. Surface temperatures of 50° C are not unusual. Infrared thermometer surveys from the air confirm this even when the viewfield includes both structures and green spaces. The differences of the urban and rural surface temperatures as function of building density is shown in Figure 8-7.

In spite of these high surface temperatures the daytime urban heat island is not spectacular. Generally, the excess of urban versus rural air temperature is only 1–2° C because the hot air created at the surface rises convectively over the city. This leads to "thermals" well-known to aviators over urban areas. These rising currents have secondary effects on clouds and rain which will be discussed below. On the other hand the

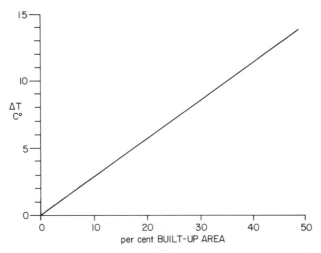

Figure 8-7.   Daytime surface temperature difference to rural sector area in relation to settlement density.

urban heat island can become quite spectacular at night. The temperature differences that develop are dependent on the general wind and cloudiness conditions. Thus the heat island is not independent of the synoptic weather situation. In windy, cloudy weather none of the micrometeorological differences can develop. They are principle features of nights with clear sky and low winds.

This can be readily seen from two sets of isotherms for the nocturnal minimum temperatures in the Washington, D. C., metropolitan area (Nicholas, 1971). Figure 8-8a shows the temperature distribution during night after a cold front passage with a blustery NW wind. Only two isotherms are noted. In contrast, Figure 8-8b shows the case of a calm, clear night. There are many isotherms, and the heat island of the city core stands out clearly.

The heat island usually shows its highest development not at the time of the minimum before sunrise but rather two to three hours after sunset. At that time cooling in rural areas is high and under clear skies inversions hug the ground. In the city convection has ceased and the warm surfaces feed heat stored in the daytime into the stagnant air. The walls of buildings also radiate toward each other rather than to the sky and hence tend to cool only very slowly. Thus temperature differences of several degrees Celsius to the rural area will exist. The values depend greatly on the size of the urban area.

It can be shown that even single large buildings (Landsberg, 1970) or

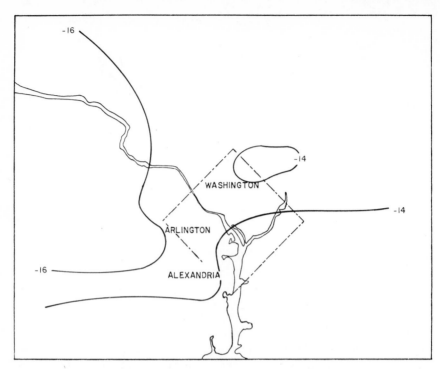

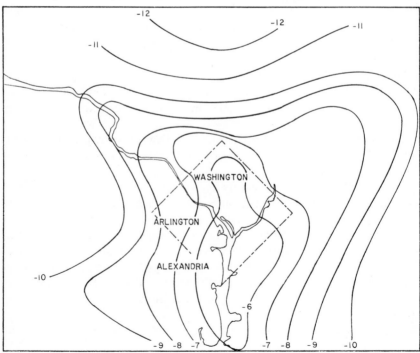

isolated shopping centers (Norwine, 1972) create miniature heat islands of about 1° C in the evening. The gradual growth of the heat island at the time of its maximum development with urban size increase has been followed in a new town during its period of growth from a hamlet of 200 inhabitants to a town of 30,000. This change is shown in Figure 8-9, indicating that maximum temperature differences of up to 8° C eventually developed. In large cities it can become even larger. Heuseler (1965) showed that for Berlin, Germany, on clear, calm nights the frequencies of urban-rural air temperatures run as follows:

Difference, °C	6.1–8.0	8.1–10	10.1–12	12.1–13.3
Percentage Frequency	14	57	10	12

The maximum was 13.3° C, the contrast of a major frontal system, and only 7% of the cases were 6° C or less.

The heat island effect has some intriguing secondary consequences. One is the lengthening of the frost-free season in higher latitude cities. In Washington, D. C., for example, the last freezing temperature in the city occurs three weeks earlier than in suburban areas. This, in turn, has an influence on the phenological development of the flora. Blooming occurs considerably earlier in the city than at the outskirts (Figure 8-10). In winter, snow often turns to rain over the warmer inner city. In the New York City area in winter, when weather conditions favor precipitation, the probability of it falling as snow is only 27–35% in the city, but 40–45% in the outlying area (Grillo and Spar, 1971).

Because of the fact that fuel requirements are highly correlated to daily temperature sums below 18° C, the so-called degree day value, the average temperature rise of 1–2° C results in from 5–15% fuel savings in large cities, compared with their hinterland. This rise in average temperature, which is, of course, different from the maximum heat island effect previously discussed, can be seen in Figure 8-11 for the rapidly growing city of Tokyo, now the largest in the world (Fukui, 1970). The trend clearly shows the effect of growth over half a century. Notable is the sharp dip in 1945. This has been attributed to the large-scale destruction of the city in World War II, which brought back the microclimate of an earlier era.

So far the primary effect of surface change on the heat island has been given the paramount role in the alteration of temperature. But it is by no means exclusive. The elimination of much of the vegetation and the rapid

Figure 8-8. Nocturnal minimum temperature in the Washington, D. C., metropolitan area (data from Nicholas, 1971) for two weather conditions. (*a*) After cold front passage, wind speed 11 m sec^{-1}, heat island effect eliminated. (*b*) Winter night with near calm conditions < 3 m sec^{-1} – notable heat island development.

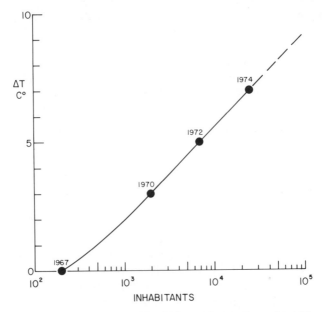

Figure 8-9.   **Increase of maximum heat island (clear, calm evenings, about 3 hr after sunset) with population increase in newly urbanized community Columbia, Maryland.**

runoff of rain also add another fundamental change. The former reduces evapotranspiration, the latter direct evaporation. Then processes, which consume much energy in rural areas, are drastically reduced in cities.

Similarly, the balance of dew is considerably changed. In the city much less dew condenses than in the open areas of suburbs and farms. This is clearly seen from a series of dew observations in and around Washington, D. C., during a summer month, as shown in Figure 8-12 (Myers, 1974). The lack of dew in the city leads, in part, to another peculiarity of the urban temperature. This is the very steep rise of air temperature after sunrise. The rise is much slower in rural areas. There radiative energy is first used to evaporate dew but in the city the same energy immediately serves to raise the temperatures of the highly absorbent surfaces.

Finally, we have to come to grips with man-made heat. This is the surplus heat of all thermal and thermodynamic processes. Lots of air is used in cooling processes, warmed and returned to the atmosphere. This has led to the use of the term *heat rejection*. More reference to this will be made below. But here only the share of the human contribution in the urban energy balance should be placed in perspective. First of all, the metabolic heat rejection of men and animals can be dismissed as totally insignificant. It amounts to only 0.1% of all anthropogenic heat rejection.

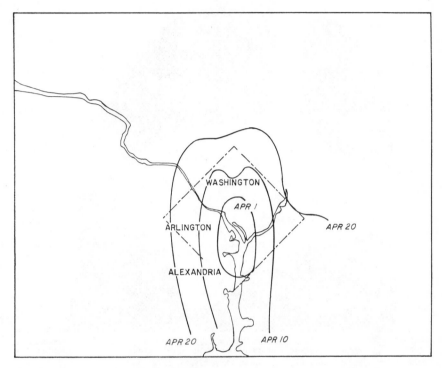

Figure 8-10. Average last day of freezing temperature in spring in Washington, D. C., metropolitan area (isochrones 10 days apart).

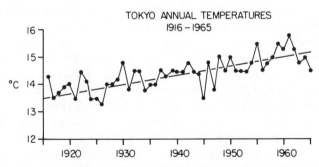

Figure 8-11. Time series of annual temperatures in Tokyo, Japan, showing rising trend brought about by metropolitan growth (adapted from Fukui, 1970).

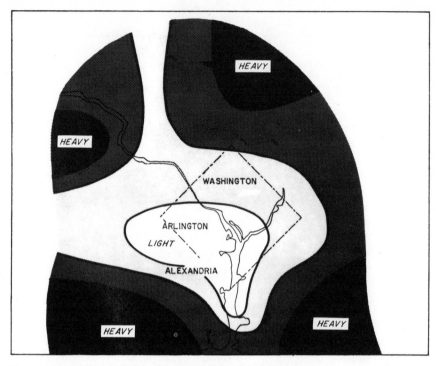

Figure 8-12. Dew distribution of noctural dew in the Washington, D. C., metropolitan area during calm, clear summer night (adapted from Myers, 1974).

In the most densely built-up areas, such as Manhattan Island, the winter heat rejection—mostly from stationary sources—is less than 0.3 cal/cm^{-2}/min^{-1}. This with the low solar elevations and frequent cloud covers is locally a substantial factor in the heat balance. In summer, even with a major fraction of the heat rejection resulting from air-conditioning, the total is below 0.1 cal/cm^{-2}/min^{-1}, and this is considerably below the energy received from sun and sky. Even in a city with such a harsh winter weather as Montreal, heat rejection at most amounts to one-third of the total energy balance, and averages about one-fifth (East, 1971). Higher efficiency in energy utilization and greater use of electric transportation may eventually reduce this component of the urban energy budget.

In periods when summer heat waves plague cities, the higher temperatures in the central cities not only cause added discomfort but increase mortality. Deaths from heat stroke and from cardio-vascular ailments can rise spectacularly. In this context it needs to be pointed out that the urban heat island is rarely a uniform temperature field with concentric isotherms around a high core value. Detailed surveys reveal a fabric of microvariations, governed by types of structures, vegetation, and distance to the edge of town, where isotherms often crowd together in front-like fashion. Thus older districts of a city with shade trees may readily show lower incidence of heat morbidity and mortality compared with newer areas, densely built up with apartment structures.

Humidities are obviously also affected by the urbanization process. The reduction in evaporation and evapotranspiration reduce the vapor pressure in the most densely built-up areas. This contributes about one half of the observed lowering of relative humidities. The other half is attributable to the temperature rise and is simply a consequence that the same amount of water vapor is further away from saturation at a higher than a lower temperature. There are no good estimates of the total amount of water contributed to a metropolitan atmosphere by combustion processes. Much of that water escapes as steam from chimneys and stacks and hence escapes the conventional measurements at 2 m height. Aloft it is simply added to the city plume of effluents, with which it is vented off and where it may enter into the complex chemical reactions that take place in the plume. Some will undoubtedly rise with convection currents and contribute to cloud formation.

Windfield. An urban area has a profoundly disturbing influence on the windfield. The basic effect is simply mechanical. Buildings and structures are obstacles in the wind path. Common sense alone would let us reason that there must be a slowdown of wind speed near the surface. Friction is substantially increased and a new turbulence structure is induced. As in the case of the windbreaks the roughness parameter z_0 rises considerably. In urban areas this element will reach values of 100–500 cm. This will reduce wind speeds to less than 50% of the gradient wind speeds. This gradient speed, governed by the pressure distribution, which is reached at only 300–500 m above a smooth surface, may not be reached up to twice that height over an urban area.

On an average, wind speeds near the surface, at a standard height of 10 m, are reduced by 20–30%. The effect of the metropolitan areas can be noted in the windfield as much as 30–40 km downwind. However, detailed wind observations indicate that weak general winds are far more affected than strong winds. For winds of 3 m/sec^{-1} or less the reduction is likely to be as much as 40%, but for winds over 6 m/sec^{-1} it may only be 10–20%. Here again the internal fabric of the city plays a major role. Channelization through the canyon streets of the cities can speed up winds parallel to the wind direction, with highest speeds in the middle of the street. If the street is at an angle, speeds on the sidewalks on the windward side may only be half of those opposite.

There are two effects of urban areas on turbulence. One is that hours of turbulence apparently increase through urbanization. The other is the change in turbulence frequency. In essence, the wind flow is chopped up. Whereas in rural, open areas the turbulence bodies are large and their wave length fairly long, in urban sectors the waves become shorter, the eddies smaller and the range from lull to gust relatively larger. This is not entirely trivial because turbulence structure has a profound effect on transport and dissipation of contaminants.

An entirely different influence on the windfield is produced by the heat island. The ascending air currents caused by the buoyant hot air created near the overheated surfaces has already been alluded to. Vertical wind speeds of 10 cm/sec^{-1} are common. Over Manhattan, even nocturnally, 20 cm/sec^{-1} have been observed and double such values in daytime (Angell, *et al.,* 1969). On days when general winds are weak these are notable alterations of the general flow field which have important effects on the release of rainfall.

The rising air current over the urban center must for continuity reasons induce a wind convergence from rural areas. This has, indeed, been observed in a number of localities, both in daytime and at night. A daytime case for Washington, D. C., is shown in Figure 8-13.

This country breeze has different character in day than at night. During the day it appears as a gentle converging flow. Although noticeable on the wind vanes, it is usually an added component to the general wind and thus hard to trace as an independent motion. Things are quite different at night. Considering that at night surface flow is quite slow in clear weather, when the intense heat islands develop in the cities and ground inversions in the rural area, any flow in the lowest level will need a pressure difference. The local temperature difference will cause an isobaric gradient of a fraction of a millibar. This is usually not enough to set up a steady circulation against the frictional resistance. But as already indicated, the isotherms, and consequently isobars, will crowd into the space not far from the edge of the city. There a miniature cold front develops and, from time to time a small cold air outbreak will invade the city. Often topographically suitable paths will be followed, especially where slopes support such an outbreak by gravity flow of cooler air. Enlightened planning and construction of urban areas can help this desirable ventilation, which may prevent the common nocturnal build-up of some air pollutants.

Precipitation. Observations in and near some cities early in the century

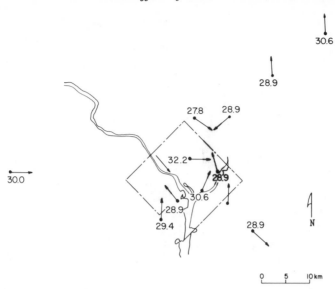

Figure 8-13. Wind convergence in Washington, D. C. during clear summer day. Centers of heat island hatched: temperatures in °C.

suggested that there might be an urban influence on rainfall. As in all instances involving precipitation, proof of an alteration or interference is very difficult. Both the nature of the measurements and the natural variability militate against reliably ascertaining the alteration. Two hypotheses, not mutually exclusive, emerged to explain an urban effect on precipitation. The first invokes the rising air currents produced by the heat island as initiators or, at least, reinforcers of rain. The other hypothesis suggests that certain chemicals in the pollutant plume of the city, if carried into existing clouds, might interfere with the precipitation process. In some instances cloud seeding might start rain, in others it might prevent rain by overseeding.

As always, observations have had to collect the facts that might verify the hypotheses. These observations leave now little doubt that the heat island can, given the right initial conditions, cause showers. There is certainly no doubt that convective clouds start over urban areas earlier than over the countryside. This is principally a summer occurrence. Midday cloudiness in that season is definitely increased over metropolitan districts. As surface heating continues these clouds can grow to the size and height which makes rain definitely possible.

There are occasionally conditions of vertical stability when only a degree or two difference in temperature at the surface will create the

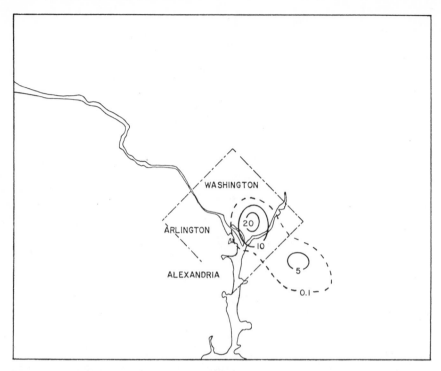

Figure 8-14.   Isolated shower initiated by Washington, D. C. heat plume (isohyets in mm).

necessary instability to produce a shower. Winds aloft will govern the point at which the precipitation occurs, often downwind beyond the city limits. These showers are not anticipated in the forecasts nor is there any precipitation over a large area in the surroundings (Harnack and Landsberg, 1975). A typical case is depicted in Figure 8-14. A total of 25 mm of rain fell from an isolated thunderstorm cell over the eastern part of Washington, D. C.

Climatological records also tell the story. In Washington the eastern sector and the rural area beyond receive about 10% more precipitation than the western section (Canfield and Woollum, 1968). There are no topographical reasons why this should be so. And, indeed, it is not a peculiarity of Washington. Many other areas show the same conditions (Changnon and Huff, 1973). Isolated showers are not the only reason for this increase. It is only easier in their case to prove the urban influence. In synoptic conditions where rain occurs naturally, the extra lift imparted to the precipitating cloud may push the cloud to considerably greater height and cause a light or moderate rainfall to turn into a heavy downpour. This

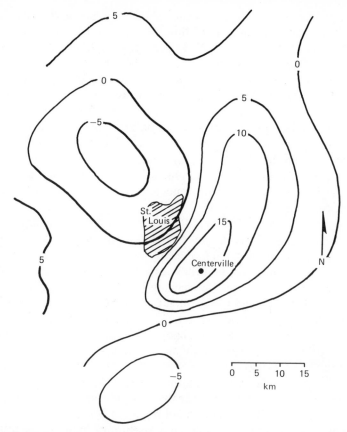

Figure 8-15. Percentage of change in summer rainfall in the vicinity of St. Louis, Missouri (1949–1968) (after Changnon and Huff, 1973).

is more apt to have an impact on slow moving frontal systems of the warm season than on the fast-moving, energypacted winter systems.

A particularly well documented case is the increase of precipitation noted east of the St. Louis metropolitan area. There over a 30-year interval summer precipitation has gradually increased until it is now 15% higher than previously (Changnon and Huff, 1973). The relative precipitation changes that have taken place are shown in Figure 8-15. Together with ordinary rainfall changes, alterations in thunderstorm frequency and hail frequency have been made plausible.

The increases of 5–15% in annual precipitation over or near urban areas can hardly be contested. Their association with the thermal plume of cities seems also well established. Where does that leave the nucleation hypothesis? Here again there is some useful evidence, indicating that this process is operative from time to time. First there is a need to deal with the possibility that an excess of condensation or freezing nuclei has an inhibiting effect on precipitation. The idea here is that too many condensation nuclei competing for moisture will cause droplets in clouds to be small. Such small drops are more difficult to coalesce into raindrops. Freezing nuclei cause subcooled liquid drops to freeze and initiate the Bergeron-Findeisen process of precipitation formation by vapor transfer. This process works well when only a few droplets freeze, but if too many nuclei are present all droplets freeze and none can grow at the other's expense. It is, of course, well nigh impossible to state what a cloud would have done in the absence of these nuclei. Hence, no valid proof can be obtained on their effect.

There are, however, a few well documented cases of snowfall produced from preexisting clouds by plumes from industrial stacks and a single case for an urban area. Some climatological observations suggest that super-cooled clouds drifting over an urban area might be stimulated to precipitate. There seem always ample freezing nuclei in urban plumes, mostly resulting from suitable molecules in automobile exhaust. But the effect is apparently considerably smaller than the summer showers.

In addition, there are the tantalizing observations of weekly cycles in rainfall in urban areas. These indicate a gradual rise of rainfall amounts from Monday to Friday and a notable drop during the weekend. The classical example was published for Paris, France (Dettwiller, 1970). Although an increase of 1/2 mm for the workdays over the weekend may not seem too impressive, if continued regularly it is a 5% increase in the yearly average. As the work week is an arbitrary human institution one cannot escape the conclusion that a manmade cause must underlie this cycle. There is no evidence that the heat island shows a weekly cycle, or if it does, it is very small. This leaves only a pollution source, which shows definite weekly fluctuations in urban areas, as a logical cause. The mechanism has not yet been discovered and thus the issue remains a puzzle.

Alterations Through Pollution

Although there has been some concern about possible climatic effects by air pollutants since the 1930s, heated debates on this topic have ranged since the early 1960s. Many of the arguments have been based first on surmises, later on models. Only in recent years have there been system-atic observational surveys, attempting to sort fact from fiction. Because of the complexity of the subject matter progress has been slow. A number of broad surveys have laid the groundwork for eliminating the worst exaggerations and advancing knowledge in an orderly fashion (Matthews, *et al.*, 1971; Singer, 1975). It is easy in this problem to ascribe certain local alterations to man-made pollutants. It is considerably more difficult to discern global effects, if any. In particular, it is essential to distinguish man-made atmospheric contaminants from those produced by nature. There are prodigious amounts of admixtures brought into the atmosphere from volcanic eruptions, forest fires caused by lightning, sea spray, and decay of organic material. In many instances the natural "background" is only incompletely known and only a few compounds are so uniquely anthropogenic that they can immediately be identified as such.

Carbon dioxide. Carbon dioxide is an end product of the combustion of all wood and fossil fuel. Once released to the atmosphere, it mixes completely with the other atmospheric gases. This gas is a good absorber of infrared radiation and as such intercepts part of the radiation outgoing from the planet's surface, principally between 12 and 18 nm. It thus conserves planetary heat and together with the atmospheric water vapor forms an invisible blanket that protects the earth from excessive cooling. From measurements in the 1870s it is well known that the CO_2 concentration in the atmosphere then was 290 ppm. Repeated measurements have shown a gradual increase.

At the end of World War II, CO_2 had increased to 310 ppm. It continued to rise. This rise has accelerated steadily and has paralleled the rapidly increasing use of fossil fuels for industrial, automotive, and domestic purposes. In 1975 the concentration stood at 330 ppm. The increase in the last years just prior to that point averaged close to 1 ppm/year. Projections of future use of fossil fuels show a continuous growth for decades to come under the pressure of rapidly expanding population and the hastening growth of industry in the world. The estimate is that fossil fuel use will grow at a 4% annual rate to the end of the century.

There are two major sinks for CO_2 in nature. The smaller one is vegetation with assimilates the gas in its metabolic processes. Only if the vegetation cover increases materially can there be an increased rate of uptake. There are only inadequate data to show whether or not there has been any net increase in plant matter over the past few decades. The major absorber of CO_2 are the oceans. They dissolve about one half of the anthropogenic CO_2. This rate is not constant and it is not certain that the oceans will continue as partial but steady eliminators of the man-made CO_2 surplus. Eventually the oceanic CO_2 will be chemically bound into solid carbonates, forming sediments on the bottom of the oceans. But even if one assumes steady absorption of half the anthropogenic CO_2, the

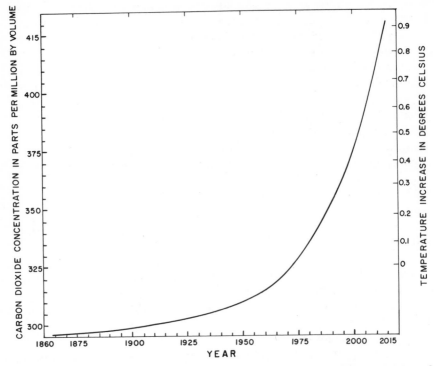

Figure 8-16. Observed and projected increase in atmospheric carbon dioxide and estimated corresponding global temperature size (after Landsberg and Machta, 1974).

fraction remaining in the air will grow so rapidly that by the year 2015 the atmospheric CO_2 will have increased by about 100 ppm. This increase was shown in Figure 8-14. Some scientists have speculated that in another century the atmospheric CO_2 might double.

It remains to explore the impact of such an increase in atmospheric CO_2 on the global climate. There is no doubt that it will raise the equilibrium temperature of the earth. The question is: how much? The only way to obtain an estimate is by using a suitable model of the atmosphere. In Figure 8-16 one such an estimate is given, corresponding to the anticipated CO_2 increase to the year 2015 (Landsberg and Machta, 1974). It is just under 1° C, which is a value comparable in magnitude for global warming from natural causes from the mid-nineteenth to the mid-twentieth century. This estimate was based on a circulation model of Manabe and Wetherald (1967). These authors (1975) have given a new estimate for the case of a doubling of atmospheric CO_2. This is based on a nine vertical layer general circulation model. It includes most major factors affecting the energy balance but replaces the ocean by a simple wet, evaporating surface. Surface albedo is considered but no cloudiness predictions are included. The shortcomings of the model will tend to accentuate the end effect of CO_2 and one need not rely too heavily on the calculated global value of a 3° C temperature increase. Much of this is concentrated at latitudes above 55° and in the stratosphere. Yet the order of magnitude is undoubtedly correct and the tendency that the higher latitudes in the northern hemisphere will be most affected by such a climatic adjustment to the changed atmospheric composition. This is in accordance with the latitudinal distribution of natural temperature changes, which have been observed in the past two centuries. Both, warming and cooling always are more pronounced in higher than lower latitudes.

The inescapable conclusion is, therefore, that anthropogenic CO_2 can lead to a significant global and especially regional climatic alteration.

Clouds and contrails. The undisputed increase in cloudiness caused by the urban heat island has already been discussed. But there are other increases in cloud formation caused directly by pollutants. These are better documented by individual case studies rather than by climatic statistics. The latter can be principally invoked for the indubitable increase of fogs in polluted areas. Among the pollutants is a fair share of hygroscopic particles. Many of these are sulfuric acid aerosols, chemically transformed from sulfur dioxide effluents. In most industrial areas fog frequency has doubled compared to the cleaner upwind countryside.

Not all fogs of this origin are resting on the ground. They are either lifted a few tens of meters by the influence of the heat island or actually form at chimney and stack height. These high fogs could technically also be properly designated as low stratus clouds. They are a common winter characteristic of industrialized valleys. They form a solid deck to the height of the usually present ground inversion of temperature. The bright sunshine above is reflected from the top of the cloud layer and cannot penetrate into the valley. Only a major upheaval with strong winds will clean both fog and pollutants out of the low places. Of course, high fogs can also occur naturally but their frequency and duration is far shorter in the absence of pollutants.

Other cloud formations are of more recent origin. They have been noted especially in the vicinity of large power-generating stations fired by fossil fuels and using cooling towers. The plant stack will emit pollutants that can act as nuclei for condensation and the cooling towers furnish ample water vapor. The combination will result in a dense, cloud-like plume. In the presence of high natural water vapor content and suitable atmospheric temperature structure, again vast cloud sheets can be initiated by the effluents. Terrain conditions can foster such formations, which have been traced from the air for a dozen to over a 100 km downwind.

Another set of cloud formations is attributable to the exhausts of high flying aircraft. Jet-powered airplanes not only produce considerable water vapor but also an uncountable number of condensation nuclei. When these exhaust products encounter appropriate temperature and saturation conditions, a long cloud trail will form. These condensation trails, or contrails for short, were first observed during World War II and not appreciated by the aircraft crew because they gave away their position and course.

Most of the contrails are short-lived and disappear by evaporation. However, a few are highly persistent. They form in a layer where nature is close to the formation of cirrus clouds. These persistent contrails are dispersed by the wind but are frequently sufficiently dense to remain visible. Near major air-traffic centers they can occasionally cover a substantial portion of the sky and may last for hours. These conditions seem to have notably increased since the introduction of passenger jets on a large scale. This started in the middle 1960s. Observations of cirrus clouds have increased near major airports in the western United States, where low clouds are relatively rare and where opportunities to observe cirrus clouds are common. Cirrus observations at Denver, Albuquerque, and Salt Lake cities showed a rapid increase of these clouds since the start of the jet age, as shown in Figure 8-17. Although the rise is only one-tenth or less for the cirrus clouds and likely to be insignificant in the energy budget of the globe, it is another effect attributable to man's activities (Machta, 1971; Machta and Telegadas, 1974). Yet the total amount of cirrus produced by jet aircraft is quite uncertain, because the amount that forms over low cloud covers cannot be observed from the ground and weather satellites can not readily distinguish natural cirrus clouds from man-made contrails. The potential seeding of the low clouds by ice crystals falling from contrails and the possibly initiated precipitation has also not been assessed.

Dust. The question whether or not man-produced dust has a measurable influence on climate remains open and controversial, because of natural dust production during volcanic eruptions, sea salt spray, and wind erosion of natural surfaces. Material originating near the surface stays only a short while in the air before it settles by gravity or is washed out. We have at best crude estimates of natural production. It amounts to about 2×10^9 metric tons annually. The quasipermanent dust contents of the atmo-

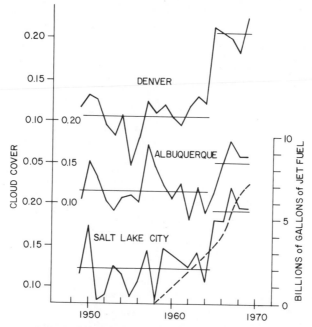

Figure 8-17. Observations of high clouds (in tenths of sky cover) at three airports as function of time (solid lines, left scales). Note rise in high cloudiness with jet fuel consumption (dashed line, left scale) (after Machta and Telegadas, 1974).

sphere is about 10^8 tons; much of it is in a size fraction of particles with < 0.1 μm diameter residing in the upper troposphere or stratosphere. There the natural processes that cleanse the material from the air are not very effective.

The man-made component of the atmospheric aerosol has been estimated at about 2×10^8 tons from agricultural activities, including wind erosion of fields, and an equal or perhaps slightly higher amount from industrial activities, and from automotive and domestic sources (Fennelly, 1976). The surprisingly high agricultural contribution can to a considerable extent be attributed to slash-and-burn methods prevalent in many parts of the world. As to how much of the man-made dust stays in the air, we have no precise answer. Some guesses have it that about 10% stays longer than a year in suspension. This would lead to a gradual accumulation of more and more small particles in the air. But actually there is now considerable evidence that local sources in the industrialized regions are being brought under control (Ellsaesser, 1975) and no global increase is proven.

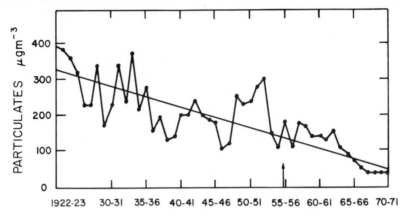

Figure 8-18. Time series of atmospheric particulate load at Kew near London, England. Arrow marks introduction of controls (Clean Air Act) (after Auliciems and Burton, 1973).

An impressive case of clean-up has been recorded for the London, England, atmosphere (Auliciems and Burton, 1973). This is shown in Figure 8-18 where the particulate load at Kew, a London suburb, is shown as a time series. Other localities have shown measurable but not as spectacular results. In still others the dust load is static. Increased industrialization and automobile traffic have balanced decreases brought about by control efforts. The agricultural contribution has remained essentially uncontrolled.

A special case again is in aerosols produced by high-flying aircraft. Some of them are carbon particles from incomplete combustion of fuel. Others originate from sulfur dioxide in the fuel which is transformed to sulfuric acid. At low stratospheric temperature this will be in solid form. Some will combine with ammonia vapors in the air to form ammonium sulfate dust (Friend, *et al.*, 1973). The elimination of these particles is slow and proceeds by atmospheric transport processes. The monitoring of debris from nuclear explosions has produced information on residence times of aerosols in various layers of the atmosphere. The information gathered and supplemented by other available data is shown in Figure 8-19. This clearly shows that in the troposphere residence time of particles is measured in days, in the higher stratosphere in years. In the layer near the tropopause, whether nominally in the stratosphere or troposphere the residence can be days or months, depending on cyclonic activity (Reiter, *et al.*, 1975). In areas of intense, active cyclones, the proximity of polar and tropical tropopause with intense jet streams, stratospheric gaps with strong vertical motions develop. Through these gaps stratospheric air

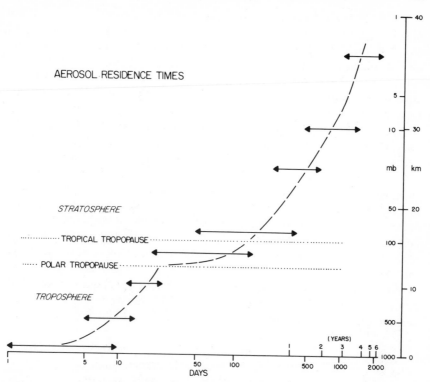

Figure 8-19. Schematic representation of average residence time of aerosols, as related to height.

parcels and their dust burden can be brought into the troposphere and eventually to the surface where the particles are eliminated (Reiter, 1975). It is the long residence time in higher stratospheric layers that has caused concern because of the ever higher flight levels of aviation.

The long residence times guarantee that the dust finds world-wide distribution in the stratosphere. This has been also the experience with debris of high-reaching volcanic eruptions. Even in the middle troposphere dust clouds can travel considerable distances, especially in the subtropical high pressure belts. Sahara dust is regularly noted in the Caribbean (Carlson and Prospero, 1972; Lushine, 1975). Better monitoring procedures than heretofore will keep track of whether or not the atmospheric aerosol load, especially in the stratosphere, is steady, increasing, or decreasing. Laser probing will become a major tool in this surveillance.

Much effort has been devoted to figure out what effect the interception of solar radiation by dust has on the global temperatures. There is, indeed, considerable absorption by low-level dust which can reach 30–40% reduction of solar energy at the surface (Collier and Lockwood, 1974; Peterson and Flowers, 1975; Wesely and Lipschutz, 1976). This same dust will also absorb outgoing long-wave radiation from the surface (Wang and Domoto, 1974; Riches, *et al.*, 1975). The net result is assumed to be a warming of the lower atmosphere. In general, irrespective of height of the dust, model calculations show that they will cause warming at the poles because of the lowered albedo (Cylek and Coakley, 1974; Shaw, 1976).

Large increases in aerosols in the high atmosphere by major fleets of supersonic transport aircraft and frequent space shuttles should lead to an increased albedo of the Earth through back-scattering of the incoming radiation. At the same time there is also absorption of both incoming solar and outgoing terrestrial radiation (Cadle and Grams, 1975). This must lead to some heating of the atmosphere at the height of the aerosol layer. On the whole, however, there should be some global cooling. Present day activities in the lower stratosphere by air and spacecraft have so far contributed only minor amounts of aerosol to the stratosphere and have remained climatically subliminal (Pollack, *et al.*, 1976).

Other effluents. The variety of pollutants spewed into the air by human activities is bewildering. There are literally thousands of compounds. Most of them have atmospheric effects principally by acting as condensation and freezing nuclei. We have already discussed the most important of these in prior sections. The troublesome fraction of these effluents is what undergoes chemical transformations and interacts with atmospheric gases.

Such interactions generally take place under the influence of sunshine. Even though all wave lengths of the solar radiation can contribute energy to photochemical reactions, the most energetic part of the spectrum is the ultraviolet. This phenomenon has long plagued the sunny regions of southern California and similar climates with industry and automobile traffic.

A classical reaction splits nitrogen dioxide, ubiquitous in urban atmospheres, and leaves highly reactive atomic oxygen and by a second reaction creates ozone:

$$No_2 + h\nu \rightarrow NO + O$$
$$O + O_2 + M \rightarrow O_3 + M$$

The ozone, which readily dissociates again, is an irritant in itself but further chain reactions with hydrocarbons from exhaust gases lead

to formation of other irritants such as peroxyacetylnitrate (PAN: CH$_3$O—O—O—NO$_2$). A number of chain reactions regenerate the NO$_2$
$$\underset{C}{\overset{\|}{}}$$
and the atmospheric result is the well-known reduction of visibility referred to as *smog*. Actually there is an analogous process in nature by photochemical action on terpenes produced by trees. This creates the blue haze, which gave the "Great Smokies" in Tennessee their names.

The paradoxical situation exists that the same type of photochemistry producing ozone in the urban air acts to destroy ozone in the upper atmosphere. There the actinic far ultraviolet rays of the sun are energetic enough to split the oxygen molecule and catalytic interaction of atomic and molecular oxygen leads to ozone formation:

$$O_2 + h\omega \rightarrow 2\,O$$
$$O + O_2 + M \rightarrow O_3 + M$$

This ozone, in turn, intercepts the shortest ultraviolet wavelengths and forms a protective blanket for the biota on earth. Many of these would be killed or injured if wavelengths absorbed by DNA were to reach the surface with high intensities. The ozone forms a layer in the stratosphere, with greatest concentration around 25 km above the surface. Formation, destruction, and transport processes combine to create maximal concentrations in high latitudes and lesser ones over equatorial zones. The ratio is about 2:1. The high latitudes show the greatest values in spring. Aside from the annual variation of ozone concentration there is a variation throughout the sunspot rhythm. Locally there are large day-to-day changes above a place. Variations of 10% or even more are not uncommon. In such a highly variable element any trends are difficult to discern.

Thus heated arguments have arisen about possible effects of man-made effluents on the ozone layer. These are essentially potential influences rather than observed ozone destruction. Yet, because some of these influences could be slow and insidious the matter can not be brushed aside as something the grandchildren of the present generation should worry about. The main concern, among other biological effects, is the possible effect on skin cancer rates among light pigmented persons. Crop plants seem to be fairly robust in their response to ultraviolet radiation. Knowledge is as yet quite inadequate as regards possible effects on beneficial insects helpful in fertilizing flowering plants.

The effluent from aircraft, under suspicion as the archculprit in ozone destruction, is nitrogen dioxide, NO$_2$. This is photochemically dissociated and the nitric oxide formed reduces the ozone to ordinary oxygen molecules.

$$NO_2 + h\nu \rightarrow NO + O$$
$$NO + O_3 \rightarrow NO_2 + O_2$$

All this looks simple and straightforward but nothing could be more deceiving. There are so many chemical species present in the stratosphere and so many reactions possible that matters have not yet been fully sorted out. Around 50 reactions play a role (Crutzen, 1974) and the reaction rates at the low stratospheric temperatures have not yet been fully determined. Besides, oxides of nitrogen can also be produced by solar proton eruptions reaching the air. This type of event undoubtedly accounts for part of the natural variations of ozone (Crutzen, *et al.*, 1975).

Man has also copiously produced oxides of nitrogen in the stratosphere by nuclear air bursts. Calculations have made production of 1–15 kilotons of NO/megaton of nuclear explosion effect plausible (Bauer and Gilmore, 1975). But observations of ozone during the period of nuclear testing in the atmosphere show very little if any influence on ozone concentrations.

Another disturbing influence on the ozone layer has been predicted from man-made chlorofluorocarbons. These are used in refrigeration systems and spray cans. They are chemically inert in the troposphere. However, in the stratosphere a chlorine atom is split off by the solar ultraviolet in the wavelengths 175–220 nm. This chlorine interacts with and destroys the ozone:

$$CF_xCl_y + h\nu \rightarrow CF_xCl_{y-1} + Cl$$
$$Cl + O_3 \rightarrow ClO + O_2$$

In this, as in the other stratospheric chemical processes, there are numerous other reactions involved. Some of them are chain reactions which make the disturbing element react further rather than eliminating it. Much needs yet to be clarified in this respect (Anonymous, 1975; Basuk, 1975).

Of course, immediately two questions arose: how the chlorofluorocarbons get into the stratosphere; and whether there are other, possibly natural, sources of chlorine, which might be involved in ozone depletion. As an answer to the first question, one can point to a number of mechanisms. One is a vertical transport by intense convective storm systems which break through the tropopause. They are known to inject water vapor into the stratosphere. Turbulent motions near the stratospheric gaps of major storm systems will exchange tropospheric and stratospheric air and their respective admixtures. Finally gradual slow diffusion processes can not be ruled out. Inasmuch as the chlorofluorocarbons are man-made compounds, the fact that about 140 ppt have been found for one of these and 75 ppt for another compound at an altitude of 12 km indicates that they are measurable in the stratosphere (Hester, *et al.*,

1975). The mixing ratio stays fairly constant to 20 km (Delany, *et al.*, 1974).

Among other potential artificial sources of stratospheric chlorine are carbontetrachloride and hydrochloric acid, both widely used. The natural sources are not all known, but volcanic eruptions and, principally, sodium chloride from the ocean must be a main source. Sea salt is an omnipresent aerosol but its effects on the chemical reactions are presently assumed to be minor.

Only further research can remove the uncertainties on ozone depletion but the effects of such reduction on surface climate can nonetheless be estimated. Fortunately, they are likely to be minor. If ozone reduction stays below 20%—and efforts will undoubtedly be made to keep it smaller because of the biological effects of the more intense ultraviolet penetrating to the surface—surface temperatures will stay unchanged. The stratosphere at the ozone level will cool but this should have only minimal effects on the general atmospheric circulation (Reck, 1976). In fact the chlorofluorocarbons would add to the infrared absorption of the carbon dioxide (Ramanathan, 1975). But the latter can be expected to be the far most climate-disturbing man-made contribution to the atmosphere.

Thermal effects. It is only in recent years that heat rejected into the air by human activities has been designated as a pollutant. One may quibble about the appropriateness of this usage but waste heat is clearly an important factor in our climate. We have already seen some of the effects, where rejected heat becomes a substantial part of the urban heat island. But in that environment other energy transactions are more important than anthropogenic heat rejection.

In areas of concentrated industrial activity, cramped into a small space, the ejection of waste steam and warmed-up water from cooling processes has another dimension. Power stations using fossil or nuclear fuels are already occasionally causing influences on the atmosphere. Public insistence upon remoteness and land policies have led to more intense development of existing sites and to plans for even greater concentration in power parks. All the heat rejected, whether through direct discharge into rivers or lakes, cooling ponds, or cooling towers ultimately ends up in the atmosphere.

Projections of future energy use are anything but reassuring. They envisage consumption of 270×10^{18} joules in 1980, 570×10^{18} J by the year 2000, and 1240 J by 2025. The major fraction of this energy will have to be dissipated by the atmosphere (Perry and Landsberg, 1976). There is no problem to accommodate these amounts on a global scale without an appreciable effect on global climate.

Table 8-3. Calculation of the Vorticity Concentration Parameter for Several Sources

Source	Radius, R(m)	Buoyancy flux, F(m⁴/s³)	Heat flux, H(m²/s⁴)	Mixing height z_1(m)	V_E(m/s)	V_∞(m/s)	V_∞/V_B
Single cooling tower sensible heat	25	3,500	10^{-2}	10^3	5.2	0.32	0.06
Cluster of 20 cooling towers sensible heat	500	70,000	10^{-2}	10^3	5.2	1.7	0.33
	5,000	70,000	10^{-2}	10^3	2.4	1.7	0.71
Strong natural convection	500	2,500	10^{-2}	10^3	1.7	1.7	1.0
Oil Burners	125	6,000	10^{-2}	10^3	3.6	1.6	0.44
Saturn V	10	1,300,000	10^{-2}	10^3	51.0	0.13	0.0025
Australian bushfires	10^{-3}	900,000	10^{-2}	10^3	13.8	1.7	0.12

Source environment

The difficulties, if any, will arise on the local or regional scale. Some estimates have been made for various cooling methods. Cooling ponds have a number of advantages. There is no immediate discharge into rivers with possible damage to the aquatic ecosystem. There can also be by-products by aquaculture in the ponds. Power plants operate at about 35% efficiency. Hence, for every megawatt of electricity produced, close to two megawatts have to be dissipated through the cooling system. It has been estimated that, for example, in the U.S. midwestern climate, the ponds will assume water temperatures of +10° C in winter and 30° C in summer. The main effect is likely to be additional fog formation. This is only probable in winter because the temperature difference between air and pond surface has to be 16.7° C for a vapor pressure deficit of 1 mb below the saturation point for water vapor. In that same region, based on available climatic data, the fog hours would nearly double (Vogel and Huff, 1975). These would be restricted to periods of weak winds. No reliable estimates can be made on plume effects, downwind icing, or snow fall.

The most common modern cooling method for power plants is with cooling towers. Models for estimating their effect on the immediate vicinity are available (Bhumralkar, 1973). They show that for existing power plants short-period temperature and moisture perturbations may be around 0.5° C and moisture additions essentially negligible. But for the proposed plants of 30,000 to 40,000 megawatts, 6 km on the side, temperatures rises of 3° C and moisture additions of 1.6 g of water/kg of air can be expected (Koenig and Bhumralkar, 1974). This is a substantial atmospheric modification and added precipitation of 5–20 cm/yr is another probable consequence.

Power parks with 50,000 MW generating capacity will dissipate 100,000 MW heat, 80% of it in form of latent heat, on an area generally less than 100 km². The energy flux is about three times that of the average incident solar radiation (340 W/m⁻²). The vertical energy flux in such a park would be about one-fifth that found in thunderstorms. Table 8-3 shows comparisons between natural energy sources, their observed effects, and man-made heat releases (Hanna and Gilford, 1975). The analogy shows that such power parks, if ever placed in operation, might trigger thunderstorms or even tornadoes. It is certainly a prospect that should shake us out of our complacency.

Outlook

It has been demonstrated beyond any reasonable doubt that man's activities already have inadvertently led to local climatic alterations. As urbanization progresses at a rapid pace, these effects will intensify and comprise larger and larger areas. Power production in small areas with massed cooling towers dissipating waste heat certainly have the potential to influence small storm systems. Both urbanization and concentrated heat rejection will increase precipitation downwind. They may also increase hail downwind to the detriment of agriculture.

But the greatest potential danger for the global climate is the accelerated growth of the carbon dioxide contents of the atmosphere. A rise of 2° C in the global equilibrium temperatures could bring about major changes in the subpolar regions of the northern hemisphere. No one can assuredly predict that these will be entirely favorable. But alterations of this magnitude have influences on the general atmospheric circulation and could well bring about considerable dislocation in rainfall distribution to the south. We are not too far from developing mathematical models which can simulate such changes and there is hope that in a decade more precise projections of the effects of such alterations can be made.

Prospects for climate control on a large scale, affecting large areas are decidedly dim. All such schemes are likely to remain in the speculative realms for decades to come. It would be better to concentrate talent, work, and funds on beneficial small-scale alterations, principally for the benefit of the farmer. Much more wide-spread use could be made of existing technology to control low-level wind speeds and surface albedos. There is still much opportunity for further improvements, especially for the control of temperatures in the atmospheric boundary layer. Additional efforts also are warranted for control of evaporation. Weather modification, especially rain making and hail control for the benefit of crops, is still very elusive. Perhaps a decade or two of research work—not misdirected operations—may bring nearer a reliable technology to achieve these ends.

References

Angell, J. K., Pack, D. H., and Hoecker, W. H. (1969). Urban influence on nighttime air flow estimated from tetroon flights. *J. Appl. Meteorol.* **10**, 194–204.

Anonymous, Freeze protection with a man-made fog, Univ. of Florida, Gainesville, Sunshine State Agricultural Research Report J. **19** (1–2), (1974), 3–6.

Anonymous, *Fluorocarbons and the Environment.* Report of Federal Task Force on Inadvertent Modification of the Stratosphere (IMOS), Gov't Printing Office (038-000-00226-1), Washington, D. C., 109 pp.

Arnold, M. D., Floods as man-made disasters. *Environ. Conserv.* **2**, 257–263.

Auliciems, A., and Burton, I. (1973). Trends in smoke concentrations before and after the clean air act of 1956. *Atm. Environment* **7**, 1063–1070.

Basuk, J. (1975). Freons and ozone in the stratosphere. *Bull, Am. Meteorol. Soc.* **56**, 589–592.

Bauer, E., and Gilmore, F. R. (1975). Effect of atmospheric nuclear explosions on total ozone. *Reviews of Geophys. & Space Phys.* **13**, 451–458.

Bhumralkar, C. (1973). Observational and theoretical study of atmospheric flow over a heated island. *Mo. Wea. Rev.* **101**, 719–745.

Borisov, P. M. (1967). Can we control the climate of the Arctic. *Priroda*, Issue 12, 63–73.

Caborn, J. M. (1965). *Shelterbelts and Windbreaks*, Faber & Faber, London, 288 pp.

Cadle, R. D., and Grams, G. W. (1975). Stratospheric aerosol particles and their optical properties. *Rev's of Geophys. & Space Phys.* **13**, 475–501.

Canfield, N. L., and Woollum, C. A. (1968). Washington metropolitan area precipitation and temperature patterns. *Tech. Memo*, Weather Bureau Eastern Region, No. 28, 32 pp.

Carlson, T. B., and Prospero, J. M. (1972). The large-scale movement of Saharan air outbreaks over the northern equatorial Atlantic. *J. Appl. Meteorol.* **11**, 283–297.

Chandler, T. J. (1970). *Selected Bibliography on Urban Climate*. World Meteorological Organization, No. 276, TP 155, Geneva, 383 pp.

Chandler, T. J. (1976). *Urban Climatology and Its Relevance to Urban Design*. World Meteorol. Organization, Tech. Note No. 149, 61 pp.

Changnon, S. A., and Huff, F. A. (1973). Precipitation modification by major urban areas. *Bull. Am. Meteorol. Soc.* **54**, 1220–1232.

Charney, J., Stone, P. H., and Quirk, W. J. (1975, 1976). Drought in the Sahara: A biogeophysical feedback mechanism. *Science* **187**, 434–435; and **191**, 100–102.

Chýlek, P., and Coakley, J. A., Jr. (1974). Man-made aerosols and the heating of the atmosphere over polar regions. In *Climate of the Arctic*, 159–165.

Collier, L. R., and Lockwood, J. G. (1974). The estimation of solar radiation under cloudless skies with atmospheric dust. *Quart. J. R. Met. Soc.* **100**, 678–681.

Crutzen, P. J. (1974). Estimates of possible variations in total ozone due to natural causes and human activities. *Ambio* **3**, 201–210.

Crutzen, P. J., Isaksen, I. S., and Reid, G. C. (1975). Solar proton events: Stratospheric sources of nitric oxide. *Science* **189**, 457–459.

Delany, A. C., Shedlovsky, J. P., and Pollock, W. H. (1974). Stratospheric aerosol: The contribution from the troposphere. *J. Geophys. Res.* **79**, 5646–5650.

Dettwiller, J. (1970). Incidence possible de l'activité industrielle sur les précipitations à Paris. In *Urban Meteorology*, World Meteorol. Organization, Tech. Note No. 108, 361–362.

East, C. (1971). Chaleur urbaine à Montréal. *Atmosphere* **9**, 112–122.

Eckholm, E. P. (1975). Desertification: A World Problem. *Ambio* **4**, 137–145.

Eimern, J. van, *et al.* (1964). *Windbreaks and Shelterbelts*. World Meteorological Organization, Technical Note No. 59, Geneva, 188 pp.

Ellsaesser, H. W. (1975). Where are we now in air pollution. *Proc. Twelfth Space Congress, Cocoa Beach, Florida, April 9–11 (1975)*, 2–5 to 2–16.

Fennelly, P. F. (1976). The origin and influence of airborne particulates. *Am. Scientist* **64**, 46–56.

Fletcher, J. O. (1968). The polar oceans and world climate. Paper presented at Symposium on Beneficial Modifications of the Marine Environment, Ntl. Acad. Sciences, Reproduced by RAND Corp., Santa Monica (1968), 60 pp.

Flohn, H. (1970). Etude des conditions climatiques de l'avance du desert. Tunis, 17 pp.

Fowler, W. B., and Helvey, J. D. (1974a). Effect of large-scale irrigation on climate in the Columbia Basin. *Science* **184**, 121–127.

Fowler, W. B., and Helvey, J. D. (1974b). Comment on Stidd (1974). *Science* **188**, 280–281.

Friend, J. P., Leifer, R., and Trichon, R. (1973). On the formation of stratospheric aerosols. *J. Atm. Sci.* **30**, 465–479.

Fukui, E. (1970). The recent rise of temperature in Japan. *Japanese Progress in Climatology*, Tokyo University of Education, 46–65.

Geiger, R. (1961). *Das Klima der bodennahen Luftschicht* (4th ed.). Friedr. Vieweg & Sohn, Braunschweig, 646 pp.

Grillo, J. N., and Spar, J. (1971). Rain-snow mesoclimatology of the New York metropolitan area. *J. Appl. Meteorol.* **10**, 56–61.

Hanna, S. R., and Gifford, F. A. (1975). Meteorological effects on energy dissipation at large power parks. *Bull. Am. Meteorol. Soc.* **52**, 1069–1076.

Harnack, R. P., and Landsberg, H. E. (1975). Selected cases of convective precipitation caused by the metropolitan area of Washington, D. C. *J. Appl. Meteorol.* **14**, 1050–1060.

Hershfield, D. M. (1962). A note on the variability of annual precipitation. *J. Appl. Meteorol.* **1**, 575–578.

Hester, N. E., Stephens, E. R., and Taylor, O. C. (1975). Fluorocarbon Air Pollutants. *Environm. Science & Technol.* **9**, 875–876.

Heuseler, H. (1965). Extreme Temperatur Differenzen Stadt-Land in Strahlungsnächten. *Umschau* **65**, 60–61.

Howard, L. (1818). *The Climate of London*, Vol. 1, London.

Jensen, M. (1954). Shelter Effect. The Danish Technical Press, Copenhagen, 264 pp.

Joos, L. A. (1969). Recent rainfall patterns in the Great Plains. American Meteorological Society, Symposium paper, October 1969, Madison, Wisconsin.

Keeling, C. D. (1976). Impact of industrial gases on climate. In *Energy and Climate: Outer Limits to Growth?* (manuscript). (NAS/GRB), 32 pp.

Koenig, L. R., and Bhumralkar, C. (1974). On possible undesirable atmospheric effects of waste heat rejection from large electrical power centers. The Rand Corporation, Santa Monica, R-1628-RC.

Landsberg, H. (1940). The use of solar energy for the melting of ice. *Bull. Am. Meteorol. Soc.* **21**, 102–107.

Landsberg, H. E. (1970). Micrometeorological temperature differentiation through urbanization. In *Urban Climates*, World Meteorol. Organizat. Tech. Note 108, 129–136.

Landsberg, H. E. (1974). Inadvertent atmospheric modification through urbanization. In Hess, W. N. (ed.), *Weather and Climate Modification*, Wiley, New York, 726–763.

Landsberg, H. E. (1975). *Atmospheric Changes in a Growing Community*. Univ. of Maryland, Inst. f. Fluid Dynamics, Tech. Note BN 823, 53 pp.

Landsberg, H. E. (1976). The definition and determination of climatic changes, fluctuations and outlooks. In Kopec, R. J. (ed.), *Atmospheric Quality and Climatic Change*, Studies in Geography No. 9, University of North Carolina, Chapel Hill, 52–64.

Landsberg, H., and Machta, L. (1974). Anthropogenic pollution of the atmosphere: Whereto? *Ambio* **3**, 146–150.

Leopold, L. B. (1968). Hydrology for Urban Land Planning—A Guide Book on the Hydrologic Effects of Urban Land Use. U. S. Geological Survey Circular 554, 18 pp.

Lushine, J. B. (1975). A dust layer in the eastern Caribbean. *Mo. Wea. Rev.* **103**, 454–455.

Machta, L. (1971). Global effects of contamination in the upper atmosphere. *Am. Inst. of Chem. Eng'rs. 64th Ann'l Meeting*, San Francisco (unpubl. paper).

Machta, L., and Telegadas, K. (1974). Inadvertent large-scale weather modification. In Hess, W. N. (ed.), *Weather and Climate Modification*. Wiley, New York, 687–725.

Manabe, S., and Wetherald, R. (1967). Thermal equilibrium of the atmosphere with a given distribution of relative humidity. *J. Atm. Sci.* **24**, 241–259.

Manabe, S., and Wetherald, R. (1975). The effects of doubling CO_2 concentration on the climate of a general circulation model. *J. Atm. Sci.* **32**, 3–15.

Matthews, W. H., Kellogg, W. W., and Robinson, G. D. (1971). *Man's Impact on Climate*. MIT Press, Cambridge, Mass., 594 pp.

Miller, D. R., Rosenberg, N. J., and Bagley, W. T. (1975). Wind reduction by a highly permeable tree shelterbelt. *Agricult. Meteorol.* **14**, 321–333.

Munn, R. E. (1966). *Descriptive Micrometeorology*. Academic Press, New York & London, 245 pp.

Myers, T. M. (1974). Dew as visual indicator of the urban heat island. Univ. of Maryland, Meteorol. Progr., M.S. Thesis, 54 pp.

Nicholas, F. W. (1971). A synoptic climatology of Metro Washington: A mesoscale analysis of the urban heat island under selected weather conditions. University of Maryland, Dep't. of Geog., M.S. Thesis, 120 pp.

Norwine, J. R. (1972). Heat-island properties of an enclosed multi-level shopping center. Preprints, Am. Meteorol. Soc., Conf. on Urban Environment & Second Conf. on Biometeorology, Philadelphia, 139–143.

Oke, T. (1973). Review of Urban Climatology, 1968–1973. World Meteorol. Organization, Techn. Note No. 134, 132 pp.

Perry, H., and Landsberg, H. H. (1977). Projected world energy consumption. In *Energy and Climate*, National Academy of Sciences, Washington, D.C., 35–50.

Peterson, J. T. (1969). *The Climate of Cities: A Survey of Recent Literature*. Nat'l. Air. Pollut. Control Admin., Raleigh, N. C., 48 pp.

Peterson, J. T., and Flowers, E. C. (1975). Interactions between air pollution and solar radiation. Int'l Conf. on Environmental Sensing and Assessment, Vol. 2, Las Vegas, 32–4, 5 pp.

Pollack, J. B., et al. (1976). Estimates of climatic impact of aerosols produced by space shuttles, SST's and other high flying aircraft. *J. Appl. Meteorol.* **15**, 247–258.

Ramanathan, V. (1970). Greenhouse effect due to chlorofluorocarbons: Climatic implications. *Science* **190**, 50–52.

Reck, R. A. (1976). Stratospheric effects on temperature. *Science* **192**, 557–559.
Reiter, E. R. (1975). Stratospheric-Tropospheric Exchange Processes. *Reviews of Geophys. & Space Phys.* **13**, 459–474.
Reiter, E. R., *et al.* (1975). Measurements of stratospheric residence times. *Arch. Met. Geoph. Biokl.* **24**, 41–51.
Riches, M. R., Peterson, J. T., and Flowers, E. C. (1975). Effects of atmospheric aerosols on the infrared irradiance at the Earth's surface in a nonurban environment. U. S. Environmental Protection Agency, Environmental Monitoring Series, EPA-65014-75-017, Research Triangle Park, N. C., 35 pp.
Ripley, E. A. (1976). Drought in the Sahara: Insufficient biogeophysical feedback? *Science* **191**, 100 pp.
Rosenberg, N. J. (1966). Microclimate air mixing and physiological regulation of transpiration as influenced by wind shelter in an irrigated bean field. *Agricult. Meteorol.* **3**, 197–224.
Schultz, H. B. (1962). The interaction of the macro- and microclimatic factors contributing to the success of wind machines for frost protection. In Tromp, S. W. and Weibe, W. W. (eds.), *Biometeorology,* Pergamon, 614–629.
Shaw, G. E. (1976). Properties of the background global aerosol and their effects on climate. *Science* **192**, 1334–1336.
Singer, S. F. (ed.) (1975). *The Changing Global Environment.* D. Reidel, Dordrecht, 423 pp.
Stanhill, G. (1965). Observations on reduction of soil temperatures. *Agricult. Meteorol.* **2**, 197–203.
Stewart, J. B. (1971). The albedo of a pine forest. *Quart. J. R. Met. Soc.* **97**, 561–564.
Stidd, C. L. (1974). Irrigation increases rainfall. *Science* **188**, 279–280.
Vogel, J. L., and Huff, F. A. (1975). Fog effects resulting from power plant cooling lakes. *J. Appl. Meteorol.* **14**, 868–872.
Wang, W. C., and Domato, G. A. (1974). The radiative effect of aerosol in the Earth's atmosphere. *J. Appl. Meteorol.* **13**, 521–534.
Wesely, M. L., and Lipschutz, R. C. (1976). An experimental study of the effects of aerosols on diffuse and direct solar radiation received during the summer near Chicago. *Atmospheric Environment* **10** (in print) (1976).
Woodruff, N. P., *et al.* (1972). *How to Control Wind Erosion.* U. S. Dep't. of Agriculture, Washington, D. C., Agric. Info. Bull. Nr. 354, 22 pp.
Yoshino, M. M. (1975). *Climate in a Small Area.* University of Tokyo Press, 549 pp.
Zych, S., and Dubaniewicz, H. (1969). Wplyw Zbiornika retencyjnego Otmuchow i hipoteza oddzialycvania Zbiornika glebinow na klimant mieskowy. *Zeszyty Nauk. Univ. Lodz, Ser. II* **32**, 3–20.

9

CLIMATE, AGRICULTURE, AND ECONOMIC DEVELOPMENT

Asit K. Biswas, Director
Biswas and Associates, Ottawa, Canada, and
International Institute for Applied Systems Analysis,
Laxenburg, Austria

During the past several decades, international organizations like the United Nations, the Organization of Economic Co-operation and Development, the various bilateral aid agencies like the Agency for International Development of the United States, the Candadian International Development Agency, and the Swedish International Development Agency, and major philanthropic institutions like the Ford and Rockefeller Foundations, have made determined efforts to improve the life styles of developing nations through economic development. Furthermore, on January 1, 1971, the United Nations launched its Second Development Decade (DD2) which was directed toward the achievement of similar goals. In spite of these development projects to improve the social and economic conditions of the developing countries, primarily clustered within a poverty belt that encircles most of Asia, Africa and Latin America, the gap between the rich and poor nations has continued to grow. This is not to denigrate the necessity and usefulness of these organizations; without them the living conditions in much of the world would probably have been far worse.

The benefits of the modern technological and industrial developments and the unprecedented postwar expansion in world economic activities helped all nations, but these benefits, unfortunately, were very unevenly distributed, depending on many different factors, including the stages of development of individual countries. This, plus the fact that the developing countries had a far larger population growth than the developed countries, both in absolute numbers and percentage increase, have made the gap between rich and poor nations progressively wider. The latest

237

demographic data, however, is cautiously encouraging. If the changing patterns of crude birth rates in both developed and developing countries, for the 20-year period 1955–1974, is considered, they indicate that the crude birth rate, on overall basis, has been steadily falling in all major regions. Thus, in the 93 developing countries, the rate appears to have dropped by nearly 13%. The maximum decline has been in Asia, and the minimum in Africa. During the same period, the crude birth rate of developed countries declined further. Even then, however, the average crude birth rate of developing countries remains quite high: nearly 2.3 times that of the developed nations.

In addition to the nature of population growth, the distribution of economic growth has been somewhat skewed in the developing countries. Typically, the upper 20% account for 55% of GNP and the lower 20% contribute only 5%. This skewness is also reflected in the concentration of land ownership. Again, typically, 20% of the richest landowners of the developing countries own 50 to 60 percent of the cropland. These percentage figures, according to FAO, are 82% for Venezuela, 56% for Colombia, 53% for Brazil, and approximately 50% for India, Pakistan, and the Philippines. Roughly 100 million small farms of the developing countries, having an area of less than 5 ha, account for only 20% of the cropland. In other words, it means that technological and industrial developments have virtually bypassed the lower 40% of the income strata of the developing countries, who neither contribute significantly to the economic growth of their countries, nor share in the benefits stemming from such growths. Naturally, economic growth cannot affect the lifestyles of the poor and the underprivileged unless it reaches the masses.

It is thus imperative that economic development should continue, at least selectively, if for no other reason than to provide an opportunity for the less fortunate, both within nations and among nations, to catch up with their more fortunate counterparts, until a better global distribution of resources is achieved. Such a development will have important consequences, including a major impact on the population growth. It is equally important that such socio-economic development take place within a long-term sustaining strategy for all mankind, with appropriate understanding of the constraints posed by the finiteness of the earth and the quality of the environment (see Chapter 6).

Climate and Development

A cursory analysis of the existing literature on economic development will indicate that very little attention, if any, has been given to the relationship between the level of economic development of a country and its overall climate. This is somewhat surprising when it is considered that most of the countries with tropical or semi-tropical climates are either poor (per capita GNP of $100–299) or very poor (less than $100). In contrast, most of the countries in the temperate climate are either rich (per capita GNP over $1000) or semirich ($300–1000). The location factor has attracted some limited interest. For example, Galbraith pointed out in 1951 that, "If one marks off a belt a couple of thousand miles in width encircling the earth at the equator one finds within it no developed countries . . . . Everywhere the standard of living is low and the span of human life is short." Similarly a decade later, a UN Report (1961) on the world social situation stated that, "If the industrialized countries are marked on a map, they will be seen to be located as a rule in colder climate than the underdeveloped countries. This correlation with climate is as good as most correlations between non-economic factors and economic development."

In spite of such statements, location factors have seldom been considered important for analysis, and for all practical purposes, have been consistently ignored. Nearly all macro- and micro-economic growth models do not explicitly consider climate as a parameter, and most of the world models, except SARUM, do not consider it either (Biswas, 1977). Neither does Leibenstein (1957) mention climate in his list of the "characteristics of backward economies" that was developed from a comprehensive survey of the works of leading economists. Thus to date the importance of climatic factors in the assessment of comparative economic development within the tropical region has been largely ignored by development theorists and technicians.

In the rare occasions when climate was mentioned as a possible contributing factor that could somehow be related to the status of development in the tropics and semi-tropics, it was often dismissed as irrelevant or of very little importance. The fact that socio-economic developments of these regions would require a better understanding of the interrelationships between the climatic variables and agriculture, was seldom seriously emphasized. Yet such understandings are essential if the principles of development are to be applied correctly to alleviate poverty on a long-term sustaining basis.

The possible relation between climate and development had not gone exactly unnoticed prior to 1950s. For example, Huntington, in his book *Civilization and Climate,* published as early as 1915, maintained that different types of climates determined the varying levels of development and civilization of the different nations of the world, since climate affected human energy, and thus achievement of the society. Huntington, unfortu-

nately, popularized the vague feeling of pessimistic geographical determinism, that is, that colonized people were somehow racially inferior to
the European stock. Similar condescending attitudes toward the natives
of the Asian and the African countries, during their pre-independence
period, were quite prevalent. There is no doubt that to some extent, these
glib sentiments were self-serving and opportunistic in nature, since they
tended to rationalize the general philosophy that very little could be done
to improve the life-style of the natives, who were often regarded and
treated as *second-class* citizens in their own countries. Many people
believed that the natives were basically lazy, and that they would not
work any harder than necessary to maintain their lowly subsistence
levels. If they were offered better economic incentives or inducements, so
the argument went, then they would only cut down their productivity so
as to earn only enough to provide for their basic living standards. In other
words, the natives were only interested in maintaining their historic low
standard of living because of their very narrow and limited economic
horizons, which were supposed to have been conditioned by generations
of poverty and subsistence living. It is interesting to note and compare that
similar attitudes prevailed between the gentry and the lower classes in
Europe during the pre-industrial and pre-liberal times. Hecksher (1935),
for example, notes that "according to the statements of many Mercantilist
writers, the more people were paid, the less they worked." Such attitudes, however, not only eased the conscience of the so-called civilized
class, the elites, but also justified, at least in their minds, the payment of
low wages, bad working conditions, and the existence of harsh regulations
to make the natives work. A cynic may be tempted to theorize that man's
behaviour tends to become basically opportunistic, unless a determined
effort is made to change it otherwise.

Unfortunately, in those days, it was reasonably fashionable to attribute
the inferiority of the natives to the climatic conditions prevailing in such
countries, as if the hot climate made people soft in the head! Thus, Sir
William Kerr Tytler (1953) in his work, *Afghanistan: A Study of Political
Developments in Central and Southern Asia*, reasoned as follows:

> What then is the reason for this peculiar mentality? To anyone who has lived
> and worked for many years in India and with the Indians, there is a very
> simple answer to this question, too simple perhaps to be wholly satisfying. It
> is the environment and particularly the climate in which the people of India
> live and have lived for countless generations.

Similar sentiments were echoed by Harvey (1947) in his work, *Outline of
Burmese History*:

> It is difficult to say what causes one race to progress and another to
> stagnate. The spiritual factor is decisive, but racial character is itself ulti-

mately the outcome of geographical environment. Every particle of our bodies comes out of the ground, and Man is, as it were, only the most complex of the plants grown by the soil. Different earths and climates grow different men just as they grow different trees. There is little stimulus to action in lands which have so easy a climate that the earth, tickled with a hoe, laughs with a harvest. Above all, a race is heavily handicapped if for centuries a murderous sun beats down upon its head, and generation after generation is born with malaria in its blood to sap the will, to destroy one working day in three, and to shorten life by decades.

Not surprisingly, there was a strong backlash from the scientific community and the general intelligentsia against the naive and racialistic theories propounded by the likes of Huntington, Tytler, and Harvey on the effects of climate on man, and thus by inference, on the status of the economic development of any nation. Such theories also served as a comforting rationale for the continued colonization of the tropical and semitropical countries by the people from the temperate zone, thus providing a cheap source of labour. The reaction of economists and geographers against such theories, however, was so complete and overwhelming that it probably contributed to an undesirable side-effect, that of general neglect of the study of interactions between the climatic conditions and the economic development of nations. That social scientists repudiated such an obnoxious theory is certainly a credit to them, but to the extent that it led to their sad neglect of logical scientific studies toward an important direction and valid goal is certainly very unfortunate. It was analogous, to some extent, to the proverbial situation of throwing out the baby with the bath-water.

A few scientists did visualize this lacuna in its overall perspective. One of these few (Kindleberger, 1965) stated that "the arguments against Huntington are telling, but the fact remains that no tropical country in modern times has achieved a high state of economic development. This establishes some sort of presumptive case—for the end result, if not the means." Unfortunately, the extent of the concern of these few scientists was only to point out the problem: they did not pursue any worthwhile scientific studies which could contribute to the formation of new development principles.

An equally important factor could have been the attitude prevalent among several social scientists who have tended either to completely ignore the relationship between climatic parameters and economic development or casually dismissed it as only fortuitous, and thus of little consequence. Seldom has climate been included explicitly in economic analyses, except for occasional considerations in location theory. Thus, for all practical purposes, climate is not discussed at all in most books concerned with theories of regional development. Even agricultural economists like Mellor (1966), and Brown (1974) do not consider climate either. Mellor's book, *The Economics of Agricultural Development* does not even have an index citation on climate. Considering the close relation between climate and agricultural production, such omission by agricultural economists is somewhat hard to understand. Since in most of the developing countries agricultural production is a major economic factor, which often decides whether it is going to be a "good" year or "bad" year, such omission is not only surprising but somewhat incomprehensible.

Few have mentioned the problem, and they have tended to dismiss it somewhat cursorily. Thus, Lee (1957) suggested "Climate and economic development in the tropics is a convenient bogeyman to be blamed for psychological difficulties whose real origin is much more personal." Similarly Lewis (1955) comments "Because economic growth is currently most rapid in temperate zones, it is fashionable to assert that economic growth requires a temperate climate, but the association between growth and temperate climate is a very recent phenomenon in human history," or "The climate hypothesis also does not take us very far." In spite of such casual dismissals, it remains that the principal failure of economics, certainly within the last three decades, has been in the area of economic development, and this has occurred irrespective of the fact that a great deal of resource has been spent in this area. As Boulding (1970) has pointed out:

> The refinements in development theory which have developed in the last generation do not seem to have carried us very far towards a real understanding of the process as a total social process, and we do not really understand what it is that makes the difference between a developing and a non-developing society.
>
> . . . One wonders whether culture-boundness may not have something to do with this relative failure. Development, like economics, has been very largely a Temperate Zone product. The complexities both of tropical ecology and of tropical societies are beyond easy access for those raised in essentially Temperate Zone culture. This is not to suggest a naive climatological determinism, but just as tropical biological ecosystems differ very markedly from those in the Temperate Zone it would not be unreasonable to suppose that the processes of social evolution would likewise produce marked adaptations to the peculiar rigors and delights of tropical climate and life style.

One can argue that the general failure of social scientists to recognize the importance of the possible connection between climate and agricultural production, and thus economic development, is, to a certain extent, another tragic result of technology transfer defined in a broad sense. The situation is somewhat comparable to the failure of several grandiose development schemes in developing countries based on well-proven and workable models in developed nations (see Chapter 6). This, however, is not surprising since virtually all of the developments in economics or economic geography have taken place in the Western World. The fundamental principles have been developed over the years, generally based on the conditions prevalent in the developed countries. Thus, many "classical" theories are being used in developing countries, even though they are primarily temperate zone products, which means that the theories are being used more generally than their validity may warrant. When these theories are superimposed on a different world, an alien culture with radically different socio-economic conditions are institutional infrastructures, the risk of fundamental error, or alternatively the magnitude of error is exceedingly high. If, for example, the underutilization of the labour force, a common condition in Asia, Africa, and Latin America, is analyzed according to traditional Western concepts of unemployment and underemployment, the resulting figures and conclusions are generally meaningless, or at best the magnitude of error is so great that it would be folly to rely on them to make any major policy decision.

Myrdal, in his monumental and classical work, *Asian Drama* (1968), consistently criticizes the biases introduced by the use and application of Western concepts, theories and models in the study of the economic problems of South Asian countries. He points out that such analyses seriously distort the results:

> The very concepts used in their (theories of classical economics) construction aspire to a universal applicability they do not in fact possess. As long as their use is restricted to our part of the world this pretense of (universal) generality may do little harm. But when theories and concepts designed to fit the special conditions of the Western world—and thus containing the implicit assumptions about social reality by which this fitting was accomplished—are used in the study of underdeveloped countries in South Asia, when they do *not* fit, the consequences are serious.

Myrdal further points out:

> For, although research, planning and public discussions that are based on Western concepts, theories and models tend systematically to bypass the complications arising from attitudes, institutions, and modes and levels of living, the relevance of these to problems of development is at least "accounted for" by interspersed reservations and qualifications and by the habitual admission that development is a "human problem."

One may legitimately ask: if Western scientists have not been very successful in developing theories of economic development that are applicable to the developing countries, why such theories have not been developed by scientists from the developing countries themselves. Herein probably lies one of the dichotomies of the whole situation. The majority of the elite in the developing world tend to be trained in the West, and in general Western thinking is considered to be more "progressive" and "scientific." Because of their training and social attitudes, these intellectuals often produce dissertations that are replete with the traditional theories of classical Western economics. Many of them are familiar with the latest abstract growth models originating from Harvard or Oxford, and very few of them question the validity of their use in the context of the socio-economic and institutional conditions of their own countries. Such uncritical acceptance of the biases of Western concepts and theories on the part of academia, is not a monopoly of any one individual country: it seems to be all-pervasive. In essence, it can be said that there is nothing wrong in living in an ivory tower, provided it is not the only place of residence. This, sadly enough, is often not valid. Thus, the biases go undetected and are perpetuated, when at the very least they should be noticed and questioned, and better still corrected.

There are other reasons which may have contributed to some degree to the overall neglect of studies of climate as it could affect economic development. Both meteorologists and climatologists have tended to stay within their disciplinary isolation, and consequently very few ventured into work on the fringe areas analysing the effects of climate on biology, economic development, or other environmental factors. Recent emergence of new study areas like biometeorology, aerobiology, or energetics may improve the situation, and could provide a better fundamental basis for theoretical development in such interdisciplinary areas. Prior to this, the study of the interrelations between climate and living organisms was primarily in the domain of physiologists (Tosi, 1975).

Many social scientists on the other hand felt that climate can be considered as a "fixed" parameter, since it cannot be changed to any significant extent. Since it could not be modified, there was a general tendency to accept climatic considerations as boundary conditions, and they were often conveniently omitted from overall analyses.

The conditions discussed before have tended to create a bias, an almost all-pervasive bias, against the consideration of climatic factors within the framework of economic development. Often the mere possibility of the consideration of such studies has brought forth accusations of subscribing to the naive and simplistic theory of climatological determinism. Such prevailing conditions, however, have not prevented a few social scientists, like Higgins (1968), Kamarck (1973), Myrdal (1968, 1974) or Streeten (1971), from pointing out the relevance of climate within the framework of economic development. Myrdal, for example, categorically states that the importance of climate in economic development has been "grossly underestimated," and states (1968, p. 2121):

> Climate exerts everywhere a powerful influence on all forms of life— vegetative, microbial, animal and human—and on inanimate matters as well . . . . Every serious study of the problems of underdevelopment and development in the countries of South Asia should take into account the climate and its impacts on soil, vegetation, animals, humans and physical assets—in short, on living conditions and economic development.

And Streeten (1971) comments:

> Perhaps the most striking fact is that most underdeveloped countries lie in the tropical and semi-tropical zones, between the Tropic of Cancer and Tropic of Capricorn. Recent writers have too easily glossed over this fact and considered it largely fortuitous. This reveals the deepseated optimistic bias with which we approach problems of development and the reluctance to admit the vast differences in initial conditions with which today's poor countries are faced compared with the pre-industrial phase of more advanced countries.

Such perceptive observations, however, are exceptions rather than the rule, and yet the correlation between climatic regime and economic development is as good as most correlations between non-economic factors and economic development. This, of course, does not mean that there is one-to-one relationship between climate and economic development, but rather that present development theories for the tropical and semitropical countries leave much to be desired. This becomes especially relevant when it is considered that countries in such regions predominantly have agriculturally-based economies, and their yields of agricultural products are direct functions of climatic parameters. Considered in such a light, the role of climate in the development process becomes a much more important factor than hitherto conceded.

The close linkage between economic development and agricultural production can be easily confirmed by analyzing the historical trends in developed countries. It should be noted that historically very few countries have managed to industrialize without initially achieving a high degree of agricultural self-sufficiency. At the risk of oversimplification, one can argue that industrial revolution requires a prior agricultural revolution, or at the very least, a concurrent agricultural revolution. According to Kellogg (1963):

> Historically, an agriculture able to provide a surplus over the needs of the farm families made possible capital accumulation for industrial develop-

ment. Industry, in turn, furnished materials and services for a still more productive agriculture. Thus has agriculture initiated the kind of industrial development that characterizes the economic growth of the so-called advanced countries. The levels of agricultural production per man hour per hectare have steadily increased as the materials of industry have been substituted for direct farm labour.

The leaders of most countries in the tropics and semitropics profess to have understood the importance of an agricultural revolution to expedite the development process of their own countries. For example, Jawaharlal Nehru, the late Prime Minister of India, emphasized that "the whole success and failure of all our planning hangs by that single thread of our agricultural production and, specially, food production." The same point was made over and over again by many leaders of the developing countries at the World Food Conference, held under the aegis of the United Nations at Rome in 1974 (Biswas and Biswas, 1975). A critical analysis of their past performances, however, indicates that very seldom has adequate priority been given to much-needed land and agrarian reforms. Much of the emphasis has often been only lip service.

The lack of self-sufficiency in food production in developing countries is a serious hindrance to their further economic development. For example, if current trends continue, by 1985 the developing world may face annual deficits of 85 million tons in normal years and over 100 million tons in years of unfavourable climate (U.N. World Food Conference, 1974). Continually escalating high prices of energy, food, and manufactured products which these countries have to import for mere survival, and the falling prices of raw materials which they export, have already created serious balance of payment problems for many of the Third World countries, and some are now in rather poor financial condition. The twin crises of energy and food hit most of the developing countries very harshly, especially between 1973 and 1975, because price rises were very swift and very great, and the economies of most developing nations were not resilient enough to absorb these types of major price increases, without major perturbations or serious deterioration of their existing social and economic systems (Biswas and Biswas, 1976).

Viewed in global terms, the food-population equation during the 20-year period 1951–1971 was quite reasonable. The production of cereal grains, the principal source of world food supply which dominates the world food economy, more than doubled, while there was a less than 50% increase in population. This means that the average cereal availability per capita increased by about 40% in 20 years. Because of regional disparities, however, this increase was very unevenly distributed; more than half was accounted for by the richer 30% of mankind, and the balance, less than

50% of the food supply, was left for the poorest 70%. Even this amount was inequitably distributed, ranging from a high per capita annual increase of 0.9% in Latin America to an actual per capita decline of 1.1% in Africa during the 1953–1971 period. According to FAO, the minimum requirement is to increase the average annual rate of food production in developing countries from 2.6% over the last 12 years to at least 3.6% during the next 12 years. In other words, if the dependence of the developing countries on imported food is not to increase, the rates of growth of food production on a sustained basis must improve above the recent trends by over 50% in Africa (from 2.5%/yr to at least 3.8%), over 40% in Asia and the Far East, 30% in the Near East, and nearly 25% in Latin America. These are no mean targets, and yet such rates of growth should be considered the minimum necessary to satisfy basic human needs: they fall far short of the overall goal of 4% annual increase in agricultural production, as enunciated by the Second Development Decade proclaimed by the United Nations. If these minimum requirements are to be met, there has to be better understanding of the interrelationship between climate and agricultural production, and thus eventually between climate and economic development.

The interrelationships between climate and soil and pest management will be briefly examined in the following sections.

Climate and Soil Management

Some of the effects of climate factors on soil loss have been discussed earlier (see Chapter 6). Thus, only other impacts will be considered herein.

The variation in precipitation in the tropical climates tends to be greater than in temperate regions. For example, in Pakistan, total annual rainfall in any given year can be expected to exceed or fall short of the mean annual rainfall by an average of 30% or more (Stamp, 1966). This is problematical from an agricultural viewpoint, since rainfall tends to be either too much or too little for crop production. The distribution of rainfall during the growing season is an equally important criterion for agricultural production. In the monsoon countries, the time of the onset of the monsoon could easily determine the difference between a good or a bad crop year. In other words, nature does not always provide the right amount of rainfall at the right time and at the right place. Some of the worst famines of Southern Asia can be attributed directly to the summer monsoon rains not starting as early as usual (Critchfield, 1960).

The magnitude of the extreme climatic fluctuations witnessed in the tropics would be clear from a few examples. In one month alone (July 1972) nearly 4,455 mm of rain fell in Luzon, where much of the high-yielding variety of agriculture of the Philippines is concentrated. It affected some one million acres of rice plantations, and reduced the yield to 1,493 kg/ha, compared to 1,717 kg/ha in 1970. It also destroyed nearly 30% of the sugar crop, which predominates the export earning of that country. Similarly, persistent drought steadily reduced the total area of millet cultivation in Chad from 1.23 million ha in 1961 to 0.80 million ha in 1972. The yield during the same period decreased from 842 to 540 kg/ha. The flow of the River Volta at Akosombo fluctuates between 350,000 cusecs at the peak to about 1,000 cusecs during the period of low flows. Because of such wide climatic fluctuations, and because a major portion of the population in these countries depends on agriculture for its livelihood, rainfall is often the central concern of the year. Hoagland (1973) suggests:

> If the question, "How do Africans live?" means how do most of them spend the majority of their time, the answer probably is "Thinking about rain." Life tends to be organized around it, in the way consumer goods are the centrepiece of Western societies.

This is especially true for rural agricultural areas. The same feeling is expressed graphically by Blixen (1975):

> The farmer who has lived through (drought) will never forget it. Years afterward, away from Africa, in the wet climate of a northern country, he will start up at night, at the sound of a sudden shower of rain, and cry, "At last, at last."

The agricultural workers of India, Pakistan, Bangladesh and Sri Lanka also harbour similar sentiments about rainfall, especially during crop seasons.

Because of such intense fluctuations in rainfall, irrigation is essential for a significant portion of the tropical countries in order to control water availability. But irrigation practices in the tropics have resulted in a problem that is rarely seen in the temperate climates. It is the spreading of water-borne diseases, and the consequent suffering of millions of human beings and animals. In the tropical and semitropical regions of the world, irrigation schemes have enhanced and often created favourable ecological environments for parasitic and water-borne diseases such as schistosomiasis, liver fluke infections, filariasis, and malaria to flourish. These have been discussed in detail in Chapter 6.

Expansion of irrigation has also caused deterioration of soil fertility and has contributed to the loss of good agricultural land, as discussed in Chapter 6.

The rainfall and temperature patterns in the tropical climates also create other problems. In some countries, where there are definite dry and wet seasons, the climatic factors tend to accentuate the problem of soil erosion. During the long dry season, there is some loss of topsoil due to wind erosion. However, far more damage is done during the onset of the rainy season. The vegetative cover, at the end of the dry season, is already at an absolute minimum. Thus when the heavy thunder shower occurs, the water does not infiltrate into the soil as well as in light steady rain, and year after year soil erosion takes place due to surface runoff. Tempany and Grist (1958) have suggested that if the heavy rains double the water flow, "scouring capacity is increased four times, carrying capacity thirty-two times and the size of particles carried sixty-four times." Fisher (1961) estimates that these processes have contributed to the erosion of nearly 150 million acres in India alone. Even considering the fact that soil is formed more quickly in the tropical region than in temperate climates—Veleger, according to Fisher (1961), estimates it to be ten times faster in the tropics—the soil formation is much too slow to replace the loss.

The situation is somewhat different in tropical forests and woodlands (Richards, 1977). They absorb large quantities of water from the soil and also give out large amounts of water vapour. The closed type of tropical forests, because of their multilayered structure, successfully intercept rainfall, and thus protect soil from direct impact. This contributes to very little runoff and soil erosion. Much of the water infiltrating into the surface is absorbed by the dense superficial networks of roots, which is approximately three times as dense as in the temperate forest (Klinge, 1973). Destruction of tropical forests, and their replacement by grasslands or other herbaceous vegetation, changes the ecosystem, and the soil then becomes exposed to the effects of sunlight, heat and rain, which increase erosion. Such destruction further reduces rapid and efficient recycling of water, and also the water holding capacity of the soil. Greater amount of surface runoff tends to increase the frequency of floods and accentuates sediment loads in rivers and streams due to increased erosion.

Tropical forest ecosystems are thus both stable and fragile. They are stable because over long periods of evolution, spanning the geological time scale, they have developed resilience which allows them to withstand climatic and other natural environmental hazards. However, faced with modern technology, the ecosystems may prove to be quite vulnerable. The ecology of tropical forests has to be much better understood before any long-term sustainable development plans can be made with any degree of confidence.

Tropical vegetations often give a deceptive impression of soil fertility. Major tropical forests are often on nutrient-poor soils, especially in terms of phosphorous and potassium. During their evolutionary process, they have become adapted to such poor soil conditions by developing complex nutrient-conserving mechanisms, so that the loss of nutrients through drainage is compensated for by nutrients from rain and dust of the atmosphere and weathering of minerals in the soil. Furthermore, since the major part of the nutrient is usually held in biomass rather than the soil, the resulting loss through drainage water is minimal. This nutrient cycle, however, is broken by the destruction of the forest, especially by burning of the trees. The loss of nutrients under such conditions is extremely high. If the forest sites in the humid tropics are to be converted into agricultural areas, inputs of fertilizers often become necessary, since they are rapidly leached away by rain, and thus are somewhat transitory in their effects (Richards, 1977). This creates two problems: agriculture under such conditions is often uneconomic, and leached fertilizers could contribute to adverse environmental effects, as discussed in Chapter 6. Richards (1977) states that "in some areas climax forests exist under conditions of nutrient deficiency so extreme that they cannot be replaced by any form of permanent agriculture, e.g., the 'campinas' and 'pseudo-caatingas' on podzolic sands in the Rio Negro region of Amazonia and the 'Kerangas' (heath) forests of Borneo."

There are other problems with tropical soil as well. Preparation of the land for planting is generally carried out prior to the onset of the rains. This means that this arduous task has to be carried out very often in what turns out to be the hottest and driest season of the year. In contrast, in temperate climates, precipitation exceeds evaporation during winter months, and consequently it is comparatively easier to work with the moist soil in the spring. In addition, the easy availability of mechanical instruments makes the job much simpler and easier than the tropical climates. Yudelman (1972) comments:

> . . . the water regime in temperate Europe differs considerably from that in tropical Africa: a combination of the pattern of rainfall and the relationship between precipitation and rates of evaporation results in droughts or floods being rare in Europe, whereas in Africa production is frequently sandwiched between droughts and floods. Consequently, soil and water management and timing of farm operations are much more important in Africa than in Europe.

Climate and Pest Management

The tropical regions are extremely rich in species of plants and animals. This becomes abundantly clear if the "World Life Zone System" of ecological classification, developed by Holdridge (1967), is considered. This multifactorial classification scheme provides a quantitative relationship between climatic parameters and the principal features of associated natural vegetation. Thus, each life zone defines a distinctive set of possible ecosystems that are unique to the given climate. Globally, approximately 120 different bioclimates can be observed under the life zone system. Of these, 39 life zones are in the tropics and another 31 in the sub-tropics, which account for the 57% of the world total. In contrast, warm temperate regions contain 23 life zones and cool temperate regions another 16, making a total of 39. And yet virtually all the industrialized countries and the high-yielding agriculture seem to be concentrated within these two temperate, mid-latitude regions (Toshi, 1975).

The situation is even more dramatic if the life zones of certain individual countries are concerned. Toshi found 32 tropical life zones in Peru, and expects another 25 subtropical life zones in the southern quarter of that country. Both Panama and Costa Rica have 12 life zones each, and Nigeria seems to have 17. In contrast, temperate countries like Holland have only 1 life zone, and the entire United States, east of the 102nd meridian, seem to have only 10.

Such diversity of species have attendant problems, especially when monoculture is considered. In the temperate climate, there are comparatively few species of plants, all but one of which have to be suppressed at any place to develop monoculture. Similarly, with regard to pests, there are fewer species in the temperate regions, and these have to be controlled for better yield from monoculture. In comparison, in the tropics and sub-tropics, many more varieties of plants and pests have to be suppressed, if monoculture is to be profitable. Suppression of more varieties of species normally tends to need more energy, and accordingly the overall management necessary to obtain good yields from monoculture becomes an even more difficult process than in the temperate climates. The situation worsens further when it is considered that farmers in the tropics tend to be much less educated than their counterparts in the temperate regions, and in addition do not have similar access to many other necessary items like fertilizers or energy, like their colleagues in more temperate latitudes.

One of the major advantages of the temperate climate over the tropical and subtropical climates is the colder temperatures of winter. The presence of frost and snow over a significant portion of the year ensures the eradication of pests, parasites and weeds that affect man, agricultural products and animals. The absence of frost in the tropics means that insect, pest and parasitic lives continue unabated throughout the year. Their life and reproduction cycles continue to proliferate without any hindrance. In comparison, in temperate zones, winter acts as the great executioner of nature. According to Wrigley (1969):

> The tropical environment which favors the fast luxuriant growth of crops and vegetation, also favors the weeds which compete for moisture and nutrients; and the parasitic fungi, insects, spider mites, eelworms and virus diseases which make for serious reductions in the crops. Without a 'close season' for plant growth, these pests may thrive all the year.

Another problem of the lowest latitudes is the short-day photoperiodic rhythm, which reduces net photosynthesis in plants, as compared to summer months of higher latitudes, when days are long in the growing season. This problem is particularly relevant in regions where night-time temperature rarely drops below 20° C. The high incidence of cloud cover could further reduce availability of sunlight during the day and heat irradiation at night. This could further reduce net photosynthesis in such areas.

Monoculture faces a high probability of attack from pests in the tropics. Even when a species of crop is well established, there is always a possibility that a new species of pest will suddenly appear. For example, the Philippines, which became self-sufficient in rice in 1967, due to the introduction of the high-yielding varieties, had to reimport rice in 1971, since the new varieties were subject to major pest outbreaks. There have been similar other serious pest problems which have seriously affected agricultural production in the tropics. Thus, the incidence of coffee rust eliminated the arabica coffee industry in Sri Lanka, and blister blight in tea was a very serious menace in India, Indonesia and Sri Lanka, until control measures were found. Other examples are the effects of stem borers and blast on rice in Asia, Phytophthora Palmivora on cocoa in Cameroon and other West African countries, cotton pests in Egypt, Peru and Nicaragua, "sudden death" of the Zanzibar cloves, "wither-tip" of the Dominican limes, and the Panama disease of the Caribbean and Latin American bananas. In other words, every cereal or crop has at least one serious pest that affects its yield.

Tropical agriculture faces other pest problems uncommon in temperate zones. One of the most severe is locusts, which are a serious threat to all foliage in Africa (except Madagascar), all of Middle East, India, Pakistan, and Afghanistan. They appear in large swarms, and can easily eat as much food in one day as some 10,000 people. Locusts also created serious farming problems in the United States until they were controlled, especially in the plains states, during the nineteenth and the early twentieth centuries. The problem of the Rocky Mountain locusts, however, was certainly much less in magnitude than their tropical counterparts. Similarly, the red-billed Quelea finch (weaver bird) presents another serious problem for tropical Africa, which has been discussed in Chapter 6.

Food losses from various pests and insects are much higher in the tropics than in the temperate latitudes, as discussed in Chapter 6. Similarly, storage of food presents another problem in the tropics. Because of high incidence of pests and insects, and presence of high temperature and humidity, food loss in storage, in the tropics, is a very serious problem Lack of investment capital does not make the problem any simpler. Furthermore, the current state of development of appropriate storage facilities that are especially suitable to the tropical climatic and socioeconomic conditions, leaves much to be desired. Temperate zone technology, even though it is well-proven and well-established in such areas, may not be most appropriate in the tropics. Transfer of technology, from temperate to tropical regions, has not been an easy problem to solve, as noted in Chapter 6.

Pest problems in domestic animals in the tropics are also serious. Properly managed, animal husbandry can play a significant part in improving both the income and the diet of the people. Raising of livestock, however, presents some difficult problems in tropical climates. Like their human counterparts, animals often have to survive at mere subsistence levels. Good pastures are often lacking, and the grasses they eat often have poor nutritive value due to the lack of essential minerals in the soils, as mentioned earlier.

Diseases also keep animal production low in the tropics. To cite just one example, the present production of beef and veal in the tropics averages to about 14 kg/head compared to about 75 kg in the temperate climates. The National Academy of Sciences, in a report on Tropical Health (1962), stated:

> Intestinal parasites are almost universally distributed in domestic animals throughout the tropical world. The economic effects are multiple and not necessarily confined to mortality in infected animals. These parasites are responsible also for retarded development of young animals, reduced yields of milk and meat, lowered wool production, and impaired working capacity of draft animals.
>
> . . . Conditions in the tropics are conducive under most circumstances for the transmission and perpetuation of gastrointestinal parasites; transmission can and does take place in most instances throughout the year, whereas in the temperate zones low temperatures serve as a barrier to transmission during the winter months.

It can be argued that the African animal trypanosomiasis is one of the major causes of the underexploitation of the land and water resources of a significant portion of tropical Africa. If trypanosomiasis could be brought under control, it has been estimated that this region could carry a supplementary cattle population of about 120 million head. This could produce an additional 1,500,000 tons of meat/year, representing a value of at least $750 million (UN World Food Conference, 1974). The tse-tse flies also are the vectors of human trypanosomiasis (sleeping sickness), and cause untold human misery. The seriousness and magnitude of the problem was recognized at the World Food Conference at Rome, and one of the main resolutions passed was on the control of trypanosomiasis (Biswas and Biswas, 1975).

Climate and Man

The problems discussed earlier naturally have eventual impacts on the human life style, including standard of living. There are certain other factors, however, which directly affect human health, creativity, and work efficiency.

The relationship between human health and economic development has not been much explored in recent times, and this indicates another "Western" bias in current theories of development. While an average worker may be considered to be healthy in the temperate zones, he is far from being in good health in the tropics for a variety of reasons, including availability of adequate nutrition (M.R. Biswas, 1978). Bad health obviously affects general attitudes to work, and hence contributes to inefficiency.

Even though the interrelation between tropical climates and health or work efficiency have not been conclusively established, several comments can be made. Because of socio-economic and climatic conditions, diseases seem to be quite prevalent in the tropical and semitropical regions. Indeed, the whole situation gives rise to a vicious cycle. Lack of appropriate development means that people do not have adequate education, nutrition, sanitation, or health care, all of which contribute to make them more prone to diseases. This in turn affects efficiency of work, which further reduces rate of development. The warm and humid climates of the tropics further worsen the situation. An example would make this point clear.

According to a survey carried out by the World Health Organization (WHO) on the extent of water supply and sewerage facilities available at the end of 1975 in 67 developing countries, only 20% of the rural population have access to safe water. If both urban and rural sectors are considered, 35% of the people are adequately served. This means that women

Table 9-1. Time Spent for Water Collection in Africa

Distance Between Water Sources and Consumers (miles)	Time Spent in Collecting Water	
	(hours)	(% of average daily working time)
0.25	0.166	2.8
0.50	0.333	5.5
1.00	0.667	11.1
2.00	1.333	22.2
3.00	2.000	33.3
4.00	2.667	44.4
5.00	3.333	55.5
6.00	4.000	66.6
7.00	4.667	77.7
8.00	5.333	88.8
9.00	6.000	100.0

and children have to spend some of their time in collecting water. Hence, if the water supply of the various regions are developed, it would reduce the water collection journey of women and children, who currently spend up to 5 hr/day collecting family water requirements. Table 9-1 shows that time spent in carrying water is a function of the distance of the source from the consumer, and also shows how it affects the daily working time of water carriers (Biswas, 1978). It shows that if the water source is about 4½ miles away, a woman would spend at least 3 hr/day carrying water, or 50% of her daily working time. If this time can be freed by providing water closer to home, it can be used for productive work.

Time and inconvenience are not the only disadvantages of long water-collection journeys in the tropics; it increases other costs as well. It has been estimated that it takes up to 12% of daytime calorie needs of most carriers in nondry areas; and in drier areas and in mountainous regions, energy spent in collecting water and firewood may take up to 25% or more of daytime calories (Cleave, 1974). Thus, elimination of water collection journey has not only important implications in terms of reduced disease propagation (since contacts with disease vectors during long water-collection journeys will be eliminated) but also in terms of nutrition, a fact often overlooked by planners and politicians.

Water development will undoubtedly reduce health hazards like cholera, typhoid, infectious hepatitis, amoebiasis, enterovirus diarrheas and bacillary dysentery. It would further reduce human contacts with vectors of water-borne or water-based diseases like schistosomiasis, trypanosomiasis and guinea worm (*Dracunaculus Medinensis*). These are primarily tropical diseases. Schistosomiasis as discussed in Chapter 6, is currently endemic in over 70 countries, affecting over 200 million people. Guinea worm infection currently affects 48 million people, chiefly in India and West Africa. Some have estimated that the incidence of *Trypanosoma gambiense* can be reduced by 80% by good water supply schemes (Bradley, 1974).

The above discussion is presented merely to indicate the complexity of the problems and the interrelations between the various sectors: development, climate, nutrition, health, work efficiency and life-style.

Man is also affected by other diseases in the tropics. Among these are malaria, filariasis, river blindness, leprosy, dengue, etc. The extent of these diseases can be realized by considering that more than 2,000 million people are now exposed to malaria (UNEP, 1977), about 250 million people have some form of filariasis (Kamarck, 1973), more than 10 million people are infected by leprosy, and some 20 million people have been blinded, totally or partially, by river blindness. While billions of dollars are being spent on research to find cures for diseases that affect inhabitants of temperate zones, a mere fraction of that total (probably much less than 10%) is being spent for research on the tropical diseases. And yet, there is no doubt that tropical diseases affect many more people than temperate zone diseases.

Lack of nutrition in the developing countries also affects work efficiency and the general attitude to work. Increasing population and lower standards of living in most countries of the tropics and subtropics means that agricultural workers, one of the most underprivileged groups, do not get adequate food, neither in quality nor in quantity. Hence, it is going to be difficult to increase the agricultural production of the developing countries, unless their farmers have better nutrition and education. Physical inputs like pesticides, fertilizers or better water control will certainly help, but in the ultimate analysis it is the agricultural workers that produce food, and they must have a better quality of life. As Myrdal (1968) perceptively comments:

> The popular theory that indigenous people are more able than Europeans to cope with the climatic stresses of the region is not established; the opposite might be true in view of the European's better nutrition and health. In any case, the sultry and oppressive climate that much of South Asia experiences all or most of the time tends to make people disinclined to work. Manual labourers, for example, habitually wield their tools with a feebler stroke and take more frequent and longer rest pauses than workers in cooler climates.

Absence of a temperate zone type of winter in the tropics may also contribute to the development of different socio-psychological conditions. The farmers in temperate zones have to manage their affairs in such a way as to carry them through a largely unproductive winter. The absence of alternate productive and non-productive seasons may create different basic attitudes towards savings and investment. Interestingly enough, similar analogy can be found with bees. Maeterlinck's classic study indicates that bees stop storing honey when they are taken to areas where continuous supply of food is available all throughout the year. To quote again from Boulding (1970):

> In the temperate zone we take for granted the rhythm of the seasons, with the constant looking forward into the future which this produces—"If winter comes, can spring be far behind?" The more disagreeable temperate climates produce demands for activity almost for its own sake. What else is there to do in the middle of the Chicago winter except work? The subtler rhythms and the more genial environment of the tropics may lead to a life style and a type of provisioning which is very different from that of the Temperate Zone.

Conclusion

Climate is an important parameter that should be considered in any theories of economic development, especially in the tropics and subtropics. The physical, social, economic, cultural and institutional conditions are very different in the tropics, compared to temperate zones. Thus, development plans for the tropical countries must consider their specific characteristics, both in terms of assets and liabilities, and then devise ways to maximize their assets and minimize their liabilities on a long-term sustaining basis. For example, tropical forests are estimated to be responsible for some 69% of the earth's biological productivity (Brünig, 1974). The question then arises how man can take advantage of this natural phenomenon. Whatever strategy is adopted, it must *not* be based on obtaining quick financial return by realization of capital, which would ultimately prove to be a self-defeating strategy.

It is important that strategies developed are compatible with the laws of nature, not against it. Hence, problems of pest control or artificial ecosystems like monoculture or reduction of forest areas to grazing lands, can often be solved only when the ecology of the balanced natural systems, which they replace, is studied and understood.

Equally important is the need for carrying out comprehensive research programs on a variety of problems associated with economic development in the tropics. Too much of the existing research is on an *ad hoc* basis, and such programs, because of their "on again, off again" nature, are neither optimal in return for the resources expanded, nor likely to produce a major breakthrough. A determined effort is necessary to make real progress.

However, call for only further intensive research is never an ideal solution. There are many areas where adequate knowledge is available, but for a variety of reasons they are not being used. For example, it should be possible to prevent much of the loss of productive soil in the tropics, but for whatever reasons countermeasures for such prevention are not being taken. Plato graphically described some 23 centuries ago how deforestation increases soil erosion and floods; and the need for terracing on sloping land to prevent soil loss was pointed out by Bernard Palissy at least four centuries ago (Biswas, 1970). Yet one wonders why such simple countermeasures are not implemented. The simple technology has been available for centuries; it is certainly widely known; preventive steps are not expensive and are urgently needed, and yet they are not used in practice. Thus research by itself is unlikely to solve any problem, unless the results can be brought to bear in the real life. As Confucius said in the fifth century B.C., "The essence of knowledge is, having it, to apply it."

References

Biswas, A. K. (1970). *History of Hydrology*. North-Holland Publishing Co., Amsterdam, The Netherlands, 336 p.

Biswas, A. K. (1977). *World Models, Resources and Environment*. Biswas & Associates, Ottawa, 23 p.

Biswas, A. K. (1978). Environmental implications of water development for developing countries. Jnl. of Water Supply & Management, **2**, No. 4, 283–297.

Biswas, A. K., and Biswas, M. R. (1975). World Food Conference: A perspective. Agriculture and Environment. **2**, 15–37.

Biswas, A. K., and Biswas, M. R. (1976). Energy, environment and international development. *Technos*. **5**, No. 1 (Jan.–Mar.), 38–65.

Biswas, M. R. (1978). Nutrition and development in Africa. International Journal of Environmental Studies.

Blixen, K. (1975). *Out of Africa*. Jonathan Cape, London.

Boulding, K. E. (1970). Increasing the supply of black economists: Is economics culture-bound? *American Economic Review* **60**, No. 2 (May), 406–411.

Bradley, D. J. (1974). Water supplies: The consequences of change. *Human Rights in Health*. CIBA Foundation Symposium No. 23, Associated Scientific Publishers, Amsterdam, 81–98.

Brown, L. R. (1974). *In the Human Interest*. Norton, New York, 190 p.

Brünig, E. F. (1974). Ökosysteme in den Tropen. *Umschau* **74**, No. 13, 405–410.

Cleave, J. H. (1974). *African Farmers: Labour Use in the Development of Smallhold Agriculture*. Praeger, New York, 166.

Fisher, C. A. (1961). *South-East Asia, A Social, Economic and Political Geography*. Methuen, London.

Galbraith, J. K. (1951). Conditions for economic change in underdeveloped countries. *J. of Farm Economics* **33** (November), 693.

Harvey, G. E. (1947). *Outline of Burmese History.* Longmans, Calcutta, India, 48–49.

Hecksher, E. (1935). *Mercantilism.* Allen and Unwin, London, 165.

Higgins, B. (1968). *Economic Development.* Norton, New York, 209–223.

Hoagland, J. (1973). Quoted by Kamarck, A. M., in Climate and economic development, Seminar Paper No. 2, Economic Development Institute, International Bank for Reconstruction and Development, Washington, D.C., 1973, 70 pp.

Holdridge, L. R. (1967). *Life Zone Ecology.* Rev. ed. Tropical Science Center, San José, Costa Rica.

Huntington, E. (1915). *Civilization and Climate.* Yale University, New Haven, Conn.

Kamarck, A. M. (1973). Climate and economic development. *Finance and Development* **10**, No. 2 (June), 2–8.

Kellogg, C. E. (1963). Interactions in agricultural development. Summary of Proceedings on Agriculture, Conference on Application of Science and Technology for the Benefit of Less Developed Countries, World Food Congress, Washington, D.C., WFC/63/BP/UNCAST, June 4–18, p. 45.

Kindleberger, C. P. (1965). *Economic Development.* 2nd ed. McGraw-Hill, New York, 78.

Klinge, H. (1973). Root mass estimation in lowland tropical rain forests of Central Amazonia, Brazil. *Tropical Ecology* 1, 29–38.

Lee, D. H. K. (1957). *Climate and Economic Development in the Tropics.* Harper, New York.

Leibenstein, H. (1957). *Economic Backwardness and Economic Growth.* Wiley, New York.

Lewis, W. A. (1955). *Theory of Economic Growth.* Allen and Unwin, London, 53 and 416.

Mellor, J. W. (1966). *The Economics of Agricultural Development.* Cornell, Ithaca, N.Y.

Myrdal, G. (1968). *Asian Drama: An Inquiry into the Poverty of Nations.* 3 vol. Pantheon, New York.

Myrdal, G. (1974). The transfer of technology to underdeveloped countries. *Sci. Am.* **231**, No. 3 (Sept.), 172–182.

National Academy of Sciences—National Research Council (1962). *Tropical Health.* National Academy of Sciences, Washington, D.C., 175.

Richards, P. W. (1977). *Tropical Forests and Woodlands: An Overview. Agro-Ecosystems* **3**, No. 3 (June), 225–238.

Stamp, L. D. (1966). *Asia: A Regional and Economic Geography.* 12th ed. Methuen, London.

Streeten, P. (1971). How poor are the poor countries. In *Development in a Divided World*, D. Seers and L. Joy (Eds). Pelican, Harmondsworth, England, 67–83.

Tempany, H., and Grist, D. H. (1958). *Introduction to Tropical Agriculture.* Longmans, London, 88.

Tosi, J. A. (1975). Some relationships of climate to economic development in the tropics. In *The Use of Ecological Guidelines for Development in the American Humid Tropics.* New Series No. 31, International Union for Conservation of Nature, Morges, Switzerland, 41–55.

10

THE FUTURE OF MAN

Aurelio Peccei, President
The Club of Rome

The concluding pages of this book are on the future of man. One should be cautious about speculating on this important but lofty subject. Dennis Gabor has already warned that man can now invent his own future, though not yet predict it. As a matter of fact, man is busily shaping it every moment of every day, while perhaps ignoring that he is doing precisely this and apparently little concerned what the ultimate result of his labours may be.

These remarks should by no means be construed as suggesting that an aloof attitude should be condoned. Quite the contrary; it seems clear that at this point in human evolution, when everything is in flux and man has become the main agent of change on Earth, one of his major obligations is to set about designing his own future, purposefully, objectively, and earnestly. He must stop simply letting the future happen, as if it were the unpredictable and uncontrollable outcome of actions and events beyond human understanding.

Unfortunately, mankind is still far from the stage of conscious future-building. Discussing the future of man can hence be a hazardous and perhaps even presumptuous enterprise; in accord with this, the discussion herein is limited to a few reflections on the grave consequences of current human unpreparedness and improvidence, and some inquiry into how such an unbelievable involution could persist in this golden age of knowledge. Finally, some suggestions have been made as to what path might be taken to bring man-made developments—which means most of what is happening—under control, and to help establish a position from which to shape the future in favour of mankind.

Musing on the future, at the end of a book that focusses on man's primary need for food, reminds me of the conclusion of a project I helped to sponsor, which was carried out in recent years in Holland. That the eminent Professor Hans Linnemann undertook to lead this worthy study is a reflection of how difficult and urgent it will probably be, in the years and decades to come, for humans to solve the basic problem they share with all other species—enough food, in the right place, at the right moment. Meteoric advances, unchallenged conquests, and all manner of shining achievements have crowned the human species as the true master on Earth, but have provided no security against hunger—and this situation is likely to continue, as far ahead as we can see. This warning, already given in unequivocal and even chilling terms by others, has just been repeated with the help of a refined model of international relations in agriculture, whose acronym, MOIRA, was the name of a goddess of destiny.

When asked whether it is possible to stamp out this blight on the human condition, MOIRA explored the intricacies of the food problem in depth and pronounced its verdict: if anything, hunger is going to increase. Before reaching this conclusion, MOIRA of course examined all imaginable combinations of the policies and strategies adopted or ventilated. What MOIRA could not take into account, however, are man's ingenuity and resourcefulness when he grasps the terms of the threats or challenges he is up against. These exceptional qualities have not yet been called into play, because man has not yet clearly sized up his new situation and its purport for good and evil.

It is a tragic irony that in a world which, theoretically, could feed even more humans than the unprecedented numbers living today, the spectre of famine is likely to continue to hover over us, haunting and striking hundreds of millions of people, many more than at any time in the past. This is surely going to happen, we now know, unless some fundamental changes are made in human society. These changes will be possible, however, only when people around the world come to perceive the conditions that make them necessary. It is an encouraging sign, though, that the more sensitive sectors of the general public are growing increasingly aware that pointed questions must now be asked in this connection. How will an ever more intricate and vitally interdependent world community be able to survive, let alone prosper, in the nuclear age, with so many hungry, desperate people in its fold? If mankind is unable to solve the food problem for all its children today, what then will happen when the human family grows by a further one or two billions?

Other questions follow in stride. To approach them responsibly, one has to consider a wider panorama than that of food and climate, and try to grasp why at the peak of its knowledge and power the human species finds itself in a more dangerous predicament than at any time during the hundred centuries of its recorded history. The key to its future can probably be found by posing and answering such a line of enquiries.

Early in 1976, two ominous pieces of news sent shock waves around the world. Apparently unrelated, both were emblematic of this age of triumphant science and technology. One concerned human proliferation; and the other, the arms race. On March 28, 1976, the Population Reference Bureau of Chicago announced that at 5:15 A.M. that day, the number of Earth's inhabitants had reached four billions. Soon thereafter, reliable sources indicated that military spending had attained a record high of $300 billion a year. Almost everybody was able to read the message heralded by these trends—that disaster will come soon. It still did not spark off any decisive movement to put a halt to them, however, and we continue our way along this disaster course. Our generation, much responsible for this state of affairs, seems paralyzed by the enormity of the problems it creates.

There now seems to be tacit acceptance that a world population of six or more billions is inevitable towards the end of this century, when today's newly born will be thinking about getting married and raising their own families in peace. The feeling exists, too, that the destructive might of our armaments is reaching such a terrifying diapason that no human power can possibly stop the havoc of their use some day, somewhere—perhaps everywhere.

People are confusedly aware that the world is drifting out of control for other reasons, moving from one bad economic or political crisis to another even more vicious. Their leaders, who are supposed to guide mankind, are so overwhelmed by immediate crises and engrossed by mutual rivalries that it is a near miracle if they do not end up by making things still worse than they are at present. As a consequence, while caught in the turmoil of drastic changes occurring at accelerating pace, mankind just hopes to succeed in muddling through, without plan or purpose, not daring to look farther than a few years ahead. Under these circumstances, the future will be marked by the host of problems we leave behind and by ever larger masses of people struggling with ultimate weapons for space and resources.

With such a heritage, the generations to come are hardly being offered a sporting chance of a normal life, let alone an opportunity of pursuing happiness and welfare comparable to ours. Although this is certainly not our intention, we are condemning them to a struggle against desperate odds. We are probably no more callous or egocentric than our ancestors who throughout history endured hardships, ploughed the land, built houses and cathedrals, and saved and dreamed for the benefit of their children and their children's children. Why, then, do we behave so differently? Why do we maintain such ethically and morally indefensible attitudes? The reason, at once so simple and yet so complex, is that our generation has "progressed" so precipitously that it has lost its bearings and now finds itself in a state of profound cultural disarray.

That mankind as a whole is in a pathological condition can be perceived by analyzing the essence and origin of its current predicament. For all the wealth of information and the stupendous knowledge it has accumulated, it has not yet been able to adjust to the revolutionary changes—true mutations—that it has wrought in its universe in the course of a few decades. Somebody quipped that it mistook *information* for *knowledge*, and this for *wisdom*; and that it enhanced its *know-how* neglecting the *know-what*.

Mankind's torrential growth in numbers, beyond anything reasonable, and the monstrous overkill capacity it has developed, both of which threaten its very existence, are proof of a profound derangement, though in different forms and mixes, in all countries—developed and developing, East and West, North and South. Other related phenomena—its tendency to create ever more complex artificial systems beyond its control, its systematic ravaging of its natural life-supporting habitat, its irresponsible manipulations of recombinant DNA and of its own genetic material—are all symptomatic of a pervasive cultural imbalance and disorder.

This is a singular human illness. We belong to a species, weak in other biological resources, that is vitally dependent on its cultural capacity. Thanks to the unique endowment of our brain and hands, we have made this spectacular ascent to stardom among all forms of life; by relying on it again we can ensure our survival and continued domination in the planet, but if our advantage is abandoned even for a short period—as is now threatened—our species is no less endangered than the orangutans, scimitar-horned oryxes, and kakapos.

Problems of cultural maladjustment exist only marginally with other species. No doubt when one of them is unable to adapt to a modification of its natural environment it is destined to suffer or even disappear. None of them, however, is in a position appreciably to change its own habitat—as man is. Moreover, they can adjust to change only or mainly by genetic evolution, supplementing their organic adaptation by developing instinct on the basis of experience. Their behaviour is therefore encoded in their genes, in such a way that a tiger always knows, for better or worse, how to be a tiger, and a swallow a swallow, an octopus an octopus.

Although man cannot rely on biological evolution, especially under the present circumstances, he possesses immense possibilities of cultural adaptation and anticipation that can be realized only if he employs his assets intelligently. In a word, he has to learn continuously what it takes to be a man; and to be a modern man is a much more complex and exacting business than we seem to have realized so far. Our fantastically expanding cultural patrimony enables us to devise new ways and means of modifying our environment and living conditions; and we have indeed already made ample use of this capacity. At the same time, however, we have failed to foresee what it takes for us to live in harmony with such changes, and indeed whether we are prepared to accept and to accomplish all that is required. We must now remedy this, and see to it that from now on our cultural evolution precedes major man-made changes instead of following them; otherwise we may forever be uncertain whether we are capable of the quality jump required not to be out of step with the realities of our own making.

The case of modern man is one of grave lopsided cultural development. Drawing from his extremely versatile cultural matrix, but exalting certain achievements and shunning others, he has developed the new science-based technologies that have given him the tools to expand his establishment and enhance his influence on the planet in a prodigious manner. Having thus incomparably transformed his terrestrial domain and his status in it, he should have modified his views and modes to suit; but he has so far failed to do so. So engrossed has he been in exercising his technological prowess, even playing and gambling with it, that he has disregarded how costly the consequences might be and has neglected to develop his other cultural assets in parallel.

The result is that everything else peculiar to man, from values to behavior, from judgment to institutions, is out of phase with his technology. Such a divorce of power and reason has thrown the human system into chaos and left man himself bewildered, wondering why in the long run his marvelous accomplishments may well cause more harm than good. He is tempted to get out of it all by falling back on old policies and practices which nowadays are quite ineffective, if not directly damaging. The vicious circle in which he is caught thus tightens a bit every year.

Several examples of the disorders of our age come easily to mind. Pride and interest in having many children lingers on, though infant mortality has been drastically reduced and social services taking care of the old are being developed. Similarly, in this new age of the satellite, of global interdependency, and of transnational integration, the national sovereign state, conceived at the time of the stage coach, remains the functional unit of the world political organization. Coeval to these outdated structures are the concepts of national defence still prevalent today, though they have lost any meaning with the appearance of The Bomb. The very existence of some 150 egocentric states of all descriptions and dimensions is such a dangerous and costly oddity, so refractory to any rationalization, that peace and prosperity are well-nigh impossible in the human family.

The list of examples could continue. While the nature, scale, and dynamics of the *problematique* has changed, human affairs are still guided by parochial or power politics, short-term expediency, piecemeal approaches, the mirage of perennial growth, and ideologies of the past. The principles and instrumentalities that used to foster development, measure economic performance, manage the monetary system, administer ever more sprawling cities, husband and allocate natural resources, and educate the young, are patently outdated and inadequate and will become increasingly at variance with reality as everything grows bigger, problems more complex, and expectations higher.

There can be no doubt that cultural mismatch is certainly not a new phenomenon. It has occurred before; existing equilibria have been shaken by the invention of new techniques or new weapons, and empires and civilizations have fallen under the stress. What is new and most worrying, however, are the brutal and shattering suddenness of the present crisis, its depth, and its planetary dimensions. Commensurate answers and a firm basis for the continuation of human ascent can be found only if mankind soon succeeds in ensuring a harmonious cultural improvement that will permit it to understand the new realities of its universe and then organize its global performance in ways consistent with the unprecedented responsibility its novel position of power places on its shoulders. To reach such a higher order of culture and organization on a global scale is the epochal, inescapable challenge facing our generation.

No doubt, further doses of technology—from the simplest and softest to the most sophisticated—will be needed to attack new and old problems and improve the standard and quality of life of four, and soon five or six, billions of people. And a new, more equitable and better functioning international economic order is definitely required to redress the world situation. Admittedly, too, all existing institutions need a thorough overhaul, and new ones are necessary, from the local and national to the regional, and global levels. Without a cultural quality jump, however, all this will be in vain, nothing will suffice to save these billions of men and women from their deepening plight.

In weighing the challenge before us, we should never forget that in our teeming, increasingly integrated societies, great numbers of people are going to acquire ever greater power, at least power of disruption and passive resistance, and that in the long run people themselves will have to be, and indeed will be, the true protagonists of their good or ill fortunes. Cultural evolution therefore has to be a worldwide phenomenon; whether we like it or not, it will no longer suffice for it to take place in some nations or regions only—or in the closed fold of the élites; it must be universal.

If the foregoing analysis of the human plight at this juncture is correct, the immensity of what must be done to retake control of our destiny need not be stressed. The way is now obvious: it goes right through the hearts and minds of people. The major change must take place not outside the human being, but within.

However vast and complex it may be, this task is not impossible. There are encouraging signs of a human, and humanistic, awakening. In different parts of the world, among ordinary citizens of diverse condition and convictions, the awareness is growing that there is some basic inadequacy in the manner the human lot is managed in this new age. Citizenries are more advanced in this respect than the political functionaries, who should know better but are so often unprogressive and locked in struggles for power. Such enhanced public consciousness is reflected by the spontaneous groups of citizens springing up everywhere, as antibodies in a sick organism, with the aim of stimulating the laggard national and international establishment. One such group is The Club of Rome.

In conclusion, the future of man depends on man himself. This may sound tautological, but on closer analysis one is forced to admit that this patent truth is in reality grossly neglected. The same concept, though, can perhaps be better expressed by saying that human future depends on human quality. At the present oversized scale of mankind and in the face of increasing planetary complexities, however, the issue of the quality of the human being is the forgotten one. The time has come to place it, urgently, in the central position that is its due.

What is human quality? In the present circumstances, it can no longer be only an expression of ethical, spiritual, and humane values, which alone can enlighten knowledge, but it must also englobe the existential capabilities of the species. But can, then, human quality be so developed as to be always on a par with the extreme alternatives—marvelous or terrible—looming up for the future? Human fate hinges on the answer that our generation and following generations will be able to give to this question. This difficult terrain has been explored recently in *The Human Quality* (Peccei, 1977), from which a quotation, mildly but still realistically optimistic, can conclude this chapter:

We have succeeded in improving the quality of athletes, cosmonauts and astronauts, of chickens, pigs, and maize, of machines, appliances and materials; we succeeded in the case of man's productivity, in his ability to read fast and his capacity to talk to computers. However, we have never tried in earnest to sharpen his perception of his new condition, to heighten his consciousness of the new strength he possesses, to develop his sense of global responsibility and his capacity to assess the effects of his actions. I am sure that, if we try, we will succeed—not least because every step made along this road will show more clearly that it is in our fundamental interest to go further in the same direction. As to whether there is any purpose in this enterprise, a mere glance around suffices to show the immense scope that exists for improving human quality.

Reference

Peccei, A. 1977. The Human Quality. Pergamon Press, Oxford, England, 214 p.

NAME INDEX

SUBJECT INDEX